TRADITIONING DISCIPLES

# American Society of Missiology Monograph Series

The ASM Monograph Series provides a forum for publishing quality dissertations and studies in the field of missiology. Collaborating with Pickwick Publications—a division of Wipf and Stock Publishers of Eugene, Oregon—the American Society of Missiology selects high quality dissertations and other monographic studies that offer research materials in mission studies for scholars, mission and church leaders, and the academic community at large. The ASM seeks scholarly work for publication in the Series that throws light on issues confronting Christian world mission in its cultural, social, historical, biblical, and theological dimensions.

Missiology is an academic field that brings together scholars whose professional training ranges from doctoral-level preparation in areas such as scripture, history and sociology of religions, anthropology, theology, international relations, interreligious interchange, mission history, inculturation, and church law. The American Society of Missiology, which sponsors this series, is an ecumenical body drawing members from Independent and Ecumenical Protestant, Catholic, Orthodox, and other traditions. Members of the ASM are united by their commitment to reflect on and do scholarly work relating to both mission history and the present-day mission of the church. The ASM Monograph Series aims to publish works of exceptional merit on specialized topics, with particular attention given to work by younger scholars, the dissemination and publication of which is difficult under the economic pressures of standard publishing models.

Persons seeking information about the ASM or the guidelines for having their dissertations considered for publication in the ASM Monograph Series should consult the Society's website—www.asmweb.org.

Members of the ASM Monograph Committee who approved this book are:

> Paul V. Kollman, CSC, University of Notre Dame
> Roger Schroeder, SVD, Catholic Theological Union
> Michael A. Rynkiewich, Asbury Theological Seminary

Previously Published in the ASM Monograph Series

David J. Endres, *American Crusade: Catholic Youth in the World Mission Movement from World War l through Vatican ll*

W. Jay Moon, *African Proverbs Reveal Christianity in Culture: A Narrative Portrayal of Builsa Proverbs Contextualizing Christianity in Ghana*

E. Paul Balisky, *Wolaitta Evangelists: A Study of Religious Innovation in Southern Ethiopia, 1937–1975*

Auli Vähäkangas, *Christian Couples Coping with Childlessness: Narratives from Machame, Kilimanjaro*

# Traditioning Disciples

*The Contributions of Cultural Anthropology to Ecclesial Identity*

COLLEEN MARY MALLON

American Society of Missiology
Monograph Series

VOL. 8

☙PICKWICK *Publications* • Eugene, Oregon

TRADITIONING DISCIPLES
The Contributions of Cultural Anthropology to Ecclesial Identity

American Society of Missiology Monograph Series 8

Copyright © 2010 Colleen Mary Mallon. All rights reserved. Except for brief quotations in critical publications or reviews, no part of this book may be reproduced in any manner without prior written permission from the publisher. Write: Permissions, Wipf and Stock Publishers, 199 W. 8th Ave., Suite 3, Eugene, OR 97401.

Pickwick Publications
An Imprint of Wipf and Stock Publishers
199 W. 8th Ave., Suite 3
Eugene, OR 97401

www.wipfandstock.com

ISBN 13: 978-1-60899-088-7

*Cataloguing-in-Publication data:*

Mallon, Colleen Mary.

    Traditioning disciples : the contributions of cultural anthropology to ecclesial identity / Colleen Mary Mallon

    x + 282 p. ; 23 cm. Includes bibliographical references and index.

    American Society of Missiology Monograph Series 8

    ISBN 13: 978-1-60899-088-7

    1. Ethnology—Religious aspects. 2. Identification (Religion). 3. Christian life. I. Title. II. Series.

BL256.M2 2010

Manufactured in the U.S.A.

*Dedicated to
my parents,
James and Rita Mallon,
and to my religious community,
the Dominican Sisters of Mission San Jose*

# Contents

*Acknowledgments / ix*

Introduction / 1

1 Towards Naming the Present / 7
2 The Notion of Tradition in Roman Catholicism: Historical Overview / 56
3 Interpretative Anthropology: Social Identity and Transformation from the Works of Mary Douglas, Victor Turner, and Clifford Geertz / 117
4 Yves Congar on Discipleship: A Thick Description of Christian Identity / 177
5 Traditioning Disciples: Ecclesial Identity and Refiguring Tradition / 225

Conclusion / 265

*Bibliography / 271*
*Index / 279*

# Acknowledgments

I WANT TO EXPRESS my deep gratitude to T. Howland Sanks, SJ, mentor and friend, who challenged me to love the questions more than the answers. Hal's passion for excellence, his love for all things theological, and his committed service as a scholar and teacher make him a truly remarkable theologian. I am deeply grateful to the remarkable women of my religious community, the Dominican Sisters of Mission San Jose, who daily inspire my love for God and commitment to our shared mission as women of the Word. I am particularly grateful to Rose Marie Hennessy, OP, and her council for their support and to Carolyn McCormack, OP, whose gentle and true spirit inspires my discipleship and mentors my teaching. Finally, I would like to express my appreciation to the American Society of Missiology for choosing this work for publication. I am grateful to the members of the selection committee for their careful review and support.

# Introduction

TRADITION AND SOCIAL IDENTITY pose a problem in contemporary discourse. The forces at work in the creation of personal and communal distinctiveness are the focus of significant study and debate. How communities used shared traditions to create and sustain corporate identity has opened new avenues of exploration into the "invention" of "imagined communities," particularly in the social sciences.[1] Yet, those engaged in the current debate warn against falling into either of the two extremes that bracket the continuum of views concerning identity. Neither *primordialism*, an essentialist view, nor *instrumentalism*, a constructed view, serves to account adequately for the complexities at work in identity formation. As Jan Nederveen Pieterse points out, primordialism fails to examine critically the assumption that ethnic groups are timeless givens, while instrumentalism "ignores the cultural character of ethnicity and the importance of symbolic resources, which are all flattened to economic choices."[2]

The complexity of the identity debate only increases as globalization both "extends the effects of modernity" and compresses "both our sense of time and our sense of space."[3] This global context, marked by boundaries both geographical and conceptual, places unprecedented emphasis on difference, diversity, and the local. Within this polycentric situation, experiences of multiple belonging imply that the sources of identity are multiple. How does the concept of tradition function in this context? How is the understanding of mission impacted by these forces? Moreover, how does a religion with a highly developed sense of the sacral nature and function of its tradition, such as Roman Catholicism, sustain both its vitality and credibility?

1. See Anderson, *Imagined Communities*; also, Hobsbawn and Ranger, *Invention of Tradition*.
2. Pieterse, "Varieties of Ethnic Politics."
3. Schreiter, *New Catholicity*, 9–11.

In the years following Vatican II, Roman Catholicism struggled to dialogue with a modern world, already gone "postmodern." In some sectors, the initial enthusiasm for dialogue waned as the real work of collaboration demanded a re-examination of practices of authority from the local parish level to the level of episcopal conferences. Vatican II's clear emphasis on the baptismal dignity of the laity blurred the rigid boundaries of roles and responsibilities with the church. Asserting a renewed identity as the People of God effectively displaced long-cherished practices and notions that had functioned as conspicuous markers of Roman Catholicism. Vatican II opened Roman Catholicism to a world which it was both prepared and unprepared to receive: prepared in that many in the church had been working to forward an ecclesial vision far beyond the narrow strictures of Ultramontanism; unprepared in that few in the church could foresee the level of ambiguity modern pluralism would unleash within the bounds of the Roman Catholic communion.

The ambiguity of the present moment continues to shape Roman Catholicism as diverse voices speak the gospel message in new and sometimes unfamiliar ways. As the boundaries of the community are stretched by new questions (women, inculturation, liberation theologies), it is increasingly clear that the former synthesis is unraveling. Classical Christian tradition is a suspect entity. Yet, as Elizabeth Johnson notes, the tradition both suppresses and sustains. The tradition "has aided and abetted the exclusion and subordination of women, but also sustained generations of foremothers and foresisters in the faith."[4] Jesus's caution regarding new wineskins echoes through twenty-one centuries of Christian discipleship.

The dilemma of tradition calls for a reconsideration of Christian tradition and its ambiguous potentials. Accordingly, the social sciences offer important insights and questions concerning human communities and the social systems that sustain and challenge group identities. Specifically, in this book I will show how a critical dialogue between cultural anthropology and the claims of the Christian community *qua* community and the character of religious belonging (i.e., discipleship) contributes towards refiguring the notion of tradition in Roman Catholicism.

The ambiguities associated with religious traditions calls for a re-examination of how traditions function both to foster and undermine religious identities. The insights of cultural anthropology help to explicate the multiple dimensions at play in social identity. When an *interpretative*

---

4. Johnson, *She Who Is*, 9.

*approach* to symbol systems is employed, as in the works of Victor Turner, Mary Douglas, and Clifford Geertz, the complexities of social identity become increasing apparent. The trajectory of thought formed by these three anthropologists is particularly useful when approaching the theological questions surrounding religious belonging because their approach to culture never reduces religion to a social epiphenomenon. Moreover, as shall be seen, when specific insights derived from these anthropologists are critically appropriated, a nuanced perspective on human social identity emerges: the risk of tradition confronts and engages any facile notion of social identity.

One of the obvious purposes of a religious tradition is the formation of adherents. Traditions could not survive without their adepts. Thus for the Christian tradition, the formation of disciples is a functional missiological imperative. Discipleship, construed as a theological category and a locus of specific practices, offers a point of entry into the question of Christian identity. An underlining assumption that informs the whole of this text is that a dialogical and dialectical relationship exists between Christian tradition and discipleship formation. The functional effectiveness of the Christian tradition (i.e., mission) lies in its ability to create, sustain, and transform disciples who take up the task of reweaving the tradition for each generation.

By analyzing a specific notion of discipleship as a case study in ecclesial identity, a critical correlation can be explored between the insights of interpretative cultural anthropology and a distinct construal of Christian social identity. Although discipleship was never the overt focus of a single text written by Yves Congar, OP, the theology of this French Dominican and major architect of Vatican II is saturated with his understanding of "the Christian mystery." An exploration of the specific markers Congar associates with Christian discipleship, both individual and communal, results in a thick description of Christian belonging that is at once particular and yet capable of speaking beyond its limitations.

The method of mutual critical correlation engaged in this study places the question of religious traditions and social belonging in a heuristic middle ground in order to allow the meanings derived from two distinct disciplines to speak to each other. This hermeneutical approach allows the meanings of interpretative cultural anthropology and theology to contend with each other over the question of religious traditioning. In this manner,

I examine the theological fruitfulness of a semiotic approach to tradition: towards refiguring the notion of tradition in Roman Catholicism.[5]

## Overview

Chapter 1 offers a descriptive review of current discourses on the contested character of human belonging and the problem posed by the notion of tradition. I describe the present globalizing context, pointing out the various discourses engaged in the project by "naming the present" both theologically and from a social science perspective. Chapter 2 explores the historical development of the notion of tradition in Roman Catholicism by examining major shifts in the understanding of tradition and the social and cultural contexts within which these changes occur. In Chapter 3 I critically appropriate social scientific insights into the functional role of human traditions from the works of Turner, Douglas, and Geertz. Each theorist offers a unique perspective on the nature of the social and the role of symbol systems within human communities. Their contributions are critically assessed in the light of the "crisis of representation" in cultural anthropology. Chapter 4 examines a broad range of the works of Yves Congar, teasing out the significant markers of Christian discipleship that inform his theology. After a review of the context and commitments that inform Congar as theologian, I do a close reading of major texts from his corpus, identifying and discussing the structures and practices within Christian tradition that Congar associates with discipleship. The chapter concludes by suggesting what ecclesial identity might look like from the perspective of Congar's notion of discipleship. This thick description of ecclesial identity highlights in particular the missional significance of discipleship construed as corporate identity in a globalized world.

In chapter 5 the findings of chapters 3 (cultural anthropology) and 4 (theology) are placed into critical correlation. On the basis of apparent *prima facie* similarity, I compare and contrast the key findings regarding the role of tradition in social identity and transformation with the key themes of discipleship gleaned from Congar's theology. I discuss the implications a refigured notion of tradition has towards *ecclesia semper reformanda* within a truly "world church," and formulate conclusions regarding the processes

---

5. Clifford Geertz informs my understanding of semiotics. I am not engaging the entire science of semiotics, nor do I intend take up the work of Saussure. Geertz describes his ethnographic style as interpretative. See Geertz, *Available Light*, 17.

of continuity and change simultaneously at work in discipleship formation and transformation. In the Conclusion I reflect on the ambiguity of Christian tradition, its revelatory potential, its historical-cultural limitations, and the risky business of Christian discipleship.

# 1

# Towards Naming the Present

Various disciplines have attempted to describe the present moment. Whether characterized as "*tiempos mixtos*"[1] or polycentric, the implications of current discourse point towards a world of heightened complexity where marginalized and oppressed voices emerge, resist, reclaim, and rename the present. To paraphrase social theorist Michael Featherstone, the West is now confronted by the "the Rest." This context challenges past understandings of social identity and traditions. While historical consciousness and ideological critique unmask the so-called autonomous, Enlightenment subject, current studies in cultural anthropology call into question essentialist understandings of ethnicity. Simultaneously, the resurgence of particular ethnic and religious enmities, often centuries old in duration, highlight the tenacity and endurance of social memories. In this light, can the symbolic sources of social identity be reduced to mere "invention," the constructed results of various and powerful economic and political forces?

This descriptive overview offers representative anthropological and theological perspectives on the contested character of human belonging and the problem posed by the notion of tradition by drawing out some of the more distinctive threads shaping the contours of the historical present. In effect, this chapter presents the reader with a series of postmodern snapshots, each frame offering both perspective and insight. More kaleidoscope than collage, this chapter will draw out distinctive themes engaging the postmodern present in order to contextualize this study.

The first half of the chapter examines how current studies in cultural anthropology understand the task of ethnography and the challenges associated with the ongoing study of traditions, social identity, and social change. The second half of the chapter examines the current theological

1. Calderon, "America Latina," 225–29.

milieu, giving particular focus to "disputed questions" surrounding the nature of Christian theology within a pluralistic, globalized world. As with all rational disciplines, social science and theology share in the legacy and aftermath of the Enlightenment. Modernity and postmodernity are major themes woven throughout this chapter.

## Towards Naming the Present: Cultural Anthropology

In order to flesh out the diversity of views in cultural anthropology, I investigate the perspectives of James Clifford, Michael Featherstone, and Talal Asad, giving an overview of their understandings of the task of cultural anthropology in the light of the current "crisis of representation."[2] James Clifford's post-Geertzian perspective points out the radical situatedness of ethnographic writing and calls into question notions of culture as unified, homogenous, and continuous. Michael Featherstone's analysis of the effect of globalization on modern and postmodern conceptions of culture calls for a critical reappraisal of the underlying assumptions informing the perception of a unified modernity versus a plural postmodernity. Finally, Talal Asad's postcolonial critique exposes the manner in which Western conceptions of history-as-progress, inherently shaped by Christian teleology, inform the tacit presuppositions of contemporary postmodern ethnographers, thus, implicating the liberal discourse of difference and displacement. Each theorist, in response to the present "crisis," offers distinctive views and identifies important ramifications for understanding social identity.

---

2. Initially coined by George Marcus and Mike Fischer in "Contemporary Problems of Ethnography in Modern World System," *crisis of representation* refers to the dilemma facing ethnographic writing in the light of serious "across-the-board questioning of the basic frameworks of description in the human sciences." Marcus continues, "Even some of our best contemporary ethnography is written within a fiction of the whole that relies on gross constructs of state and economy that are relatively insensitive to the ways that those working in traditions of macro-system description, the Marxists or even the latter-day heirs of Parsons, have been revising their own classic frameworks of social theory. Writing about modern predicaments of ethnographic subjects in terms of mid- or early twentieth century, or even nineteenth century, visions and conceptual vocabularies of the world system, vitiates the powerful function of ethnography to represent the world with a certain currency. Thus, it also lessens the capacity of ethnography, in future perspective, to constitute a historical document in the making, keenly sensitive to its own times." Marcus, *Ethnography*, 34.

## James Clifford

In *Predicament of Culture*, James Clifford describes the task of anthropology as a profoundly complex enterprise, the result of multiple intersections of cultural traditions.

> Ultimately my topic is a pervasive condition of off-centeredness in a world of distinct meaning systems, a state of being in culture while looking at culture, a form of personal and collective self-fashioning. The predicament—not limited to scholars, writers, artists, or intellectuals—responds to the twentieth century's unprecedented overlay of traditions.[3]

Accordingly, the exotic is no longer found at great distance. Indeed, "the 'exotic' is uncannily close."[4] The mixing of peoples as a result of voluntary or forced migration, travel, and via media channels compresses distance while simultaneously heightening difference. As will be seen in the development of this chapter, the renewed interest in difference is both applauded and viewed with suspicion. The flux of traditions, traveling in what has been described as cultural flows,[5] has a destabilizing effect, calling into question social identity and the cultural sources from which communities construe (or construct) identity. From Clifford's perspective the notion of an essentialized other is no longer tenable. "'Cultural' difference is no longer a stable, exotic otherness; self-other relations are matters of power and rhetoric rather than of essence. A whole structure of expectations about authenticity in culture and in art is thrown in doubt."[6]

This new globalized terrain is far more than geographical in scope and nature. Ultimately the task of the ethnographer can be characterized as one of recording the glimpses of a participant observer. Once considered a much more unified and transparent science, cultural anthropology has repositioned the ethnographic lens, casting about introspective glances to expose the not-so-disinterested presuppositions of the ethnographer-scribe.[7]

---

3. Clifford, *Predicament of Culture*, 9.

4. Ibid., 12.

5. "'Flow' is a term that has come to be used in sociology, anthropology, and communications science to denote cultural and ritual movements, a circulation of information that is patently visible yet hard to define. Flows move across geographic and other cultural boundaries, and like a river, define a route, change the landscape, and leave behind sediment and silt that enrich the local ecology." Schreiter, *New Catholicity*, 15.

6. Clifford, *Predicament of Culture*, 14.

7. "Ethnography, a hybrid activity, thus appears as writing, as collecting, as modernist collage, as imperial power, as subversive critique. Viewed most broadly, perhaps, my

While some find the new stance more biographical of the scientist than descriptive of the would-be subject of inquiry, the postmodern predicament demands a new, disabused understanding of power/knowledge and its function in the ethnographer-informant relationship. Can the ethnographer authentically describe and analyze the cultural system of a particular people? Who among the informants is the authentic voice of the group? Whose story matters and how does the ethnographer choose from among possible informants? These questions chasten any naïve sense that what is ultimately chosen for observation and analysis by the ethnographer is somehow free from the issues of power and interest.

> I began to see such questions as a pervasive postcolonial crisis of ethnographic authority. While the crisis has been felt most strongly by formerly hegemonic Western discourses, the questions it raises are of global significance. Who has the authority to speak for a group's identity or authenticity? What are the essential elements and boundaries of a culture? How do self and other clash and converse in the encounters of ethnography, travel, modern interethnic relations? What narratives of development, loss, and innovation can account for the present range of local oppositional movements?[8]

Clifford maintains that the new emerging subjects of ethnography are authoring cultural histories that resist easy transcription. These emerging histories require new ways of telling.[9] There is no one, single path of proceeding because there are "several hybrid and subversive forms of cultural representation, forms that prefigure an inventive future."[10] This new terrain is least served by a sovereign, universally applied methodology. While it may not be possible for ethnographic writing to completely avoid reductive dichotomies or essences, the discipline demands that ethnographic representations offer more than ahistorical abstractions.[11]

---

topic is a mode of travel, a way of understanding and getting around in a diverse world that, since the sixteenth century, has become cartographically unified." Ibid., 12.

8. Ibid., 8.
9. Ibid., 17.
10. Ibid.
11. "It is more than ever crucial for different peoples to form complex concrete images of one another, as well as of the relationships of knowledge and power that connect them; but no sovereign scientific method of ethical stance can guarantee the truth of such images. They are constituted—the critique of colonial modes of representation has shown at least this much—in specific historical relations of dominance and dialogue." Ibid., 23.

To this end, Clifford endorses Michel Foucault's and Gilles Deleuze's "'toolkit' of engaged theory,"[12] where theory functions less as a system and more as "an instrument, a *logic* of the specificity of power relations and the struggles around them."[13] This demands analysis of the particular situation as well as its historical precedents. While Clifford is well aware that there has always been variety in ethnographic method, he contends that for a significant portion of the twentieth century ethnographic fieldwork functioned as the normative *modus operandi*: writings from field experiences received authoritative status in the research community. "Intensive fieldwork, pursued by university-trained specialists, emerged as a privileged, sanctioned source of data about exotic peoples."[14] The present crisis surrounding the authority of ethnographic texts asks,

> . . . how is unruly experience transformed into an authoritative written account? How precisely, is a garrulous, overdetermined cross-cultural encounter shot through with power relations and personal cross-purposes circumscribed as an adequate version of a more or less discrete "other world" composed by an individual author?[15]

---

12. Ibid.
13. Foucault, *Power/Knowledge*, 145.
14. Clifford, *Predicament of Culture*, 24.
15. Ibid., 25. Clifford discusses four modes of ethnographic authority: experiential, interpretative, dialogical, and polyphonic. Experiential authority rests in the notion, exemplified in Dilthey, that through shared coexistence, the ethnographer develops an intuitive "feel," a sense of a people through "a kind of accumulated savvy" (35). Interpretative anthropology critiques naïve claims of experiential authority and introduces the necessary distinction between experience and interpretation. Through a process of "textualization," unwritten aspects of cultural life, "behavior, speech, belief, oral tradition and ritual come to be marked as a corpus, a potentially meaningful ensemble separated out from an immediate discursive or performative situation" (38). The textualization process by which experience is made into narrative generates an "integrated portrait," and as such tends to submerge or even erase the discursive quality of actual fieldwork. Thus, Clifford notes, "Paradigms of experience and interpretation are yielding to discursive paradigms of dialogue and polyphony" (41). Dialogical ethnography focuses primarily on two aspects: the intersubjectivity of all speech and the immediate performative context of all discourse." Both dialogical and polyphonic models of ethnography struggle to produce a research method and product that captures the multiple authors of ethnographic discourse. In these models the question of how to "stage" the dialogue or the words of indigenous informants becomes critical to the goal of extending authorial authority. Even the notion of "informant" begins to lose its sense. Because ethnography includes all four of these processes, attempts to present a coherent picture of the data require "a controlling mode of authority" which "is now inescapably a matter of strategic choice" (54).

## Social Identity

The concerns surrounding ethnographic authority highlight the postcolonial critique of power and cultural identity. Clifford's assessment of colonial domination in the aftermath of the myth of development and the collapse of nationalism is both positive and negative. Indigenous populations have experienced both ruin and revival. Accordingly, "the forces of 'progress' and 'national' unification . . . have been both destructive and inventive."[16] Local peoples actively resist, expressing a power that is uniquely theirs from resources, both explicitly and latently, present within the culture.

> Many traditions, languages, cosmologies, and values are lost, some literally murdered; but much has simultaneously been invented and revived in complex, oppositional contexts. If the victims of progress and empire are weak, they are seldom passive.[17]

Given the "pervasive condition of off-centeredness" spoken of earlier, the notion of identity as a cohesive, single, and essential reality, received whole from one generation to the next, is a shaky, if not indefensible, proposition. In a world of high mobility and social interfacing, where "difference is encountered in the adjoining neighborhood, the familiar turns up at the ends of the earth,"[18] cultural identities are more fluid than static, more syncretic than pure, more invented than received. As Clifford maintains, "identity, considered ethnographically, must always be mixed, relational, and inventive."[19]

## Traditions

Traditions, fundamentally linked to the concept of identity, have also received considerable critical attention in the last thirty years. As with identity studies, historical and cultural reviews of traditions have disclosed the highly contested nature of traditioning processes, undermining any substantial identity claims made on the basis of tradition. For Clifford, and anthropologists who follow his line of thought, the overriding concern centers on the myth of continuity within cultural traditions.

> Intervening in an interconnected world, one is always, to varying degrees, "inauthentic": caught between cultures, implicated

---

16. Ibid., 16.
17. Ibid.
18. Ibid., 14.
19. Ibid., 10.

in others. Because discourse in global power systems is elaborated vis-à-vis, a sense of difference or distinctness can never be located solely in the continuity of a culture or tradition. Identity is conjunctural, not essential.[20]

Clifford is suspicious of attempts to retrieve a purified tradition via historical investigation. These "questionable acts of purification" are simply not possible to achieve. Access to the original sources is highly problematic. Only fragments are available and any reweaving of disparate sections constitutes a reinvention of tradition rather than a recovery of tradition. Currently, it is no longer possible to assume the continuity of culture and tradition, although Clifford makes a careful disclaimer: the current ethnographic emphasis on the inventive potentials of cultural resistance may understate the effect of the homogenizing forces at work globally and even fail to acknowledge local expressions of cultural continuity and retrieval.[21]

Still, Clifford remains an optimist at heart. The rejection of universalizing metanarratives and the embrace of local fragments signal not the destruction of culture, as feared by Levi-Strauss, but the construction of culture by means of inventive processes. Levi-Strauss's account of the dissolution of difference into the solvent of "an expansive commodity culture" betrays a European bias towards a unified notion of human history. Clifford maintains that the defeat of difference does not dissolve various human histories into a homogenizing culture. Throughout the world evidence indicates that what is emerging is not homogeneity, but a new type of diversity. Ulf Hannerz from the University of Stockholm notes,

> The people in my favorite Nigerian town drink Coca Cola, but they drink *burukutu* too; and they can watch *Charlie's Angels* as well as Hausa drummers on the television sets which spread rapidly as soon as electricity has arrived. My sense is that the world system, rather than creating massive cultural homogeneity on a global scale, is replacing one diversity with another; and the new diversity is based relatively more on interrelations and less on autonomy.[22]

Traditions function differently in newly globalized contexts. Traditions are "cut and retied," making identity "inventive and mobile." Traditions "need

---

20. Ibid., 11.
21. Ibid., 15.
22. Ibid., 16–17.

not take root in ancestral plots; they live by pollination, by (historical) transplanting."²³

From Clifford's perspective the notion of a primordial identity is no longer tenable in a globalized world. Identities are not received from within coherent, integrated traditions; they are constructed from the fragments and pieces of social life and constitute an ad hoc composition. Change so marks the present that attempts to claim continuity with the past is fictive and functions rhetorically to support the illusion of connection. Clifford's description of the ethnographic predicament articulates a significant viewpoint within cultural anthropology. The next section explores globalization's impact on cultural identities and traditions from a different understanding of the postmodern moment.

## *Michael Featherstone*

In *Undoing Culture*, Michael Featherstone focuses primarily on the effects of globalization on modern and postmodern conceptions of culture. Featherstone is convinced that the very idea of "unified" culture (associated with modernity) versus "fragmented" culture (associated with postmodernity) represents social constructions of culture that demand critical evaluation. Featherstone argues that modernity is neither unique nor homogenizing. Historical analysis of the sources of modernity, or more correctly global modernit*ies*,²⁴ indicate that globalization is not a product of modernity. Quite the opposite: global modernities are among the many products resulting from the phenomenon of globalization.

### PRIVILEGED CULTURE PRODUCERS

Featherstone maintains that each and every society has a group of specialists ("priests, artists, intellectuals, educators, teachers, academics") who

---

23. Ibid., 15.

24. "It is also important to examine the ways in which globalization has produced both the modern and postmodern, in the sense that the power struggles between nation states, blocs and other collectivities gradually became globalized as more and more parts of the world were drawn into the competing figuration of interdependencies and power balances.... [T]here is an important spatial and relational dimension to modernity which is lost when we conceive it as coming out of one particular time and place with all others necessarily condemned to traverse the same route.... It might, then, be advisable to speak of global modernit*ies*, with the emphasis given to the plural forms." Featherstone, *Undoing Culture*, 5–6. See also Featherstone, *Global Culture*; and Featherstone, Lash, and Robertson, *Global Modernities*.

participate in the production of a common understanding of culture.²⁵ Though all members participate in the production of culture to a certain extent, each person participates within a particular range of options, circumscribed by numerous factors including historical situation, individual capabilities, and socio-politico-economic conditions. These factors contribute to the "power potential" available to individuals and groups as culture producers. Cultural specialists possess considerable power potential towards the production and circulation of cultural goods. Moreover, "our overall sense of the value, meaning and potential unity or crisis-ridden nature of a culture will depend not only on the conditions of social life we find ourselves in, but on the conditions of those who specialize in cultural production as well."²⁶ Seemingly, a crucial, critical dialogue is necessary between the privileged producers of postmodernity and their publics.

Featherstone builds from the work of Daniel Bell, who argues that the modernist shift from the Protestant ethic to play, pleasure, and consumption occurred because of an alliance between modernism and consumerism.²⁷ The present postmodern situation is both an extension of and a reaction to modernism: reaction in so far as postmodernism represents the reversal of the exhausted project of modernity; extension in so far as postmodernism remains in alliance with consumerism.

> The confident belief in an ordered social life, coupled with ever-extending progress, has been seen to have reached its limits and a reversal has set in. Hence postmodern theorists have emphasized fragmentation against unity, disorder against order, particularism against universalism, syncretism against holism, popular culture against high culture and localism against globalism . . . Postmodernism and consumer culture are both often taken as signs that we are going through dramatic changes which are altering the nature of the social fabric as a result of double relativization: of both tradition,

---

25. Ibid., 3.
26. Ibid.
27. Ibid., 73. Featherstone makes a distinction between "modernity" and "modernism." Modernity is associated with a "relentless detraditionalization" that effectively replaced the Christendom metanarrative with a rational Enlightenment metanarrative. Modernism is the artistic countercultural reaction against the dominating rationality of modernity. "This comforting narrative in which culture necessarily follows the unfolding 'logic' of scientific, technological and economic change is however complicated by the development of countercultural artistic and intellectual movements, as well as the persistence, transformation and renewal of religion and the sacred in many aspects of life (not the least being nationalism) . . ." Ibid., 72.

and the "tradition of the new" (modernism), with the latter resulting in a questioning of all modes of fundamental values . . .[28]

This situation of "double relativization" demands that serious attention be paid to the generalizations and assumptions that inform it. Questions must be raised: Whose crisis is this? What is the relationship between the cultural specialists and ordinary people? Featherstone does not suggest that cultural specialists are intentionally duplicitous in their manipulation of cultural products. He does want to emphasize that cultural specialists are themselves embedded in the cultural/social world they hope to interpret. These interpretations are made readily available to wider audiences via the media.[29]

Seemingly, postmodernism can only be fully understood when it is contextualized within the "practices, interdependencies and interests of cultural specialists, academics, artists, critics, and cultural intermediaries, who struggle to provide interpretations and explanations of the social world." Without this understanding "we cannot assume that the crises detected by cultural specialists necessarily are the general social and cultural crises claimed."[30]

## Globalization and Cultural Complexity

Featherstone's analysis of modernity and postmodernity sets the stage for his discussion of globalization. Although Featherstone ultimately critiques the perception of postmodern cultural complexity in contradistinction to modern cultural simplicity, he begins his analysis by examining how the occurrence of "cross-overs" impacts a present sense of global complexity and confusion. The phenomenon of "crossing-over" occurs when forms of culture, previously separated and contained by secure boundaries, flow over into new realms producing new hybrids and syncretisms. From this perspective, culture provides a bound context of tacit knowledge, allowing internal social interactions to occur with relative coherence. With the advent of cultural flows the possibility of miscommunication increases significantly.

---

28. Ibid., 74.

29. "Hence there is the possibility of the bandwagon effect, a thirst for new and fashionable concepts with which to make sense of experience, which may actually be used to re-form and reinterpret existing experiences and develop new sensibilities." Ibid.

30. Ibid., 75.

Culture, which once seemed invisible, as it was habitually inculcated into people over time and became sedimented into well-worn social routines, now surfaces as a problem. Taken-for-granted tacit knowledge about what to do, how to respond to particular groups of people and what judgment of taste to make, now becomes more problematic. Within consumer culture newspapers, magazines, television and the radio offer advice on how to cope with a range of new situations, risks, and opportunities—yet this only adds to rather than reduces complexity.[31]

The global experience of "cross-over" cannot be seen as a one-way flow of Western goods, commodities, images and information. This perception is too obviously scripted from the "assumed master concepts of tradition, modernity and postmodernity, largely propelled by economic changes."[32] Global processes, although dominated by the West, are truly multipolar, with competing centers becoming increasingly apparent. Featherstone identifies two ways of conceptualizing global processes. In the first, a particular culture extends itself throughout the globe, engulfing and assimilating different cultures until one single culture dominates the world. In the second, world cultures are compressed and brought together such that they are literally piled one on top of the other; lacking any organizing principle, cultures are juxtaposed at various points of contact. The latter description conjures an image where "there is too much culture to handle and organize into coherent belief systems, means of orientation and practical knowledge."[33]

Featherstone argues that the second image of cultures-in-contest on a global field more effectively handles the data of cultural life in a postmodern, postcolonial world. The perception that "there is too much culture to handle" resurfaces the question of complexity. This is a description that demands investigation. Does the present "complexity" imply a past "simplicity"?[34] The critique of modernity asks how the very notions of "unity" and "the social" functioned within the historical and political processes of its time. Was it always more an ideal than a reality, used to validate the newly emerging political entity known as the nation-state? Will further

31. Ibid., 5.
32. Ibid.
33. Ibid., 6.
34. "What does this assertion of complexity suggest about our image of cultures as more simple and integrated in the past? How were such images possible and sustainable? How far does this point toward the need to develop a new set of cultural concepts with which to reconceptualize the role of culture in social life"? Ibid.

examination of these assumptions lead to a more diversified understanding of modernity itself? Featherstone answers affirmatively and remarks that it is important to view past conceptions of globalization from a post-colonial perspective in order to have a sense of how modernity and definitions of culture were generated at a particular cost. The present situation of massive overlying of traditions, previously described by J. Clifford, is not a fairly recent phenomenon: the rest of the world has always been a part of the West. The unitive images of modernity projected by the West effectively suppressed the real presence of difference and complexity. A concept of culture is needed that

> . . . not only discovers increasing complexity in the current phase of globalization, but also looks at previous phases of globalization and its relationship to modernity. Here we can think of the need to investigate the ways in which particular European notions of culture were generated within modernity which presented its culture as unified and integrated, which neglected the spatial relationship to the rest of the world that developed with colonialism, in effect the dark side of modernity that made this sense of unity possible.[35]

## The Spatial-Relational Dimension of Modernity

Featherstone's desire to reclaim the spatial-relational dimension of modernity stems from his conviction that the global field has always been primarily a dialogical space, not simply a monological space. The globe, planet Earth, as a finite space, provides a field of interaction between social aggregates, human communities. These collectivities both *form a global world* and are *formed by a global world*.[36] Building on the work of Georg Simmel, Featherstone points out that development of "nation-states" is a particular historical expression of this world-forming, world-formed relationship.[37] It is a "dominant particular" in the words of Anthony King.[38] In Featherstone's view there are a variety of responses to globalization, a variety of "global modern*ities*," and this process can be traced beyond the twentieth century to the post-Reformation era. Nation-states were never

---

35. Ibid., 12.
36. Ibid., 112; emphasis added.
37. Ibid., 109–10.
38. Ibid., 123. See King, "Times and Spaces of Modernity."

"born whole." From the beginning they have been the product of hugely divergent forces, circumstances, and relationships.[39]

According to Featherstone, globalization is *not* producing a worldwide monoculture. Those who maintain this are seriously misreading modernity. These notions of modernity lack a "spatial and relational dimension" because they conceive modernity "as coming out of one particular time and place with all others necessarily condemned to traverse the same route."[40] At the same time, Featherstone does maintain that a global culture is emerging. "Nation-states do not just interact; they form a *world*." The global context formed by the interrelational dealings between nation-states results in ways of being a world participant that supersede the interests and control of any one nation-state, however dominant.[41]

The existence of these "processes and modes of integration," actively forming what some call a "third culture"[42] is not the result of a totalizing master process.

> The various combinations, blends and fusions of seemingly opposed and incompatible processes such as homogenization and fragmentation, globalization and localization, universalism and particularism, indicate the problems entailed in attempts to conceive the global in terms of a singular integrated and unified conceptual scheme. Appadurai has rejected such attempts at theoretical integration to argue that the global order must be understood as "a complex, overlapping, disjunctive order."[43]

While the global context is an interactive, dialogical space, the "dialog partners" are not equal participants; the global relationships are asymmetrical. Nation-states and other cultural collectivities confront each other in the

39. "All sorts of contacts were occurring between nascent proto-nation-states through the Church, dynastic ties and other forms of association, which helped to develop a cultural complex of interchanges and transactions; this acted as a developing field or ground within which nation-states could begin to form their identities. For the vast majority of nation-states which emerged in the nineteenth and twentieth centuries this international cultural complex, or transnational field, formed a gradually extending world whose significance became increasingly salient with the intensification of contact." Featherstone, *Undoing Culture*, 144.

40. Ibid., 5–6.

41. Ibid., 112.

42. Featherstone speaks of the development of "third cultures," referring to "sets of practices, bodies of knowledge, conventions and life-styles that have developed in ways which have become increasingly independent of the nation-states." Ibid., 114.

43. Ibid., 118. See Appadurai, "Disjunction and Difference," 32.

global arena already enmeshed in webs of interdependencies and power relations. Culture clashes are an inevitable part of this global situation. In fact, these very clashes may have the effect of promoting and solidifying boundary divisions between competing collectivities. Thus, the notion that globalization is homogenization simply does not do justice to the full range of "cultural responses which continue to deform and reform, blend, syncretize and transform, in various ways, the alleged master processes of modernity."[44]

> The process of globalization, then, does not seem to be producing cultural uniformity; rather it makes us aware of new levels of diversity. If there is a common global culture it would be better to conceive of it not as a common culture, but as a field in which differences, power struggles and cultural prestige contests are played out. Something akin to an underlying form which permits the recognition and playing out of differences along the lines of Durkheim's non-contractual aspects of contract, or Simmel's analysis of the taken-for-granted common ground underpinning social conflict. Hence globalization makes us aware of the sheer volume, diversity and many-sidedness of culture. Syncretisms and hybridizations are more the rule than the exception . . .[45]

Featherstone gets at the fiction of an integrated modernity (in contrast to a disjunctive postmodernity) by asking, "Who is producing postmodernism?" He suggests that the globe has been a diverse field of interaction ("cross-over") for centuries where nation-states collide and connect in an arena that never has been homogeneous. Featherstone's perspective on globalization problematizes integrated notions of tradition and social identity. He argues that the present experience of "too much culture to handle" is not new. Modernity's deployment of integrating and unifying strategies are simply extended by postmodern arguments that fail to unmask the illusion of an integrated modernity. By analyzing modern/postmodern distinctions, Featherstone raises the question of how categories are authorized in discourse. Talal Asad offers a further critique of how Western categories function, suggesting that the improvisational character of Western cultural logic operates uncritically in current liberal discourse.

---

44. Featherstone, *Undoing Culture*, 113.
45. Ibid., 13–14.

## Talal Asad

Talal Asad employs postcolonial critique in his analysis of Western hegemony, focusing on the presence of real systemic forces in the present global context.[46] Asad is suspect of post-Geertzian anthropologists and facile claims that local peoples appear to be active agents of their own histories, resisting the hegemonic forces of global economic systems, employing diverse, latent cultural strategies, and ultimately creating new, hybrid social and cultural forms that "speak back" to the homogenizing threat of Westernization. The heart of Asad's argument lies in his claim that Christianity has structured the West's understanding of history. Beneath modern notions of history making lies a religious geology concerning subjectivity and agency that requires careful assessment. Particularly, Asad questions the assertion prevalent among contemporary historians and anthropologists that local people are the active agents and subjects of their history. Asad "remain[s] skeptical" of a "notion of history [that] emphasizes not only the unceasing work of human creators but also the unstable and hybrid character of their creation."[47]

This view of "the unceasing work of human creators" finds its source in the idea of progress, an eighteenth-century hybrid of older Christian conceptions of historical time as salvation history, philosophies of pure reason, and secular, empirical practices.[48] As a result of this fusion, a particular understanding of history making as a teleological quest for "the new" emerged, and became woven into the fabric of tacit knowledge informing the Western mind.

> . . . one assumption has been constant: to make history, the agent must create the future, remake herself, and help others to do so, where the criteria of successful remaking are seen to be universal. Old universes must be subverted and a new universe created. To that extent, history can be made only on the back of a universal

---

46. "It is an old empiricist prejudice to suppose that things are real only when confirmed by sensory data, and that therefore people are real but structures and systems aren't. There are systemic features of human collectivities that are real enough even though you can't see them directly—for example, life expectancies, crime ratios, voting patterns, and rates of productivity. . . . Various kinds of social practices are inconceivable without such representations. . . . I am concerned with how systematicity (including the kind that is essential to what is called capitalism) is apprehended, represented, and used in the contemporary world." Asad, *Genealogies of Religion*, 6–7.

47. Ibid., 2.

48. Ibid., 17.

teleology. Actions seeking to maintain the "local" status quo, or to follow local models of social life, do not qualify as history making.[49]

## SUBJECT, AGENT, IDENTITY

The notion of subject-agent as locus of self-conscious identity in a self-directed actor poses significant problems for Asad. There is considerable evidence that self-consciousness does not offer complete access to a unified center of being. "One does not have to subscribe to a full-blown Freudianism to see that instinctive reaction, the docile body, and the unconscious work, in their different ways, more pervasively and continuously than consciousness does."[50] More importantly for Asad, much of the rhetoric of subject-agent fails to account for the context within which agents interact. This omission misses two important points. First, an agent's act at some point is subsumed, or becomes a part of a web of actions, caught up in the actions of other agents. Thus "beyond a certain point, an act no longer belongs exclusively to its initiator."[51] Second, the rhetoric of subject-agent fails to acknowledge "the politically more significant condition that has to do with the distribution of goods that allow or precludes certain options."[52] Some options are possible and others are not. Some people can make choices; others, given their context, cannot: they lack the means. Asad maintains that the inability to make choices does not impinge on subjecthood or consciousness. "The *structures* of possible actions that are included and excluded are therefore logically independent of the consciousness of actors."[53]

> Another way of putting this is to say that the systematic knowledge (e.g. statistical information) on which an agent must draw in order to act in ways that "make history" is not subjective in any sense. It does not imply "the self." The subject, on the other hand, is founded on consciousness of self. My argument, in brief, is that contrary to the discourse of many radical historians and anthropologists, *agent* and *subject* (where the former is the principle of effectivity and the latter of consciousness) do not belong to the same theoretical universe and should not, therefore, be coupled.[54]

49. Ibid., 19.
50. Ibid., 15.
51. Ibid.
52. Ibid.
53. Ibid.
54. Ibid., 16.

Asad's understanding of agency is tied up with "authorizing practices." A social identity can be analyzed into its different aspects (gender, class, regional aspects) without dissolving the essential unity of the entity. "The unity is maintained by those who speak in its name, and more generally by all *who adjust their existence* to its (sometimes shifting) requirements."[55] Asad goes further, asserting that those who avoid essentialism "as the gravest of intellectual sins" need to understand that "certain things are *essential*" to social identities.[56]

> To say this is not equivalent to saying that the project (or "India") can never be changed; it is to say that each historical phenomenon is determined by the way it is constructed, that some of its constitutive elements are essential to its historical identity and some are not. It is like saying that the constitutive rules of a game define its essence—which is by no means to assert that the game can never be subverted or changed; it is merely to point to what determines its essential historical identity, to imply that certain changes (though not others) will mean that the game is no longer the same game.[57]

### Authorizing Space

In Asad's study of Western hegemony, the notions of locality and mobility play a significant role. Critiquing postmodern anthropologists' easy celebration of uprootedness and displacement, Asad notes that the description "local" does not escape determination by the dominant discourse. Both physical and conceptual space is authorized. "Everyone can relate themselves (or is allocated) to a multiplicity of spaces—phenomenal and conceptual—whose extensions are variously defined, and whose limits are variously imposed, transgressed and reset."[58] The two most influential forces organizing space today are modern capitalist enterprises and modernizing nation-states. Asad maintains that these powers realize their dominance not through a discourse of homogeneity, but through a discourse of difference and mobility. The European impulse/sensibility is one of opportunistic improvisation: the ability to make a given situation work to their own advantage, using the available resources. "What is essential is the Europeans' ability again and again to insinuate themselves into the

---

55. Ibid., 16–17; emphasis added.
56. Ibid., 18.
57. Ibid.
58. Ibid., 8.

preexisting political, religious, even psychic structures of the natives and to turn those structures to their own advantage."⁵⁹ Asad exposes how this very sensibility operates (apparently uncritically) in liberal discourses of difference and displacement. He points out that the threatening aspects of mobility are not unfamiliar to Hannah Arendt. Arendt is

> . . . aware of a problem that has escaped the serious attention of those who would have us celebrate human agency and the decentered subject: the problem of understanding how dominant power realizes itself through the very discourse of mobility. For Arendt is very clear that mobility is not merely an event in itself, but a moment in the subsumption of one act by another. If people are physically and morally uprooted, they are more easily moved, and when they are easy to move, they are more easily rendered physically *and* morally superfluous.⁶⁰

Probably the clearest example of how the West authorizes space can be seen in Asad's discussion of the word "local" and its use in ethnography. "Local peoples" connote relatively cohesive groups who are not simply locatable; they are considered bound to their geographical space. Local people are limited, enclosed, and rooted. People who are not rooted in a local space are either displaced, marginalized, and dislocated, or they are thought to be sophisticated, international, and global.

> Thus, Saudi theologians who invoke the authority of medieval Islamic texts are taken to be local; Western writers who invoke the authority of modern secular literature claim they are universal. Yet both are located in universes that have rules of inclusion and exclusion. Immigrants who arrive from South Asia to settle in Britain are described as uprooted; English officials who lived in British India were not. An obvious difference between them is power: the former become subjects of the Crown, the latter its representatives.⁶¹

The authorization of space represented by this example highlights Asad's conviction that knowledge about local peoples is hardly ever "local knowledge." Asad remains suspect of anthropological representations that imply that such knowledge is "simply universal in the sense of being accessible."⁶²

---

59. Ibid., 11. Asad is quoting Greenblatt, *Renaissance Self-Fashioning*.
60. Asad, *Genealogies of Religion*, 11. See Arendt, *Origin of Totalitarianism*.
61. Asad, *Genealogies of Religion*, 8.
62. Ibid., 9.

Asad's postcolonial critique of Western hegemony raises important questions for the present practice of anthropology. Western notions of history, forged in the context of the Christian religion, imbue the present dominant forces of nation-state and international commerce with a teleological sensibility. The effect of these systems on non-Western peoples and cultures is not neutral, nor are the forces of resistance as significant as some analysts would lead us to believe. Western cultural communicators, including ethnographers, venture into pre-existing structures of other cultures, transforming peoples and places. The notion that ethnography is representative of other peoples fails to critically assess the tacit assumptions informing the science of anthropology as both a Western product and tool.[63]

Asad's critique engages fundamental suppositions surrounding the modernizing project, exposing implicit assumptions that continue to operate in postmodern ethnography.

> . . . the European wish to make the world in its own image is not necessarily to be disparaged as ungenerous. If one believes oneself to be the source of salvation, the wish to make others reflect oneself is not unbenign, however terrible the practices by which this desire is put into effect . . . . But the question I want to raise here is this: to the extent that such power seeks to normalize other people's motivations, whose history is being made? Note that my question is not about the authenticity of individual agency but about the structure of normal personhood (normal in both the statistical and the medical sense) and the techniques for securing it. I ask whether improvisation becomes irrelevant when the agents are non-Europeans acting within the context of their own politically independent state to implement a European project: the continuous physical and moral improvement of an entire governable population through flexible strategies. Whose improvised story do these agents construct? Who is its author, and who is its subject?[64]

Ethnography in a postcolonial world must come to fuller awareness regarding modernity: "its peculiar historicity [and] the mobile powers that have constructed its structures, projects and desires."[65]

63. Leaving the question of a common humanity open, Asad notes that older anthropological theories attempting to explain human diversity in the context of a single human nature ended up distinguishing the *truly* human from the *developing* human; yet another example of how dominant power rules by means of the practice of differentiation. Ibid., 21.

64. Ibid., 12.

65. Ibid., 24.

Asad's attention to the hegemonic function of Western culture highlights the thoroughly inculturated character of categories such as tradition and social identity. Instead of celebrating the resistant energies of subjugated peoples, Asad observes that identity, in current discourse, whether modernity's integrated self or postmodernity's constructed self, continues to serve Western dominance. Of particular interest is Asad's distinction between subject and agent and the way authorizing practices function in social identity.

### *Summary: Cultural Anthropology and the Present*

Clifford, Featherstone, and Asad offer insights into the complexity of the ethnographic task in the twenty-first century. The study of human cultures, once considered a rigorous yet fairly unified science of immersion into the otherness of exotic peoples, has unraveled under the scrutiny of postmodern and postcolonial critique. This dissembling impacts the study of culture, traditions, and human identity at a most basic level. Concepts of culture as a homogenous, unified, and continuous entity are no longer tenable. Global mobilization, as tourist or refugee, and the proliferation of mass media/technology compresses time and space, as multiple "dominant particulars" encounter each other on the global field. Whether this has been the case since the post-Reformation, as Featherstone would have us believe, or this is a continuation of modernity's usurpation of "the Rest" by the West's mobile powers, as Asad maintains, remains to be seen. Moreover, while Clifford can rightly claim that the radical situatedness of the ethnographer problematizes both the process and product of anthropological fieldwork, ethnographers are not alone in their status as participant observers. Identity, once a very clear and accessible notion, has been made strange by an important distanciation. Postcolonial and postmodern critiques expose the plural, often conflictual, forces simultaneously at work in the construction/construal of social identity. If, as Asad maintains, there are certain essentials to social identity, an enduring grammar that connotes historical identity, the ability to recognize this identity may be less about sameness of expression and more about the ability to perform within the boundaries of the cultural grammar. This being said, it must be stressed that this type of "local knowledge" may be far less accessible than has been previously thought.

## Towards Naming the Present: Theology

The postmodern context presents important challenges to Christian theology: decentralization, globalization, and fragmentation effectively undermine the intellectual framework that has served as the vehicle of Christian proclamation. Moreover, "the irruption of the poor"[66] onto the stage of history has unmasked the complicity of Western theological formulations with the status quo of oppressive social and political regimes. Christian theology experiences both moral and intellectual upheaval: the sure foundations of modern theological projects are jettisoned by postmodern critique, resulting in a range of responses from fundamentalism to *a*theology.

In order to draw out some of the distinctive threads comprising present theological discourse and their implications for a renewed understanding of Christian tradition, social identity, and change, the contributions of David Tracy, Roger Haight, and Robert Schreiter are considered. Each of these theologians maintains a commitment to the public role of theology; therefore, issues concerning epistemology, common humanity, and the plausibility of universal truth claims inform their theological projects. David Tracy's lucid analysis of the present, decentered moment highlights the significant values at stake for the various perspectives at play on the global horizon. Roger Haight's theological method offers an important contribution towards establishing what Karl Rahner saw as a critical task for post-Vatican II theology: the need to formulate the fundamental substance of the Christian message and the "formal criterion for deciding what really can and what really cannot belong primordially to a supernatural revelation."[67] Robert Schreiter's work on the effect of globalization on "context" in theology directs attention to the boundary between the global and the local where processes of identity formation are explored offering new possibilities and challenges. Each of these viewpoints, while certainly not exhaustive of the current theological landscape, helps to locate and amplify the questions surrounding the notion of tradition, identity, and change in Christianity.

---

66. "What we have called the 'major fact' in the life of the Latin American church—the participation of Christians in the process of liberation—is simply an expression of a far-reaching historical event: *the irruption of the poor*. Our time bears the imprint of the new presence of those who in fact used to be 'absent' from our society and from the church. By 'absent' I mean: of little or no importance, and without the opportunity to give expression themselves to their sufferings, their comraderies, their plans, their hopes." Gutierrez, *Theology of Liberation*, xx.

67. Rahner, "Fundamental Theological Interpretation," 725.

## David Tracy

David Tracy is known for his commitment to the public nature of theology, and argues his case by grounding theology in an "analogical imagination."[68] Through a method of *mutual critical correlation* Tracy brings the questions of the present situation into conversation with the Christian fact (tradition). Since the present situation offers answers as well as questions, Tracy's method explores and evaluates through critical correlation the questions and answers available within both the situation and the Christian tradition.[69] As a public theologian Tracy seeks to find the social-rational grounds for a conversation between theology and the polis. Recent moves in theology towards intratextuality by postliberal theologians foster the segregation of religion from the public domain, thereby undermining religion's transformative social role and relegating theology to "the reservations of the spirit."[70] Convinced that the truth claims of religion have a place in the public domain, Tracy engages critical social theory, social-political movements, and Western philosophical traditions in his active pursuit of securing the public role of theology.[71]

In *On Naming the Present* Tracy limns the current situation in Western society and theology. Describing the present moment as "polycentric," Tracy notes that few people have understood the impact of this decentering. "A fact seldom admitted by the moderns, the antimoderns, and the

---

68. Tracy, *Analogical Imagination*, 408–10. Tracy proposes an "analogical imagination" as similarity-in-difference, in contrast to a "dialectical imagination." Both analogical and dialectical languages have been used as "second-order, reflective language" in Christian theology (408). Tracy argues that true analogy, that which remains open to the negative moment, resisting "a relaxed univocity and a facilely affirmative harmony" is more adequate to the task of theology in a pluralistic world" (410).

69. For an excellent overview of David Tracy's thought, see Sanks, "David Tracy's Theological Project."

70. ". . . if one recalls the theological principles of Martin Luther King's struggle in the civil rights movement, one will realize how religious symbolic resources have in fact functioned as important factors in American society. Martin Luther King, through his personal appropriation of the symbolic resources of his religious and cultural heritages, was able to articulate, and to express in action, otherwise unnoticed and untapped ethical resources for the societal struggle for social justice. . . . It is difficult to envisage King or Niebuhr or Murray willingly accepting a privatization of religion. Indeed it is impossible. Yet it is all too possible to imagine many contemporary theologians eagerly moving to some local 'reservation of the spirit.' Less, obviously, perhaps, than those artists who accept their marginalized status in society, but no less fatally, theologians can also rest easily on the reservation." Tracy, *Analogical Imagination*, 13.

71. See in particular Tracy, "Theology, Critical Social Theory."

postmoderns alike—even with all the talk of otherness and difference—is that there is no longer *a* center with margins. There are many centers."[72]

There is a sense of disorientation in the present moment. Clear and distinct notions of identity and purpose are rare and, in the light of postmodern critique, suspect. The irruption of pluralism, experienced in the migrations of peoples displaced by violent conflict or relocated as a result of available work and opportunity, results in new mixings and combinations of peoples in social-cultural interactions. As the experience of difference escalates, coping strategies emerge.

> We live in an age that cannot name itself. For some, we are still in the age of modernity and the triumph of the bourgeois subject. For others, we are in a time of the leveling of all traditions and await the return of the repressed traditional and communal subject. For yet others, we are in a postmodern moment where the death of the subject is now upon us as the last receding wave of the death of God.[73]

With all evidence pointing only to increased diversification, Tracy attempts to name the present moment, which he believes is aptly described by Clifford Geertz as "an age where no one will leave anyone else alone—ever again."[74] Tracy characterizes the present situation from three different viewpoints: modern, antimodern, and postmodern.

> For *modernity*, the present is more of the same—the same evolutionary history of the triumph and taken-for-granted superiority of Western scientific, technological, pluralistic and democratic Enlightenment. For *antimodernity*, the present is a "time of troubles"—a time when all traditions are being destroyed by the inexorable force of that same modernity. . . . For *postmodernity*, modernity and tradition alike are now exposed as self-deceiving exercises attempting to ground what cannot be grounded: a secure foundation for all knowledge and life.[75]

---

72. Tracy, *On Naming*, 4. Tracy engages modernity and the rational debate, particularly as it has evolved in the works of Jurgen Habermas. Tracy critically appropriates the thinking of Habermas, noting that theologians interested in engaging in public theology with a method of correlation can learn much from critical theory, particularly, "a critical *social* theory where 'rationality' and 'modernity' are analyzed together and where the materialist and intellectual links between the two categories are clarified." Tracy, "Theology, Critical Social Theory," 21.

73. Tracy, *On Naming*, 3.

74. Tracy, "Theology, Critical Social Theory," 25.

75. Tracy, *On Naming*, 3.

## Tracy on Moderns

For Tracy, the tragedy of modernity is the impoverishment of reason. Reason, evacuated of its promised Enlightenment, surrendered its "communicative, emancipatory role to a merely technical reason in a culture increasingly dominated by techno-economic concerns."[76] Tracy finds Habermas' theory of communicative action an important contribution to the debate on rationality because, unlike positivism, Habermas situates his work in both a historical and social theory of modernity. Positivism, inherently ahistorical, "is intellectually a spent force"; yet it exerts "culturally as powerful a force as ever."[77] The fallacy of positivism is the reduction of reason.

> Where positivism reigns, history is empty of real time and becomes at best a bad infinity: an infinity of more of the same. The sameness is clear: only science (understood positivistically) can count for inquiry; reason is reduced to a purely technical function; technology continues with neither direction nor hope as its genuine liberating possibilities are mixed, without reflection, into a dominating and leveling power over all.[78]

The hope of rational communication between reasoning persons in the public domain where questions of human well-being are meaningfully engaged is undermined by the mutation of cultural classics into consumable goods. Yet, there is much about the project of modernity that needs to be defended: reason as a basis of communication; true political democracy; radical cultural pluralism (a la William James).[79] At the same time, the critique of modernity must dismantle the myth of progress and embrace a new, concrete view of history: the concrete struggle of persons and societies, history as interruption.

Modern, liberal theology contributed greatly to significant questions surrounding questions of finitude, anxiety, and death. Yet, Tracy notes, the proposed answers must "become explicitly historical and political" to be credible in the current moment.

> Their [modern theology] accomplishments are real and retrievable, especially in the personal realm. But can personalism conquer in a culture ridden with possessive individualism? Can Christian hope

---

76. Ibid., 8.
77. Ibid., 7.
78. Ibid.
79. Ibid.

be reduced to the ahistorical individual of modernity? Can reason be understood outside its historical, cultural, and social context? Can resistance be active if the empty time of modernity relentlessly invades all consciousness to render all consolation merely private?[80]

Tracy challenges modern sensibilities to new understandings of subjectivity and history. The autonomous self is sheer illusion, as is an easy modern universalism devoid of true time. "We need a new theological understanding of both self and the present time again. We need historical subjects with memory, hope and resistance."[81]

## Tracy on Antimoderns

In sharp contrast to the modern sensibility are the *antimoderns,* characterized as those who react against the modern program of Enlightenment rationality that reduces all traditions to myth and symbolic reserves to economic choices. "For the antimoderns, ours is a time to retreat to a past that never was and a tradition whose presumed purity belies the very meaning of tradition as concrete and ambiguous history."[82] Antimoderns recognize the vacuous nature of the modern project and its attempts to level all traditions and claims to authority. Communities, denied of their symbolic resources, are left vulnerable to the onslaught of a consumer culture and the logic of a market economy that knows no bounds. Antimodern responses to the present situation are a clear indication that the once perceived antiquated and childish adherence to traditions is now a formidable reaction to the meaningless void created by modernism. The rise in fundamentalisms throughout the world religions, as well as the development of a neoconservative (postliberal) response in theology, manifests this antimodern resistance. Rather than asking how this is possible in a "modern" world, Tracy maintains that

> . . . the more reasonable question is how could this not happen in a time where there is no true time and to subjects deprived of their traditions of memory and hope? Human beings cannot but ask the limit-questions that religious traditions pose and respond to. The human demand for personal and historical meaning will not so easily be pushed aside."[83]

80. Ibid., 10.
81. Ibid., 11.
82. Ibid., 3.
83. Ibid., 11–12.

There is a quirky twist in this fundamentalist reaction. While all the values of modernity are rejected, the products of modernity are completely embraced. Thus fundamentalists have no conflict of conscience in the use of technological and industrial means to forward their worldview. But they are adamant in their religious rejection of any of the "ethical and political values of modernity (individual rights, pluralism, a democratic ethos, a trust in public reason)."[84]

> The power of fundamentalism in our day should teach the rest of us at least this much: on the one hand the human demand for historical significance and personal meaning will not be put off as easily as modernity, with its deadening social-evolutionary teleology, assumed; on the other hand, there are values in the modern experiment which all non-fundamentalists should deliberately defend: the value of the rights of the individual, the freedoms of press, religion, assembly, and representation won by the great bourgeois revolutions: the affirmation of scientific inquiry without scientism; the demand to reflect critically on technology rather than mindlessly embracing it; the affirmation of pluralism and dialogue; the defense of a public realm; a trust in democratic processes.[85]

Another response to modernity that Tracy locates with the antimoderns is the postliberal movement in current theology. Representatives of this constellation of the theological reflection include George Lindbeck, Hans Frei, and Stanley Hauerwas. Postliberal theologians adopt a line of thinking from the later Wittgenstein and develop a cultural-linguistic model for theological reflection. Postliberals understand Christianity to be one of many life forms with its own narrative and language rules. Any attempt at correlating the Christian language game with other language games (philosophical, cultural) threatens to compromise the integrity of theological claims made by the community. For postliberal theologians theology does not have a public, apologetic role; theology does not function to explain the reasonableness of Christian truth claims. Christian truth claims are publicly available only as witness: for those who have the eyes to see and the ears to hear.

> How, as modern Christians often put it, does one preach the gospel in a dechristianized world? . . . The postliberal method of dealing with this problem is bound to be unpopular among those chiefly

---

84. Ibid., 12.
85. Ibid.

concerned to maintain or increase the membership and influence of the church. This method resembles ancient catechesis more than modern translation. Instead of redescribing the faith in new concepts, it seeks to teach the language and practices of the religion to potential adherents. This has been the primary way of transmitting the faith and winning converts for most religions down through the centuries. In the early days of the Christian church, for example, it was the gnostics, not the catholics, who were most inclined to redescribe the biblical materials in a new interpretative framework. Pagan converts to the catholic mainstream did not, for the most part, first understand the faith and then decide to become Christians; rather, the process was reversed: they first decided and then they understood. More precisely, they were first attracted by the Christian community and form of life.[86]

There is much that recommends the postliberal project in theology.[87] Clearly, the focus on the biblical narrative as a source of Christian identity, and the expression of Christianity as a visible life form with specific practices, contributes towards the revivification of symbolic sources of tradition and community so necessary for communal life. But, as Tracy notes, the postliberal retrieval of the tradition is partial and, as such, threatens the very reality it seeks to revive and sustain. Our histories and our traditions are not neutral; moreover, they are implicated. In a post-Holocaust world there can be no claims for or flight to a guiltless tradition. If Christianity is to be faithful to its original grace, it will have to divest itself from its triumphalist trappings and embrace a renewed self-understanding, disabused of notions of an innocent past.

> For the memory of the Christian is, above all, the memory of the passion and resurrection of the Jesus Christ. It is the dangerous memory (Metz) which is most dangerous for all those who presume to make his memory their own. And that memory releases the theological knowledge that there is no innocent tradition, no innocent classic, no innocent reading. That memory releases the moral insistence that the memory of the suffering of the oppressed—oppressed often by the church which now claims them as its own—is the great Christian countermemory to all tales of

---

86. Lindbeck, *Nature of Doctrine*, 132.

87. ". . . the neoconservative sees through the emptiness of the present and the poverty of the modern subject. The neoconservative knows that a present without a past memory and tradition is self-illusory and self-destructive." Tracy, *On Naming*, 13.

triumph.... Christianity is always a memory that turns as fiercely against itself as against other pretensions to triumph.[88]

## Tracy on Postmoderns

Postmodern critique engages modernity and challenges its secure foundations of knowledge and power. Postmodernism unveils the fallacy of first principles in philosophical reflection and exposes the power relations that saturate all epistemological claims. Modernity's facile universal claims are deconstructed and laid bare as the dominant particular of the West.

Postmodernism's greatest achievement is the deconstruction of the modern self.

> As the postmoderns make clear, however, the modern self, unfortunately for its foundationalist pretensions, must also use language. And the very self-deconstructing, non-grounding play of the signifiers in all languages will assure that no signified—especially the great modern signified, the modern subject—will ever find the pure identity, the clear and distinct self-presence it seeks or the totality it grasps at. That self-grounding, self-present modern subject is dead: killed by its own pretensions to grounding all reality in itself.[89]

Postmoderns "offend" modern sensibilities by calling forth the repressed and suppressed voices of the other, disturbing the self-assured sameness of moderns. Through strategies of resistance, postmoderns act via disassembling. "Otherness, difference, and excess become the alternatives to the deadening sameness, the totalizing system, the false security of the modern self-grounding subject."[90] Postmodern energies are driven toward decomposition. The logic of their argument undermines reconstruction. At the outer limits of postmodern critique are the death of philosophy and subsequently the impossibility of shared rationality, a view favored by the proponents of the "new historicism." J. Wentzel van Huyssteen notes,

> The denial by the new historicists of any reality beyond the contingencies of history thus logically implies the rejection of foundationalism, realism, and of the transcendentalized subject: the self is capable of experiencing only that which can be experienced within historical space and time. It can know neither foundations tran-

---

88. Ibid., 14–15.
89. Ibid., 16.
90. Ibid.

scending history, nor realities that can be known objectively, nor universal subjective structures inherent in all persons.[91]

Tracy finds the postmodern desire to "deconstruct the *status quo* in favor of the *fluxus quo*" problematic in that the strategy of resistance hailed in postmodern critique is not possible without an agent of resistance.[92] Tracy maintains that concrete agents of resistance are found in the communities and individuals engaged in conflict with oppression and marginalization. The truly *other* has yet to be approached by postmoderns: indigenous, subjugated peoples, the poor and oppressed, other world religions and cultures, and "the terrifying otherness lurking in our own psyches and cultures."[93] In the otherness of death-dealing poverty lie the resources of memory and hope.

> Those others, especially the poor and oppressed in all cultures, now speak, unlike the postmoderns, as historical subjects of both resistance and hope. They insist that the future as both promise and judgment must interrupt all presentness even beyond the postmodern exposures of the false sense of the presence of modernity.[94]

The emergence of a "new historical subject in the Western center" will only be possible through solidarity with "the concrete other and the different in all the other centers."[95]

Western theology—modern, antimodern, and postmodern—remains narrow and insulated, removed from the predicaments of those who suffer. The interruptive memory of the poor and oppressed manifests difference that elicits an ethical-religious response. "These are the concrete others whose difference should make a difference. For through them the full and interruptive memory of the gospel is alive again among us."[96]

Tracy's analysis of the present polycentric moment has important implications for a revised understanding of Christian tradition and its relationship to ecclesial identity in changing times. If Western Christian tradition is to escape its present monologue and enter into meaningful conversation with the other as concrete historical subjects, there will have to be significant shifts in modern, antimodern, and postmodern affinities. Moderns

91. Van Huyssteen, *Shaping of Rationality*, 65–66.
92. Tracy, *On Naming*, 16.
93. Ibid., 4.
94. Ibid., 17.
95. Ibid., 21.
96. Ibid.

will have to surrender their elitist epistemological claims and acknowledge a variety of modes of reason, conversation, and praxis, thus expanding the boundaries of consultable traditions. Antimoderns must become disabused of their all-too-innocent reading of tradition and relinquish claims of possessing an identity they continue to seek in the retrieval of tradition, memory, and practice. Finally, postmoderns will move from conversation about difference to solidarity with the concretely different: the poor and oppressed, acknowledging the role that traditions play in funding social identity in oppressive and life-threatening contexts.[97] "The true present is the present of all historical subjects in all the centers in conversation and solidarity before the living God. The rest is whistling in the dark."[98]

## *Roger Haight*

> Theology is a pluralistic discipline. There are many different theologies in terms of content; all Christian theologians are not saying the same thing. But the pluralism extends much further than content, for there is no common agreement on the method of theology.[99]

Roman Catholic theology since the early 1960s has experienced a "crisis of method." With the advent of new voices, particularly those from the underside of history, and the intentional opening of the Roman Catholic Church to the modern world, the theological enterprise became exceedingly complex and conflictual. Feminist and liberation theologians championed new points of entry for theology. Questions surrounding biblical studies and interpretations generated renewed interest in the nature of revelation and its relationship to faith. Comfortable and familiar interpretations of Catholic faith, particularly in relation to authoritative teaching, became suspect and even implausible.

For Roger Haight, the present context offers both crisis and opportunity for Christian theologians. Haight explores the implications of historical criticism on the Christian tradition, arguing in *Dynamics of Theology* for a methodological framework adequate to the task of theology today.

---

97. Ibid.
98. Ibid., 22.
99. Haight, *Dynamics of Theology*, 169.

## Four Loci of Theological Method

Haight anchors his theology methodologically in four loci: faith, revelation, scripture, and the symbolic nature of theological language. Fundamentally, his theology is rooted in the human experience of revelation: mediated religious experience with transcendental reality. In this sense, religious experience cannot be construed as only human; it is a mediated experience of the divine. This encounter does not give information about God; it is an experience of/encounter with God. The very nature of revelation therefore demands interpretation and reinterpretation. The *experience* of revelation is transhistorical and transcultural but the interpretations of revelation are profoundly embedded in history and culture.[100]

Theological formulations, never immutable, are historical and cultural construals of religious experience. Their intelligibility is determined by their context. Revelation, itself, is not cognitive. To "know" the object of faith is to undermine the very reality of faith, which according to Haight "is a universal human phenomenon."[101] Faith is intrinsically related to human freedom, which is so much more than the freedom to choose; it is a defining characteristic of the human being.

The phenomenology of human existence reveals the universal human dynamism towards being. Action is directed human quest for new being: in action, humans are drawn toward being and resist non-being. It is precisely experiences that threaten human existence that show, by negative contrast, the human quest for being. Ultimately, human resistance to such experiences affirms that "no finite object, no coherent set of inner-worldly values, can supply what is demanded by the logic of human action, for this can only be infinite and absolute being."[102] Faith is constitutive of the human because, despite the absence of an object appropriate to action's inner logic, human beings still make choices. Values, meaning systems, and truths are accepted and embraced because they provide an integrating unity and order human existence. These cohesive elements in culture function as objects of faith, "because faith is the clinging commitment to those objects, truths and values which give meaning to human existence at its most fundamental level."[103] According to Haight, the ultimate question is not an affirmation or negation of faith; the ultimate question is

---

100. Ibid., 68–89.
101. Ibid., 15.
102. Ibid., 17.
103. Ibid., 18.

"*which* faith to choose."[104] Thus, although faith and revelation are not forms of knowledge, they do have cognitive dimensions: "by an existential faith and an engaged participation one encounters transcendent reality as given, as present."[105]

Revelation, as encounter of transcendent reality, is always a mediated, symbolic encounter. Religious symbols are both finite and disclosive. They are particular, limited, and culturally framed expressions that simultaneously invite participation and, ultimately, transformation. "A religious symbol is anything finite that discloses and points to what is other than itself and strictly transcendent, but which at the same time makes that transcendent other present by participation in it."[106] A symbol is never just a symbol for Haight. "As Tillich says, symbolic truth is not less but more than literal truth."[107] When theological construals are reduced from symbols to signs, God language suffers irreparable damage. The very presence of this danger highlights the *dialogical* and *dialectical* character of theological discourse. Theology, today, must give an account of itself, and in this sense theology is apologetic. Because all God language is historically and culturally framed, theological formulations, as confessional expressions, must effectively communicate their relevance to present historical moment.[108]

For Christian theologians the question of how to "interpret or reinterpret reality on the basis of the received symbols of the past" poses a fundamental task of theology.[109] Since theology today is necessarily a pluralistic enterprise, there are vast and growing differences in both theological content and method. How is it possible to maintain that such a vast array of viewpoints authentically interpret the original revelation? Haight suggests that the situation calls for a new way of thinking about theological method. Those who reject the task of reinterpretation of past symbols, doggedly holding to a revelational positivism, cannot offer an intelligible account of Christian faith. Neither can those who through a radical liberalism reduce theology to anthropology. Both of these options fail to adequately account for Christian faith and must be rejected. The plural nature of human life requires that theologians abandon the search for a single adequate method

---

104. Ibid.; emphasis added.
105. Haight, *Jesus*, 10.
106. Ibid., 134.
107. Ibid., 144.
108. Ibid., 2.
109. Ibid., 169.

or school of thought in theology and work to define adequate guiding principles that can direct the work of theology in various, divergent contexts. Haight, therefore, develops "principles . . . general enough to be inclusive of a variety of methods in theology, yet specific enough to provide guidelines that may be directive in the concrete task of theology."[110]

## Hermeneutics and the Religious Tradition

Because Christianity is a religion of tradition, hermeneutics must play a critical role in its theological methods. Christian theologians have a double loyalty: to the past expressions and to the present interpretation of Christian faith. Moreover, in our pluralistic context, theologians must explain how it is possible to say different things and still be in continuity with the original revelation. Given this, Haight argues for the necessity and the possibility of interpretation. He then explores the structure and goal of interpretation. Interpretation of past religious symbols is necessary because the mere repetition of past formulas and meanings in new situations constitutes a reformulation that "interprets and changes their meaning."[111]

> The necessity of ongoing reinterpretation stems from the way human existence is bound to the world, the concrete, material and historical world, for all of its knowledge. It is this contextuality of all human knowing that grounds the historicity of all linguistic expression and construal of meaning that in turn gives rise to historical consciousness. . . . This inevitably entails that new meaning is always being extracted from the symbols of the past and added to them by the very fact of their being received in and adjusted to new conditions.[112]

As the community moves through history, new situations pull new meanings from traditional symbols. Moreover, growth in social awareness can offer critical assessment of previous formulations exposing past and present complicity in systems of oppression. Failure to engage in this critical assessment threatens to jeopardize the community's fidelity to the original revelation. This raises the question of the actual possibility of interpretation. Can fidelity to an original revelation be maintained over centuries of time and across boundaries of diverse cultures? How is it possible to "explain how new and different interpretations of Christianity can also preserve the

110. Ibid., 170.
111. Ibid., 171.
112. Ibid.

intrinsic meaning of original revelation"?[113] Haight argues that despite the doubts of cultural anthropologists and historians, "one must affirm the possibility of human communication universally across whatever cultural differences. It is possible because in fact it happens however infrequently."[114] The acknowledgement of this fact is foundational to Haight's hermeneutical theory. It is the basis for asserting that humans can communicate across time and space. The possibility of interpretation of religious symbols demands that the interpreter have a capacity to experience transcendence. "[T]he interpreter experiences today, now, the reality which the symbol mediates."[115] Interpreters bring both their immediate social, historical context and "some prior experience and understanding of the transcendent meaning and content of the symbols he or she interprets. This derives of course mainly from membership in the tradition."[116] Thus the reality mediated by past symbols can be and is made available to the present. In this sense, Christians can claim continuity in religious experience. But this continuity is always a "sameness-in-difference," mediated by the dialectical nature of symbols.

> The key to the issue of sameness and difference in the reinterpretation of traditional symbols lies in the dialectical structure of symbols themselves. This dialectical structure must be understood in terms of a dynamic process of communication. The symbol is not the thing symbolized, for that is transcendent and other. Yet the symbol makes present and mediates the transcendent which is encountered in religious experience. The element of sameness cannot be reduced to any objective formula. Its content in the end must reside in existential experience, an encounter which transcends every linguistic symbolic formula, and thus is open to be expressed in a plurality of symbolic formulas.[117]

Fidelity of interpretation is never simply a fidelity to past expressions of faith. The new interpretation must authentically represent an experience of the transcendent in connection to traditional symbols since "they are the data for reinterpretation."[118]

Haight maintains that interpretation is dialogical in process and dialectical in structure. As a dialogical process, interpretation starts with the

---

113. Ibid., 175.
114. Ibid., 176.
115. Ibid., 177.
116. Ibid.
117. Ibid., 178.
118. Ibid.

subject matter of religious interpretation, which is nothing less than "reality itself." Haight notes that fundamentalists make the mistake of believing that "truth lies in the symbols themselves, on pieces of paper, in texts, in revealed propositions, in beliefs masquerading as faith." But the subject of religious interpretation is truth, "an existential category; truth is the quality of the way human subjectivity relates to reality, that is, in a way that corresponds to the way reality is."[119] In a dialogical process, interpretation of the really real is thematized by a guiding question. In theological reflection these questions arise from the situation and history of the interpreter. Dialogue is characterized as a give-and-take between respondents. The interpreter therefore needs to attend to historical and exegetical studies when attempting to interpret religious symbols. Critical analysis of symbols challenges interpreters to be faithful to the past in a manner that respects the nature of the symbol: symbols do not explain, they mediate the transcendent.

> Like parables they are meant to disclose a transcendent reality which, because it is transcendent, cannot be reduced to historical reality in the terms of cause and effect. The symbol is not the symbolized; a symbol mediates something else other than itself. To understand a religious symbol as an historical narrative robs it of its symbolic and transcendent value.[120]

The dialogical aspect of interpretation is particularly evident in the fact that all interpreters are subject to their own unique history, culture and social world. This is critical to Haight's understanding of the task of theology. The interpretation of the subject matter of religious symbols (the really real) is, in the end, determined by the present context.

> The issue of final meaningfulness and truth mediated by the symbols cannot be determined by past testimony; it can only be finally interpreted and judged now and in the context of the horizon of today's consciousness.[121]

The dialogical process underscores interpretation as theoretical act and concrete expression. Reinterpretation has a dialectical structure that simultaneously asserts sameness and difference, old and new, continuity and change. It is not possible to claim that original symbols and their

---

119. Ibid., 181.
120. Ibid., 183–84.
121. Ibid., 184–85.

reinterpreted expressions are exactly the same; neither is it possible to claim that they are essentially disparate expressions. Religious symbols and their reinterpretations are caught in a dialogical dialectic of sameness-indifference. They are similar to the extent that they mediate an encounter with transcendent reality; they are different at a thematic level "because *conceptual understanding is precisely that which is changed in reinterpretation.*" When the dialectical structure of interpreted religious symbols is ignored the communicative vitality of the symbols are reduced to either religious fundamentalism or mere anthropology.[122] The inherently revelatory function of the symbol is undermined, flattened and evacuated of is transformative potential.

The interpretation of Christian religious symbols requires attentiveness to their intentionality. Religious symbols draw individuals and communities into experiences of transcendence: they both communicate encounters with transcendent reality and inform all other knowledge about the world. In this sense, religious symbols are transformative, not informative. "The goal of interpretation then is to unlock that which is symbolized from the past and to release it into present-day consciousness."[123] When this happens, the community experiences new possibilities and empowerment in the context of ever changing historical situations. The goal of interpretation is the communication of transcendent reality through religious symbols whose meanings are not exhausted. In new contexts, religious symbols function by creating new meanings, new interpretations of transcendent reality.

### Three Guiding Criteria for Theology

In the light of this understanding of the hermeneutics of religious symbols, Haight suggests three criteria for guiding the task of theology in a pluralistic milieu. "Interpretation must be faithful, intelligible and empowering."[124] The task of theology requires that theologians faithfully engage the Christian tradition, mining past symbols for their transformative potential in the present moment. The resulting interpretation of the Christian symbol system must be intelligible within the current context. Moreover, the interpretation must not simply make sense, it must empower Christian discipleship, moving the membership towards active conversion. These three

---

122. Ibid., 185–86; emphasis added.
123. Ibid., 187.
124. Ibid., 188.

criteria offer general guiding principles towards deciding "what really can and what really cannot belong primordially to a supernatural revelation"[125] within the context of radical pluralism.

The hermeneutical task, reinterpreting tradition in new situations, has consequences for social identity and change. As new relationships within the symbol system are explored, pressed by questions and concerns of ultimacy, old configurations and the social identities they fostered may lose significance, creating a sense of loss. However, as Haight has argued, if the hermeneutical task is not engaged there is equal danger that the implausibility of older symbolic construals will undermine the Christian community's transformative witness. The risk of tradition cannot be avoided. In the final section, Robert Schreiter's work on globalization, ecclesial identities, and traditions will expose the depth of risk involved as Christianity moves from a European church to a world church.

## *Robert Schreiter*

Robert Schreiter contends that the most significant issue facing theology today is not theology's conversation with postmodernity, but its engagement of globalization. In *The New Catholicity*, Schreiter explores various currents in contemporary cultural and theological discourses and shows how globalization forms, deforms, and re-forms the multiple contexts of theology.

With the advent of Vatican II, renewed interest in the local church refocused ecclesiological studies and exposed the universalizing impact of dominant Western theologies. Western theologies failed to recognize the contextual character of their gospel reflections: the embedded character of their theology within a particular social and cultural matrix.[126] Western theologies were simply local theologies carried into new contexts in much the same manner that Western exports made their way beyond the perimeters of Europe and North America.[127] Schreiter maintains that "Christian theology itself might be seen as a series of local theologies."[128]

---

125. Rahner, "Fundamental Theological Interpretation," 725.

126. Schreiter, *New Catholicity*, 2.

127. Karl Rahner noted that prior to Vatican II "the actual concrete activity of the Church in its relation to the world outside of Europe was in fact (if you will pardon the expression) the activity of an export firm which exported a European religion as a commodity it did not really want to change but sent throughout the world together with the rest of culture and civilization it considered superior." Rahner, "Fundamental Theological Interpretation," 717.

128. Schreiter, *New Catholicity*, 2.

In response to the inadequacies of Western theologies, two significant types of local theologies emerged: contextual and liberation theologies. Although much links these two forms of theology, they are marked by significant difference in focus. Contextual theologies tend to emphasize cultural identity, while liberation theologies emphasize the need for social reform.[129] Yet, whether engaged in cultural analysis to recover identities violated by colonization or engaged in social analysis to transform oppressive social structures, both contextual and liberation theologies have been limited by modern analytical methods based on uncritical notions of subject, agency, and gender.[130] This inadequacy is further complicated by globalization and the new critical attention that the whole notion of context is now receiving. Schreiter maintains that globalization changes the notion of context in three ways: contexts are now *deterritorialized*, *hyperdifferentiated*, and *hybridized*.[131] Contexts are less circumscribed by geographical boundaries than by "boundaries of difference."

> A boundary of difference highlights issues of difference rather than elements of commonality as the basis for identity. In places where identities are contested, and in situations of ethnogenesis, boundaries of difference can indicate what elements of identity will play key roles in the construction of a theology. One frequently sees this in early stages of a new contextual theology: certain elements of difference are given more salience than will be the case later on in the development of that theology.[132]

Contexts are hyperdifferentiated such that the experience of compression of time/space and the mixing of diverse peoples creates new networks of relationships. Thus, people participate in a variety of social and cultural contexts, resulting in the phenomenon of multiple belonging. "Multiple

---

129. Ibid., 117.

130. With the exception of some feminist theologies.

131. Schreiter, *New Catholicity*, 26; emphasis added. Because of globalizing processes today, what constitutes the contexts of theology is also changing. The compression of time and space means that territory becomes in many instances a less useful organizing concept than in the past. Boundaries of territory are replaced by boundaries of difference. The intensity of intercultural contact not only heightens the sense of difference, but also leads to a greater need to differentiate, to account for difference. Those differentiations then combine and recombine in processes of hybridization. All of this is to say that context and culture are made exceeding complex as people experience belonging in multiple contexts (or conversely, not belonging anywhere), and find themselves struggling to negotiate their place in the world. See ibid., 46.

132. Ibid., 26.

belonging is behind the discourse of 'multiculturalism,' in which people struggle to find a way of dealing with a variety of cultures, or fragments of cultures, occupying the same space."[133]

Finally, cultural contexts are (and probably always were) hybridized. This realization exposes the predominance of an integrated concept of culture within modern studies of social life and interaction. The idea of culture as whole and integrated still informs much of theology's dialogue with the social sciences; globalization demands that this notion be re-examined. "The purity of culture was probably always more an aspiration than a reality, but in a globalized world it becomes increasingly untenable as a concept."[134]

Before exploring further Schreiter's understanding of globalization's effect on religious identity and traditions, it is important to describe in more detail his view of globalization.

SCHREITER ON GLOBALIZATION

Schreiter characterizes globalization as "the increasingly interconnected character of the political, economic, and social life of the peoples on this planet."[135] Differing somewhat from M. Featherstone, Schreiter maintains that, although the seeds of globalization were present throughout the process of colonization, "there are distinct differences in its late twentieth-century manifestation."[136] Three factors contribute to this distinctiveness: the political shift from a bipolar to a multipolar world; the economic collapse of socialism, resulting in a single world economy: neocapitalism; and the network advancement of communications technologies.[137]

> The convergence of these three phenomena—a multipolar world, global capitalism, and communications technologies—creates what is known as globalization. In defining globalization, I would like to draw upon the reflections of two sociologists, who have reflected not only on globalization, but on the role of religion within globalization as well: Roland Robertson and Peter Beyer. Globalization, as defined here, is the extension of the effects of modernity to the

133. Ibid.
134. Ibid., 27.
135. Ibid., 5.
136. Ibid.
137. Ibid., 5–8.

> entire world, and the compression of time and space, all occurring at the same time.[138]

Schreiter describes globalization as both extension and compression, yet globalization as an extension of modernity "is not simply the imperial reach of the West in a new guise."[139] The globalization process creates plural forms of modernity: global modernities.[140]

As noted earlier, globalization stimulates the multiplication of boundaries both geographical and conceptual. The compression of time and space, "symbolized in the computer chip," facilitates the flow of information, goods, and peoples at an increasingly rapid pace.[141] Compression simultaneously blurs boundaries while establishing new lines of networked relationships. "If boundaries play an important role in the semiotics of identity by helping us define who we are by who we are not, they are now so crisscrossed by globalization processes that they seem to have lost their identity-conferring power."[142]

But it is the space between the global and the local that is most appealing to Schreiter. Adopting Roland Robertson's term "glocal," Schreiter asserts that the theological implications of globalization are most accessible at the interstices where the global meets the local.

> Neither the global, homogenizing forces nor the local forms of accommodation and resistance can of themselves provide an adequate explanation of these phenomena. It is precisely in their interaction that one comes to understand what is happening.[143]

Globalization provides the most salient framework for theology; more so than postmodernism. Schreiter posits that one way of accounting for the appearance of postmodernisms is the *experience of risk* that pervades

---

138. Ibid., 8.

139. Ibid., 11.

140. "This is particularly evident in Asia. In Japan, for instance, modernization has brought not secularization so much as new religions, the latest wave of which address personal therapeutic needs. Modernity introduced into China seems to help spur a revival of Christianity and to some extent Islam, although other internal factors of China's immediate past history must also be taken into account. Such a creation of modernities would be consistent with other forms of production in the globalization process: plural forms that resemble one another yet are embedded in and reflect local cultures." Ibid.

141. Ibid.

142. Ibid.

143. Ibid., 12.

Western sensibilities: risk born of " a process of reflexivity" that "curves back upon the West."[144]

> This is most evident in the influx of former colonial people into Britain, France and Portugal, creating multicultural societies in previously monocultural situations. But what reflexivity brings as well is a sense of contingency or risk that has long been the experience of countries on the periphery. The risks . . . create a profound sense of unease and contingency in lives that modernity had promised to insulate from such vulnerabilities.[145]

With master narratives undermined, globalization offering progress without a *telos*,[146] and technical reason failing to offset a pervasive sense of anxiety, the stage is set for the emergence of various forms of postmodernism.[147]

> It may express itself in an anarchism that denies all value, or in a burrowing into a specific community or way of life as an enclave providing insulation against the contingencies one faces. Or, in the flood of information, it may seek the authoritarian ways of a guru who appears to be able to make the whole thing stop.[148]

Thus, postmodernism is less a viable framework for the task of theology and more expressive of particular, local responses to globalization. Furthermore, it is vital "not just to account for postmodern theologies as forms of contextual theology found in the West, but also to situate them within the larger situation of what is happening to context in the world today."[149]

---

144. Ibid., 13.
145. Ibid.
146. "The values that drive global systems are matched by ideals that are held up to those who encounter these global systems. Beyer identifies these ideals as progress, equality, and inclusion. As with values, these ideals have two faces. Progress (as with value, innovation) connotes improvement, but change in itself does not mean betterment. Equality is an important Enlightenment ideal for all of those who have suffered from a hierarchical society. But equality must be more than an abstract ideal. . . . Inclusion touches on the deepest human yearnings for belonging. But if inclusion means a complete erasure of difference, does it still remain an ideal? What all this points to is that neither values nor ideals lead to a better society in and of themselves. Larger questions about the goals or *telos* of society must be answered." Ibid., 10.
147. Ibid., 13.
148. Ibid.
149. Ibid.

According to Schreiter, religion does not function as a *global system* in the way that science, economics, or education does.[150] Global systems, as characterized by Peter Beyer, share certain commonalities and are propelled by *values* (innovation, efficiency, technical reason) and by *ideals* (progress, equality, inclusion).[151] While world religions may share some of these principles, they certainly do not embrace all of them, and in fact, reject outright some of these values and ideals. According to Beyer, religion functions not as a global system, but as "antisystemic global movements."[152]

> In its antisystemic action, religion engages in what Beyer calls "religious performances," i.e., providing religious answers to problems created by global systems. In so doing, religion as an antisystemic movement can provide a *telos* that a global system lacks, offering a vision of coherence and order.[153]

Extending Beyer's concept, Schreiter borrows the phrase *global theological flows*, which "are religious discourses that while not uniform, or systemic, represent a series of linked, mutually intelligible discourses that address the contradictions or failures of global systems."[154] As mobile discourses, global theological flows travel from their particular cultural context and, through the function of mutual intelligibility, they are received and adapted according to specific challenges within other cultural contexts. Schreiter names four possible global theological flows: theologies of liberation, feminist theologies, theologies of ecology, and theologies of human rights. He notes that the "ubiquity" of these flows may make them the most likely candidates for "new 'universal' theologies."[155]

> They are universal theologies in their ubiquity and in their addressing of universal, systemic problems affecting nearly everyone in the world. Each is rooted in its own context, but these four flows enjoy a mutual intelligibility within their discourses and to a great extent even among them. As we look for new models of

---

150. Ibid., 14.
151. Ibid., 9–10. See also Beyer, *Religion and Globalization*.
152. Schreiter, *New Catholicity*, 16.
153. Ibid.
154. Ibid. "They are theological discourse, that is, they speak out of the realm of religious beliefs and practices. They are not uniform or systemic, because of their commitment to specific cultural and social settings that are experiencing the same failure of global systems and who are raising the same kind of protest."
155. Ibid., 20.

universality that are not simply the extension of one culture or one rationality (however excellent or commendable these may be), it is worth attending to these global theological flows as possible ways of articulating the universal.[156]

The particularity of global flows remains significant. Local contexts are not simply passive when faced with the powers of globalization. Jonathan Friedman notes that local cultures exert forces that he terms "cultural logics."[157] Adapting this notion, Schreiter names three strategies that represent kinds of cultural logics functioning in theology: antiglobalism, ethnification, and primitivism.[158] Antiglobalism aggressively strikes out to establish boundaries against "the onslaught of globalizing forces."[159] Ethnification, a creative identity-constructive activity, employs selective memory towards establishing lost identity "amid the experience of social change and cultural instability."[160] Primitivism is also a constructive activity in which a hallowed past is recovered as a compass "to find a frame of reference and meaning in order to engage the present."[161] Each of these three cultural logics represents theological strategies for coping with the challenges of globalization.

Schreiter's perspective on globalization highlights the importance of the boundary space between the global and local. Global theological flows, emerging from particular contexts, travel into new situations where the discourse encounters sameness and difference, reception and resistance. The "glocal" perspective offers significant data towards both the possibility of intercultural communications and the incommensurability of cultures. The complexity of the process by which messages are received and adapted follows below as Schreiter's understanding of syncretism and synthesis is explored.

## Religious Identity and Globalization

Schreiter gives extended attention to the complexities of religious identity in a globalized context. As a theologian Schreiter has dual loyalties: the original message and its intelligible articulation in the present moment.

156. Ibid., 20–21.
157. Ibid., 21. See Friedman, *Cultural Identity*.
158. Schreiter, *New Catholicity*, 21.
159. Ibid.
160. Ibid., 23.
161. Ibid., 25.

Since all God-experience is mediated and all theology is inculturated, Schreiter employs semiotics of culture to limn the structure and process of such intercultural communication. From the vantage point of cultural semiotics, the communicative event can be understood as the transmission of a *message* via a series of *cultural codes* and *signs*.[162] The challenges surrounding the communication of a religious message embedded in cultural codes is dramatically heightened in a globalized context. Concepts of culture that fail to engage globalization are extensively critiqued for their inadequacy, yet leave little hope of formulating a definition beyond dispute.[163] For the purposes of his work, Schreiter adopts a tripartite understanding of culture: culture is *ideational, performance,* and *material*.[164]

> Culture [has] *ideational* elements (worldview, values, rules about behavior), *performantial* elements (rituals and roles), and *material* elements (language, symbols, food, clothing, housing, and other artifacts).[165]

Beyond a descriptive definition, notions of culture have been developed within specific contexts. Older, modern notions speak of culture as an integrative matrix from which an essential, unified, and homogeneous identity is absorbed. These integrated concepts of culture proved to be highly successful toward describing "culture as a patterned system in which the various elements are coordinated in such a fashion as to create a unified whole."[166] Although integrated concepts of culture predominated in

162. ". . . semiotics of culture may be defined as a method by which culture is studied as a communication structure and process. It focuses on *signs* (Greek: *semeia*) that carry *messages* along the pathways (*codes*) of culture. The purpose of the circulation of those messages within the culture is to create *identity*, which involves building group solidarity and incorporating new information as it comes to the culture." Ibid., 29–30. See also Schreiter, *Constructing Local Theologies*.

163. "As is well known, there is no definition of culture that is widely agreed upon. This is due in part to the sheer complexity with which human communities surround themselves. . . . But the inability to define culture is also due in part to the fact that we come to culture with such different questions and interests. And as we do so—looking for material causes, social processes, patterns of domination and hegemony, or webs of meaning—we pursue methods that take us to our goal, reconfiguring the roadmap along the way. Cultures appear to be infinitely malleable, amenable, to so many different interpretations. We think that we have captured them in one shape, only to have them metamorphose into another." Schreiter, *New Catholicity*, 47.

164. Ibid., 29.

165. Ibid., 79.

166. Ibid., 47–48. "The model of such an integrated concept of culture is the traditional society, relatively self-enclosed and self-sufficient, and governed by a rule-bound

anthropological studies throughout the nineteenth and early twentieth centuries, the shortcomings of this approach are now well documented (cf. James Clifford, above.) Modern concepts of culture foster the illusion of integration in the face of rogue elements of difference and dissensus. The myth of integration threatens to essentialize identity, giving the impression of a more cohesive culture than actually exists. These concepts "deal better with issues of cultural identity than with the challenges of social change."[167] Moreover, when integrated concepts of culture inform the intercultural hermeneutics[168] of theologians, questions surrounding the relationship between faith and culture become more problematic.

> How might Christian faith be inculturated in a new context without displacing some (integrating) aspect of that culture altogether? The culture of the evangelizer is often so closely identified with faith itself that the two become inseparable. When that happens, the culture being evangelized is displaced or destroyed. One has to become Western in order to become Christian.[169]

Globalized concepts of culture emerged in the later twentieth century, offering an alternative view. Both globalization and postcolonial critique contributed to this new perspective, emphasizing the contingent, constructive, and contested character of cultural identities. Globalized concepts of culture reject claims of an easy homogeneity. Culture is inventive, "constructed on the stage of struggle amid asymmetries of power."[170]

> Globalized concepts of culture, drawing especially on postcolonial and globalization theory, propose cultures as a ground of contests in relations where we struggle with sameness and difference, comparability and incommensurability, cohesion and dispersion, collaboration and resistance. Diversity and difference are of great

---

tradition. Such societies are small-scale, characteristic of the *Gemeinschaft*, with face-to-face relations being the principle form of interaction."

167. Ibid., 53.

168. "Intercultural refers to communication across a cultural boundary. Cross-cultural refers to generalization that can be made about intercultural communication, based on the analysis of different intercultural encounters. When applied to hermeneutics, two dimensions are reflected here. Intercultural hermeneutics, narrowly understood, is concerned with the quality and integrity of the individual communication event. Cross-cultural hermeneutics is concerned with the long-term effects—on both the message and the interlocutors—of multiple communication events. Both intercultural and cross-cultural dimensions need attention." Ibid., 29.

169. Ibid., 53.

170. Ibid., 54.

importance. The exercise of power in all its asymmetrical force never goes unnoticed.[171]

Globalized concepts of culture are better suited to account for the phenomena of change, although Schreiter notes that the very situation of coexisting and incompatible cultural logics make it difficult to formulate theories regarding change.[172] Globalized notions of culture more adequately describe the present moment: "fragmented, conflictual and disoriented."[173] They are ordered towards exposing the inherent asymmetries of power in human relations. Globalized concepts of culture offer theologians both opportunity and challenge. The absence of a *telos* in global change threatens to make innovation, uncritical and indiscriminate, the order of the day. Moreover, the rhetoric of incommensurability undermines imaginative possibilities towards non-dominative universals.

Both integrated and globalized concepts of culture inform current theology's engagement of the character of religious belonging,[174] influencing the discussion of syncretism, synthesis, and religious identity.[175] Schreiter maintains that analysis of the process of intercultural communication demonstrates that "syncretic processes and synthetic processes are likely the same."[176] Intercultural hermeneutics highlight the fact that speakers and hearers have very different goals in the communicative event.

> The speaker is concerned with getting a message to the hearer in such a manner that the hearer comes to understand the message in the same way as does the speaker. In other words, the speaker is concerned with the transmittal of the message in its integrity. The hearer, on the other hand, is preoccupied with trying to make sense of the message—that is, relating it to other knowledge within the

---

171. Ibid., 71–72.

172. Ibid., 58.

173. Ibid., 57.

174. Schreiter notes that modern concepts of culture have informed Roman Catholicism since Vatican II evidenced by its emphasis on "the dignity of cultures, the role of culture in bringing human beings to their fulfillment, and the right of a people to their own culture. The concern for the evangelization of cultures that so marked the pontificate of John Paul II, with its implied optimism about the human ability to change a culture, would imply a belief in its patterned character." Ibid., 53.

175. Schreiter notes that syncretism in religious discourse most often functions pejoratively, describing a miscommunication of the religious message while syncretism in the social sciences refers to "the formation of new identities out of cultural elements that are at hand, usually from more than one culture." Ibid., 63.

176. Ibid., 71.

hearer's universe. . . . The speaker is on the alert for any alteration of the message that might compromise its integrity; the hearer is trying to make the message fit into an identity. The speaker is on the watch for syncretism; the hearer is struggling for synthesis.[177]

Since messages travel by means of cultural codes, in intercultural communication there is a constant process of re-encoding that requires ongoing dialogue and discussion before both speaker and hearer can satisfactorily determine that a message has crossed over.

> The speaker alone, then cannot decide finally that the message has been transmitted in its integrity. . . . Meaning is established in social judgment, in the intense and repeated action between speaker and hearer.[178]

While concerns surrounding the transmission of the message are not to be dismissed, Schreiter's analysis points out that the process by which a message becomes lodged within a new culture is far more complicated than establishing simple transference or congruence. There is an innate indeterminacy in the message itself. "That means that every detail and every aspect has not been made completely explicit. Furthermore, no message can be transmitted without using a code, and different codes will highlight different aspects of the message."[179]

The indeterminate character of the message can pose problems for the speaker who harbors particular concern for the integrity of the message. This is where global concepts of culture can be particularly helpful. Speaker concerns parallel the commitments of integrated concepts of culture. There is an elusive and, ultimately, delusional striving for purity of expression. Globalized notions of culture recall the culturally and historically contextualized condition of all messages.

> [T]he Gospel never comes to a culture in pure form; it is already embedded in the less-than-pure culture of the speaker, the treasure carried in vessels of clay. Invocations of pure culture or even pure Gospel are not apposite, since here on earth at least, they do not exist. Introducing such ideas of purity into the syncretism discussion, then, does not lead to the fidelity to the Gospel which we seek.[180]

177. Ibid., 68.
178. Ibid., 70.
179. Ibid., 79–80.
180. Ibid., 71.

Moreover, globalized concepts of culture remain sensitive to the asymmetries of power in human relations and communication. Emerging Christian identities may draw premature condemnation of syncretism, short-circuiting the process of identity formation.

Schreiter contends,"... new Christian identities should be examined not just to be assured that they are not wrong, but also to see how they may be more profoundly right than we had imagined."[181]

## Summary: Theology and the Present

In this section I have reviewed three theological perspectives. It is important to point out that each of the theologians reviewed holds that theology is a public enterprise. Even in a radically plural world, an account can be given for the reasonableness of Christian truth claims. Attempts to limit the reasonableness of Christianity solely to an intra-ecclesial language game are rejected by all three theologians primarily to safeguard the fullness of Christian faith and to affirm shared human rationalities.[182]

Schreiter's analysis of the effect of globalization on local contexts highlights the convergence of multiple forces, some conflictual, some synthetic. Compatibility and incommensurability *both* mark the boundary space of the "glocal," making intercultural communication challenging but not impossible. Haight takes this communicative possibility forward across theological time and space through a hermeneutical theory attentive to the dialectical structure of symbols. Religious experience of transcendental revelation is mediated via symbols lodged with particular traditions. An existential encounter with the transcendent is mediated by, not fossilized within, the symbol system. This dialectic of sameness and difference allows for the possibility of plural orthodox theological interpretations of the one, original revelation. Tracy's insightful analysis points out that, deprived of their symbolic sources of identity, people will create the traditions they require however fictional or implausible. The critique of symbol systems and their function in social memory offers Christian theology a new prophetic challenge. If the dangerous memory of Jesus is the fundamental memory "that turns as fiercely on itself as against other pretensions to triumph," then a rehabilitated notion of tradition as destabilizing "countermemory

---

181. Ibid., 73.

182. Attempts to deny the possibility of shared rationalities fundamentally undermines Christianity's claim of universal saving revelation and in selecting these three theologians I indicate my own commitment to the public nature of Christian theology.

to all tales of triumph" may serve towards the critical recovery of a transformative tradition.[183]

## Conclusion

This chapter has offered a descriptive overview of important dimensions within the question of social identity and traditions in the fields of cultural anthropology and theology. Among the significant points highlighted, the contested and conflictual character of human social identity has been explored as well as the current argument concerning compatibility versus incommensurability of cultural exchange. The dilemma of tradition's function in the construal/construction of social identity has also been underscored. In the following chapter, the notion of tradition in Roman Catholicism will be explored through twenty centuries of Christian history. This historical overview will help to familiarize the reader with the nature of the debate of tradition, particularly in its relationship to the Christian scriptures and the ecclesial community.

183. Tracy, *On Naming*, 15.

2

# The Notion of Tradition in Roman Catholicism

*Historical Overview*

Tradition within the Roman Catholic communion is a many-faceted reality with a long and sometimes conflicted history. Tradition (big T) connotes for many a singular, authoritative, and timeless deposit of faith, universal in its claims and applications. This chapter locates this particular construal within the larger history of tradition. The continuities and discontinuities between the multiple understandings of tradition will help to provide a picture of the Roman Catholic Church's ongoing struggle to articulate its understanding of the church's role in the mystery of revelation. While an immutable deposit of faith is very difficult to warrant in a postmodern world, nonetheless the ongoing reflection of the church on the mystery of revelation (tradition) does make authoritative claims on members. These claims, as truth claims, reach beyond the bounds of the Christian communion and necessarily engage other traditions. It is equally important to affirm the historically contingent and culturally embodied character of this mediated revelation. All talk of God is necessarily symbolic and propositional formulas concerning God and God's intentions, as representational construals, are subject to the ongoing review, critique, and renewal of the believing community. This chapter lays the foundation for understanding how such construals function authoritatively in shaping and sustaining Christian identity. Since tradition and Christian life are in a dialogical and dialectical relationship, any changes in the self-understanding of the church prompts changes in the church's understanding and use of its tradition. This chapter explores how the church over the centuries has understood its own tradition and the historical and cultural circumstances that precipitated changes in that understanding.

## Ancient Church

The Roman world of the Ante-Nicean period formed the social and cultural milieu in which the nascent Christian communities sprang up, predominantly in diverse, urban centers throughout the Empire. Christianity, approximately 250 years old, was no longer a new religion: it was one of the many *religiones* informing a polytheistic society in which multiple gods permeated the world as real presences to be acknowledged and reckoned with.[1] The plurality of religions fostered a variety of local forms of worship that "stressed (even idealized) social cohesion and the passing on of tradition in families, in local communities, and through the memories of proud cities and nations bathed in centuries of history."[2]

Christianity, with its explicit prohibition against idol worship, represented a real threat to a polytheistic Empire dependent on the good pleasure of the many gods.[3] The persecutions of this period were largely due to the change in the imperial style of local government: servants of the emperor concluded that the flourishing Christian communities need to be checked, curbing their potential for runaway growth.

Within this often-hostile context, Christianity struggled to secure its distinctive character. Clearly, the marginal status of the early church did not inhibit its growth and infiltration throughout the Roman Empire. At the same time, the unique local contexts of these communities shaped the expression of Christian faith and offered substantial challenges to the communities, forcing them to clarify their self-understanding. These

---

1. The gods formed a pantheon of hierarchically ordered, otherworldly powers mirroring the hierarchical ordering of social life. Philosophers worshipped the high gods, aspiring to escape the body and all material encumbrances while average people worshipped lesser gods who hovered closer to the earth and assisted those who paid due attention. Far from abstractions, gods shared the same physical space with humans and became significant forces of social cohesion at regional levels. Brown, *Western Christendom*, 18–33.

2. Ibid., 20.

3. Peter Brown notes, "It takes some leap of the modern imagination (saturated as it is by later centuries of Christian language) to understand the novelty of seeing every human being as subject to the same universal law of God and as equally capable of salvation through the triumphant or the studious conquest of sin, brought about through permanent and exclusive membership of a unique religious group. Salvation meant, first and foremost, salvation from idolatry and from the power of the demons. . . . All past tradition was re-interpreted by such teaching. In polytheist belief, the lower ranks of gods had been treated as ambivalent, moody creatures, capable of being spiteful and manipulable on some occasions and generous and powerful on others. The Christians attacked such gods, not by denying their existence: they existed; but they were equally evil. All gods, even the highest, were malevolent and unreliable." Ibid., 26–27.

foundational expressions of Christianity, referred to as "the rule of faith" and claiming distinctive apostolic origins, inaugurated a new religious tradition, giving the early church a sense of identity and purpose.

For Ante-Nicean Christians, the importance of the rule of faith came into particular focus as the nascent community expanded geographically and diversified ethnically. Christian distinctiveness manifested itself throughout the Empire despite local nuances and emphases. Given large expanses of territory and culture, still, common beliefs and rites of worship united the Christian churches of the second and third centuries. The rule of faith that emerged from various locales at this time witnessed to its unifying function. From Lyons to Alexandria, "the rule of faith," "*regula fidei*," "the canon of truth," "the teaching of the Church," all local expressions of Christian faith, nonetheless bore remarkable resemblances.[4]

In making this assertion, it must be emphasized that early Christian teachings were markedly diverse during this formative period. Social and cultural conditions fostered the coexistence of diverse viewpoints even on matters of significant theological importance.[5] In this time of theological diversity, arguments based on received apostolic tradition played an important role in the early church's self-understanding. Although Irenaeus of Lyons and Origen of Alexandria reflect significant differences in their theological expressions, their adherence to the rule of faith as the prime interpretative tool of the Christian community is consistent.

## *Irenaeus of Lyons*

The conflict of interpretation within the church of Lyons forged Irenaeus' understanding of the relationship between the scriptures and the rule of

---

4. "The similarity in content is striking. Each might be a preliminary draft for the later and more succinct 'Apostles' Creed.' Here is evidence, within a period of about forty years, from places as far apart as Gaul, the Roman province of North Africa, and Alexandria, to support Irenaeus' contention that the Church 'believes these points just as if she had but one soul, and one and the same heart, and she proclaims them, and teaches them, and hands them down, with perfect harmony, as if she possessed only one mouth'. This is in strong contrast with the widely differing systems of the Gnostic teachers. Irenaeus' point is the simple and compelling one that the unanimity of Christian teaching in so many different places is evidence that it is derived from one source and genuinely represents the original teaching." Jay, *Church*, 1:44.

5. J. N. D. Kelly notes that the idea of revealed truth "as a sacrosanct inheritance from the apostles" did not prevent diverse theological reflection of the meaning and import of Christian revelation. "Only gradually, and even then in regard to comparatively few doctrines which became subjects of debate, did the tendency to insist upon precise definition and rigid uniformity assert itself." Kelly, *Early Christian Doctrines*, 4.

faith. His concern for the content and transmission of the Christian faith flowed directly from his context: the threat of Valentian gnostic interpretations of the Christian mystery. Valentinian gnostics posed a particularly difficult challenge: although baptized and in full communion with the Christian community of Lyons, these believers held secret, unauthorized assemblies for those considered spiritually elite. These gnostic seekers offered an alternative reading of the Christian story and taught an elaborate cosmology that undermined the unity of God and the incarnation of the Word.[6]

## THE RULE OF FAITH

In *Adversus Haereses,* Irenaeus refutes gnostic claims and uses the rule of faith as a tool to describe the manner in which a right reading of scripture can be attained. The rule of faith is "a kind of 'narrative creed' telling the theological story of Christ the Word."[7] Both the scriptures and the rule of faith are apostolic gifts given to the worldwide church, which, "although scattered throughout the world," preserves true teaching "as if occupying but one house."[8] True teaching is always an apostolic gift because it is "the doctrine that is proclaimed, accepted, guarded, preached, taught, transmitted."[9]

Distilled from the scriptural witness and liturgical life of the Christian community, the rule of faith has a dialogical relationship with the scriptures and provides for the "one right reading" of the scriptures in the church. Scripture and the rule of faith "are less mirror images of one another than conversation partners each of whom amplifies and corrects the insights of

---

6. Irenaeus *Adversus Haereses* 3.6–15 (scriptural witness to one God) and 3.16–23 (scriptural witness to one sole Christ).

7. Donovan, *One Right Reading?*, 11.

8. "For, although the languages of the world are dissimilar, yet the import of the tradition is one and the same, for the churches which have been planted in Germany do not believe or hand down anything different nor do those in Spain, nor those in Gaul, nor those in the East, nor those in Egypt, nor those in Libya, nor those which have been established in the central regions of the world." Irenaeus *Adversus Haereses* 1.10.2.

9. "As a second-century writer he [Irenaeus] assumes the objective, unchanging nature of truth, independent of the interpreter, a truth that is contained in the Rule of Faith and yet at the same time exceeds the grasp of human reason. Hence, he will develop a methodology that embraces both supreme confidence in the truth proclaimed by the Church and full awareness of the limits of human speech about God." Donovan, *One Right Reading?*, 12.

the other.[10] Accordingly, failure to interpret the scriptures with the received rule of faith results in heretical distortions. The interpretative frameworks of Gnosticism cannot offer a true reading of the Christian scriptures because they lack congruence with the rule of faith. Gnostic cosmologies fail to consider the historical events of the life of Jesus, transposing his life into a "fable." Moreover, the rule of faith is true teaching because it has been "traditioned" (handed down) by the authentic teachers of Christian faith, the apostles. Subverting gnostic wisdom, Irenaeus asserts that sound doctrine is not mysterious and secret; it is available to all through affiliation with sound teachers.

> In this order, and by this succession, the ecclesiastical tradition from the apostles, and the preaching of the truth, have come down to us. And this is most abundant proof that there is one and the same vivifying faith, which has been preserved in the church from the apostles until now, and handed down in truth.[11]

The rule of faith operates as a unifying principle among the various Ante-Nicean churches. The understanding of tradition, particularly as articulated by Origen of Alexandria, reflects both substantial agreement with and creative departure from the viewpoint of Irenaeus of Lyons, confirming catholic diversity-in-unity in its ancient ecclesial manifestation.

## Origen of Alexandria

Origen's context differed significantly from Irenaeus. Alexandria, a major center of commerce and culture, was also the heart of intellectual life in the Roman world. The son of a Christian martyr, Origen studied the Greek classics as a student of Clement of Alexandria and at a very young age became the leader of an important philosophical school. Renowned for his teaching, Origen sought to present Christianity as true *gnosis*: the key to all human knowledge and experience.[12] Origen's *Peri archon* (or *De principiis*,

---

10. Ibid., 11. Donovan prefers to speak of the "dynamism" of the rule of faith expressed by Irenaeus in the language of tradition. She notes that the notion of development in tradition is foreign to the second-century mind and therefore cannot adequately describe the role of tradition in the early church. Ibid., 12.

11. Irenaeus *Adversus Haereses* 3.3.3.

12. Scholars have disputed Origen's understanding of *gnosis*, a few contending that his understanding of secret knowledge placed him outside of Christian orthodoxy. But the consensus of scholars now points out that Origen affirmed the rule of faith and, through his allegorical method, speculated on the mysteries that remained unanswered in the Christian scriptures. See Harris, *Origen of Alexandria's Interpretation*.

"On First Principles") is a work of Christian speculation intended to attract intellectuals to faith. Written for the educated, Origen's speculations are firmly rooted in a loyal adherence to the rule of faith and scriptural witness. Yet, clearly for Origen, the rule of faith is not the product of philosophical speculation; it is that which is handed down and received from the apostles. That which is handed down has authority for Origen: scriptures, oral tradition, and customs.

> . . . in the same way we find many who think they hold the doctrine of Christ, some of them differing in their beliefs from the Christians of earlier times, and yet the teaching of the church, handed down in unbroken succession from the apostles, is still preserved and continues to exist in the churches up to the present day, we maintain that only is to be believed as the truth which in no way conflicts with the tradition of the church and the apostles.[13]

### THE RULE OF FAITH AND CHRISTIANITY AS "TRUE GNOSIS"

Origen notes early in book 1 that among believers there are questions concerning the faith. The fact that those "who profess to believe in Christ hold conflicting opinions" leads Origen to "lay down a definite line and an unmistakable rule" which the apostles preached in the plainest terms to all believers.[14] Origen believes that the rule of faith provides a basic framework of Christian faith, establishing the boundaries of Christian belief in distinction from gnostic claims. Moreover, Origen is convinced that important questions regarding the nature of God, Jesus Christ, and the Holy Spirit remain open and need to be addressed by means of an allegorical reading of the sacred scriptures.

> The grounds of their [apostolic] statements they left to be investigated by such as should merit the higher gifts of the Spirit and in particular by such as should afterwards receive through the Holy Spirit himself the graces of languages, wisdom, and knowledge.[15]

Origen maintains that there are doctrines revealed to the apostles that remain unspoken, "their intention undoubtedly being to supply the more diligent of those who came after them, such as should prove to be lovers of

---

13. Origen *On First Principles* 1.2.
14. Ibid.
15. Ibid., 1.3.

wisdom, with an exercise on which to display the fruit of their ability."[16] Convinced that Christianity is true *gnosis*, Origen believes that God's economy provides for the learned among believers to advance through spiritual investigation. Origen does not create an alternative story that diminishes or denies the historical events of the birth, life, death, and resurrection of Jesus. He does not make a *gnostic tradition* his starting point; there is an undisputed received tradition, embodied in the teachings of the apostles who handed down certain facts and practices central to the Christian community. But this tradition does not explain everything. Philosophy serves Christian faith toward increasing knowledge of the concealed *gnosis* of the Christian scriptures. The duty of "sanctified reason" is to plumb the faith received by the church in the grace of the Spirit; the model for this search is Christ himself who adapted his message to the ability of his audience. The truth communicated by Christ to the apostles through the parables must be sought by capable believers, guided by the rule of faith and the gifts received through the Holy Spirit in the "graces of language, wisdom, and knowledge."[17]

For Origen and Irenaeus, the rule of faith is the non-negotiable foundation of Christian life and faith. The Christian mystery revealed in the scriptures cannot be made to speak of God outside of the framework of the apostolic teaching, the rule of faith; to do so substitutes a different story for the story of Jesus. With the advent of Constantinian Christianity, new challenges and questions began to shape the church's understanding of its tradition, precipitating the convening of worldwide synods. Augustine's understanding of the unitive relationship between the church, scripture, and tradition highlights how this new factor in catholic ecclesial life shaped an emerging dimension within an understanding of tradition.

## *Augustine of Hippo*

With the advent of Constantine's victory in 312, the marginal status of Christianity was dramatically reversed. By 325, Constantine had gathered the first worldwide assembly of Christian bishops at Nicaea, allowing the "Christian church to see itself, face to face, for the first time, as the privileged bearer of a universal law."[18] Constantine gave the Christian church peace, wealth, and the ability to expand its influence. From the perspective of the

16. Ibid.
17. Ibid.
18. Brown, *Western Christendom*, 21.

once marginalized church, the ensuing Christianization of the Empire effected nothing less than the victory of Christ over the demons: dislodging evil spirits, their altar, temples, and cults through public exorcisms.[19]

This was the Roman world of Augustine of Hippo. In the hundred years separating Irenaeus and Origen from Augustine, the once suspect Christian minority gained majority status and Christian discourse entered into the political and social framework of the Roman world. The gathering of bishops in regional synods and worldwide ecumenical councals added a new dimension to the notion of tradition in the early church. Along with the apostolic transmission of the scriptures and the rule of faith, the present practice of the worldwide church, as defined and promulgated at ecumenical councils, represented authoritative expression of a living tradition.

Tradition: Past and Present Normative Witness

Augustine, in accord with other patristic writers, maintains a unitive understanding of church, scripture, and tradition. He focuses these three aspects of Christian life through the lens of apostolic unity expressed by the agreement of the worldwide church in general council. True doctrine is founded on scripture as it is interpreted by the tradition: the past and *present* normative witness of the universal church. Accordingly, Augustine contends that a general council of the universal church has greater authority than the decisions of local churches. The protracted disruption of the Donatist schism provided Augustine the opportunity to fully develop this argument.

The Donatists' insistence on the rebaptism of apostates resulted in a schism that violently divided the church of North Africa. While scholars have shown that the Donatist controversy was a highly complicated disturbance, influenced by historical, social, and economic factors,[20] the major theological dispute around the rebaptism of penitent apostates effectively created an alternative Christian community, one that considered itself the pure and true church. Augustine argues that the custom of rebaptism called for by Cyprian and a synod of African bishops was later reconsidered by

---

19. Peter Brown notes that for the ordinary Christian, monotheism was not so clearly established. Many maintained their local beliefs and participated in rituals for the "lower powers." "In their universe other, more familiar powers, the protectors of more human activities, had not been pushed aside by the austere and exclusive presence of the One God of the Christians…For so widespread a mentality to change, to any significant degree, so as to share the intransigence of more 'advanced' more strict, Christians, the society and culture of the Roman empire itself had to change." Ibid., 37.

20. See in particular M. A. Tilley, *Bible in Christian North Africa*.

the universal church and rejected because it put into question the validity of the saving baptism of the Lord. The Donatists' error lies in their inability to accept the teaching of the universal church.[21] The authority of a local synod is superseded by the decisions of the worldwide church gathered in an ecumenical council.[22]

The hierarchy of authorities employed by Augustine does not necessarily undermine the authority of local bishops; it places local episcopal authority within its universal context. The local church must attend to the wisdom and teaching of the universal church. Augustine argues that even the most revered of bishops can make mistakes.

> . . . if Peter, I say, could compel the Gentiles to live after the manner of the Jews, contrary to the rule of faith which the Church afterwards held, why might not Cyprian, in opposition to the rule of faith which the whole Church afterwards held, compel heretics and schismatics to be baptized afresh?[23]

Similarly, earlier theological conceptions can be corrected by later generations when greater light is brought to a question.[24]

Augustine's notion of tradition and its function within the Christian church reflects the era in which he lived. Disputes were much more frequent in a church newly ascended to the status of the one true religion of the Empire. Regional disputes and jealousies now had a new theological platform on which to rage, as the christological controversy between Alexandria and Antioch so pointedly illustrates. Since disputing parties made similar claims to be in continuity with the scriptures and the revered teachers of the past, arguments marshalling these authorities continued to

---

21. Augustine *De Baptismo* 3.2.2.

22. Ibid., 3.10.4.

23. Ibid., 2.2.2.

24. "[B]ut that all the letters of bishops which have been written, or are being written, since the closing of the canon, are liable to be refuted if there be anything contained in them which strays from the truth, either by the discourse of someone who happens to be wiser in the matter than themselves, or by the weightier authority and more learned experience of other bishops, or by the authority of Councils; and further, that the Councils themselves, which are held in the several districts and provinces, must yield, beyond all possibility of doubt, to the authority of universal Councils which are formed for the whole Christian world; and that even of the universal Councils, the earlier are often corrected by those which follow them, when, by some actual experiment, things are brought to light which were before concealed, and that is known which previously lay hid, and this without any whirlwind of sacrilegious pride, without any puffing of the neck through arrogance, without strife of envious hatred, simply with holy humility, catholic peace and Christian charity." Ibid., 2.3.4.

play a significant role in disagreements, but they were no longer sufficient. The churches were encountering questions that demanded time and careful consideration at local and regional levels, and which at times required the gathering of ecumenical councils to resolve the conflict.[25] The past and the present participated in the church's understanding of tradition.

## Vincent of Lerins

Late antiquity, which some scholars locate as early as the mid-300s, was a time when the past mattered in a particular way to the present. "The past was very real to the men and women of late antiquity: as they saw it, it had not so much to be remade as to be reasserted."[26] Both pagans and Christians alike made appeals to tradition to ground their connections to an authentic past. Gaps in the scriptural stories were filled by imaginative recreations of persons and events. Apocryphal stories and legends began to embellish the historical record filling out the details of untold stories: Mary's childhood and death, the journeys of the apostles, the adventures of disciples such as Paul's follower, Thecla. Scholarly accounts of conciliar decisions, as well as "a flowering of legend, homiletic, and poetry cover[ing] the bare bones of Scripture with human detail and unbridled embellishment," gained in popularity.[27] Late antiquity, the time of Vincent of Lerins, was a time of particular diversity and creativity,[28] when the notion of tradition took on density and definition.

---

25. "For how could a matter which was involved in such mists of disputation even have been brought to the full illumination and authoritative decision of a general Council, had it not first been known to be discussed for some considerable time in the various districts of the world, with many discussions and comparisons of the views of the bishops on every side? But this is one effect of the soundness of peace, that when any doubtful points are long under investigation, and when, on account of the difficulty of arriving at the truth, they produce difference of opinion in the course of brotherly disputation, till men at last arrive at unalloyed truth; yet the bond of unity remains, lest in the part that is cut away there should be found the incurable wound of deadly error." Ibid., 2.2.5.

26. Cameron, "Remaking the Past," 2. Cameron notes that the need to claim the past for one's own purposes was experienced by Christians and pagans alike. Christian histories were written that cast Constantine as the new Moses, freeing his people from the slavery of paganism. These works contributed toward a Christian cosmology that located humanity's purpose within a universal history of creation. See also Eusebius, *Life of Constantine*.

27. Cameron, "Remaking the Past," 7.

28. "We see in late antiquity a mass of experimentation, new ways being tried and new adjustments made. The process of myth-making and development of new identities inevitably implied the shaping of the past according to current preoccupations." Ibid., 16.

This context shaped Vincent of Lerins' *Commonitories*, resulting less in a careful report, and more in a deliberate casting of the present in terms of a hallowed past. Writing shortly after the Council of Ephesus (431), Vincent offers a report on Christian faith "first by the authority of the divine Law; second by the tradition of the Catholic church."[29] The scriptures are the "divine Law" received from the apostles, but this divine origin does not eliminate a vast number of conflicting interpretations. Therefore, "because of the great distortions caused by various errors, it is necessary that the trend of the interpretation of the prophetic and apostolic writings be directed in accordance with the rule of the ecclesiastical and Catholic meaning."[30] Irenaeus's "one right reading" had found its fifth-century expression in Vincent of Lerins.

Yet, the ecclesial character of this "one right reading" changed significantly in the next three centuries. As an interpretative framework, tradition, expressed in the rule of faith, continued to supply the theological grammar for orthodoxy and, thereby, the basis for catholic unity. However, by the fifth century, catholic unity had an organizational and institutional structure. No longer an eccentric Jewish sect struggling to maintain its distinctiveness in a religiously plural world, Christianity, the established religion of the disintegrating Empire, struggled to ward off the constant threat of idolatry. Paganism, especially in the West, remained an encroaching threat to orthodoxy.[31]

### The Vincentian Canon: "What has been believed everywhere, always and by all"

In this light, Vincent of Lerins's assertion that, "In the Catholic Church itself, every care should be taken to hold fast to what has been believed everywhere, always and by all" appears more apologetic than categorical. Vincent's overriding concern for true interpretation leads him to adopt three hermeneutical principles: universality, antiquity, and consent.[32] In

---

29. Vincent of Lerins, *Commonitories*, ch. 2.

30. Ibid.

31. "By contrast, from Augustine onwards, a succession of Latin preachers and legislators tended to stress the fact that the idols, though broken in public, lingered tenaciously in the hearts of all too many Christians. Paganism was not simply a *superstitio*, a bankrupt dispensation that lay outside the Church: paganism lay close to the heart of all baptized Christians, always ready to re-emerge in the form of 'pagan survivals.'" Brown, *Western Christendom*, 99.

32. Vincent of Lerins, *Commonitories*, ch. 2.

chapter three of *The Commonitories* he explains that the common faith of the universal church is to be preferred over particular expressions of a local church, specifically those of breakaway communities. Errant communities fail to cling to the universal faith of the church and allow novel expressions to subvert the truth. Truth lies in the ancient ways. Should the corruption of error attempt to infect the whole church, the faithful Christian "will endeavor to adhere to the antiquity which is evidently beyond the danger of being seduced by the deceit of some novelty." Yet, if deeper investigation should reveal error even in the ancient source, then the believer must go still further into the past to earlier ecumenical councils. Should there be no councils beyond a certain point, the faith of those who preceded the present generation is to be examined and their various viewpoints compared.[33]

Western Christianity of late antiquity employed a conserving rhetoric of tradition reinforcing the sense that what is now has always been so. The often-acrimonious struggles of the earlier Christian church to articulate its faith were remembered and narrated from this perspective. Thus, historically, politically, and theologically complex disputes were rendered as clear-cut conflicts between orthodox believers and duplicitous heretics. Tradition, in this light, functions to support the notion of the deposit of faith as a precious entity, vulnerable to corruption, and only truly secure in the hands of the proper ecclesial authorities.[34] Commenting on 1 Timothy, Vincent explores what Paul means when he admonishes Timothy to "keep that which is committed."

> What is "committed"? It is that which has been entrusted to you, not that which you have invented; what you have received, not what you have devised; not a matter of ingenuity, but of doctrine; not of private acquisition, but of public tradition, a matter brought to you, not created by you; a matter you are not the author of, but the keeper of; not the teacher, but the learner; not the leader, but the follower. This deposit, he says, guard. Preserve the "talent" of the Catholic faith unviolated and unimpaired. What has been

---

33. "[T]hose who, though they lived in various periods and at different places, nevertheless remained in the communion and faith of the One Catholic Church, and who therefore have become reliable authorities." Ibid., ch. 3.

34. As Peter Brown points out, the triumphalism of this rhetoric betrays a deeper insecurity stemming from the perception that demonic forces continue to besiege the Christian community. "The master narrative of Christianization, as it was explicitly propounded in many circles in the Latin west, was not one of definitive triumph. It was one in which an untranscended past perpetually shadowed the advancing footsteps of the Christian present." Brown, *Western Christendom*, 99.

entrusted to you may remain with you and may be handed down by you.[35]

The conserving character of tradition does not eliminate progress and growth, but novelty must be avoided by maintaining an organic continuity with the past. Thus, there is progress, "even exceedingly great progress," but never change. Understanding, knowledge, and wisdom grow, but always within the limits that conserve their essential character as Christian faith. "Progress means that each thing grows within itself, whereas change implies that one thing is transformed into another."[36]

## *Tradition and the Ancient Church*

Tradition in the ancient church took on different expressions and import depending on the changing historical and cultural circumstances. Although the scriptures and the rule of faith formed the canonical center of the religious tradition, there emerged an ecclesial sense that the authoritative teaching of the apostles is as much a present reality as a past legacy when the universal church reflects on current questions and ambiguities. This is because the church is a sacred reality, and as Augustine recommends, when in doubt about particular questions that do not have clear answers within scripture, the belief and practice of the church should be followed "because scripture itself bore witness to this church and its authority."[37] Thus, scripture, tradition, and the church enjoyed a perichoretic relationship that only deepened and expanded within the context of the Western Middle Ages.

## The Medieval Church

The notion of tradition in the medieval church reflects the integrative mentality of the age: holistic, synthetic, yet differentiated. The scriptures, church, and tradition remained intimately linked in the ecclesial understanding of God's communication of saving grace. George Tavard notes that medievals were not scriptural fundamentalists; they maintained a strong contrastive sense between the divine origin of the scriptures and the frail, inadequate human means by which the scriptures were brought into

---

35. Vincent of Lerins, *Commonitories*, ch. 22.
36. Ibid., ch. 23.
37. Eno, "Doctrinal Authority," 144.

existence.³⁸ At the same time, this distinction did not imply a gap or chasm between the Word of God and the church. These entities in the medieval mind were distinct yet, cohesive. The relationship between church and scripture was not functional; it was "a mystery of mutual inherence."³⁹

This relationship of coinherence between scripture, tradition, and church is important and difficult to examine because critical analysis and confessional differences in the contemporary church shape and inform current scholarship.⁴⁰ Today, theologians agree that the modern debates surrounding the relationship between scripture and tradition were foreign to the medieval mindset, although elements of the contemporary question of tradition (authority, scripture, tradition, church, magisterium, continuity, infallibility/indefectibility) had a place in the thinking of the great medieval theologians. While in a medieval context these elements were essentially synthetic, in a modern context they have been posed as separate, even competing and opposing.

In order to glimpse the "sacred canopy" that encompassed the medieval world, it is important to take in the contours of this cosmos. Medieval people lived in a world that formed a richly textured, complex, and highly interconnected world; theirs was an integrative, hierarchically ordered worldview.⁴¹ All creation had a place in a divinely appointed cosmology: each part woven into the fabric of the whole, integral and necessary although differentiated by the value of its function.⁴² The desire to mirror

---

38. "Whatever may be implied here, medieval writers commonly saw a sharp distinction between the power of Christ manifesting himself through Scripture and the inadequacy of the inspired authors. Abelard pushed this to a paradox: 'What cause is there for surprise if in the Gospels also some elements have been warped by their writers' ignorance'? The power of Christ breaks through in spite of that. The medieval mind was not fundamentalist." Tavard, *Holy Writ*, 14.

39. Tavard quotes Rupert of Deutz: "The true river, the river of living water, is Holy Scripture and the true Catholic doctrine. That woman—the Church—drew it from the well of truth, which being in the midst of herself, makes her the garden of the Lord." Ibid., 15.

40. A review of the literature on this question in the mid-twentieth century reveals the nuances of these commitments and their inevitable impact on the perspectives developed and argued. See the analysis of Oscar Cullman's work on apostolic tradition by Congar, *Tradition*, 38–42.

41 This is not to diminish the profound diversities or to deny the social, political, and cultural ferment of the time. This will be more thoroughly explored below in the discussion of the fourteenth century. See Chenu, *Nature, Man and Society*.

42. The medieval synthesis achieved in Christendom articulated a worldview where all creation formed a God-ordained, harmonious whole. In this schema a prince is hierar-

the harmony of divine wisdom in the world led to a proliferation of synthetic works: "summas, cathedrals, and the encyclopaedic programme of the twelfth century."[43]

Within this economy, the scriptures enjoyed the highest place; to the medieval mind, all saving truth could be located in the scriptures. Even when doctrinal truth appeared outside of the scriptures, as in the case of some oral tradition, attempts were made to show how it was intended within the scriptures. Extra-scriptural writings and traditions, passed on via liturgy and devotions, participated in the coinherence of scripture and church. In this context, there was no difficulty extending to these expressions the privileges of scripture. Moreover, the scriptures as God's Word must be comprehended anew in each age. The Holy Spirit, vivifying the life of the church, secured this understanding through theological reflections found in commentaries, patristic writings, canons, and decretals. These extra-scriptural writings and expressions also participated in the authority of scriptures, *auctoritas*. Thomas Aquinas's view of *auctoritas* helps to limn the medieval notion of tradition.

## *Aquinas and Tradition*

Thomas Aquinas locates *auctoritas* within his understanding of God's saving relationship with the world. For Aquinas, God is the Life Principle, the Communicator of all life, physical and spiritual. In the created world these two life processes move simultaneously towards their designed completion in God. God creates bodily existence through human generativity and God creates the *collectio fidelium*, the church, by means of sacred doctrine. The communication of spiritual life from the Divine source is the gift of salvation: the life of God (Truth) communicated to the human soul. God's communication of truth is always and everywhere a mediated communication. Thus, God, *auctor*, the source of all life and truth, manifests God's saving design through the cooperation of human intermediaries, *auctoritas*.

---

chically superior to a pauper, but the pauper has intrinsic value as well. The design of the universe is God-given: each is in its place as God wills and this will is salvific. Thus, the faithful living out of the unique position of each within the divine scheme amounts to human cooperation with God's action in the world. Congar, *Tradition*, 86.

43. Ibid. These integrative projects were often planned and executed in a manner that corresponded to details gleaned from the biblical narrative. Scripture thoroughly informed the medieval religious imagination, thereby informing all of life in a world that knew no separation between the sacred and the mundane.

> There was clearly one true *auctor*, one absolute *auctoritas*, God; but all that to which God gave the gift of being true, as expressing his truth and his will, became thereby an *auctoritas* whose exact position in time there was no need to plot with exactitude; the essential thing was that part of divine truth that it incorporated for us.[44]

Thus, the media of God's saving truth participate in the divine authority: a derived authority such that the value of the mediating entity results from its connection to its Source. As such these *auctoritates* are not absolute; they are not the Source. Nevertheless, in the economy of salvation *auctoritas* offer humanity a true communication of God's life, and, limited as these mediations may be, they deserve the respectful obedience due their Divine Source.[45]

## SACRA DOCTRINA AND THEOLOGY

Thomas makes an important distinction between sacred doctrine and theology. While theology's object is the highest form of philosophical reflection, the object of sacred doctrine lies beyond the grasp of human reason. Thus, sacred doctrine is holy wisdom whose origin and term is the Triune God.[46] Sacred doctrine, as holy wisdom, is both content and the action of communicating the truth. Thus, in the saving economy, whereby spiritual life is generated in the human soul, the act of teaching becomes integral to furthering the divine mission. Truth produces salvation in human souls. Holy teaching mediates the communication of this saving truth. For Thomas, tradition with regards to the rule of faith is not so much about knowing how the content of tradition is conveyed and established in the sense of historical precedents. Tradition, as rule of faith, is the living magisterium: those entrusted to teach and transmit the testimony of the

---

44. Ibid., 90.

45. Thomas points out that the argument from authority is the most appropriate when one deals with sacred doctrine. Because the premises of sacred doctrine are held through revelation, these premises can only be accepted on the authority of those who received the revelation. Although the argument from authority is the weakest argument when dealing in the science of human reasoning, it is "most forceful when based on what God has disclosed." Thomas, *Summa Theologiae* I-I.8 *ad* 2.

46. "Now holy teaching goes to God most personally as deepest origin and highest end, and that not only because of what can be gathered about him from creatures (while philosophers have recognized, according to the epistle to the Romans, *What was known of God is manifest in them*) but also because of what he alone knows about himself and yet discloses for others to share. Consequently holy teaching is called wisdom in the highest degree." Thomas, *Summa Theologiae* I-I.6 *res.*

tradition.⁴⁷ Thus, the *auctoritas* of the magisterium derives from its participation in the great framework of divine government.

### *Tradition and Christendom*

The survey thus far has outlined the manner in which the notion of tradition evolved over the first twelve centuries of Christianity. The dialogical relationship between scripture and tradition reached a particular flowering in the context of medieval Christendom. Linked to ecclesial authority in a constitutive manner, tradition as a medium of *sacra doctrina* communicated salvation. Holy wisdom, whose origin and term is the Triune God, created truth within the human soul by means of the holy teaching, the living magisterium. The *perichoresis* of scripture, tradition, and church reflected the highly integrative context of Christendom. Yet, disjunctive forces, seemingly suppressed, were soon to converge in a new moment of Christian history.

## Fourteenth Century to the Reformation

The medieval synthesis was never without its discontents. The institutional church prior to the Gregorian reforms was in such a state of corruption that the period from 800 to 1048 could best be described as "undoubtedly its lowest."⁴⁸ Congar notes that beginning in the eleventh century, religious ferment expressed itself in several movements critical of established ecclesial structures in the name of a purer form of Christian life.⁴⁹ These movements can be seen as the ongoing reaction to the development of an ecclesiology based on papal primacy. From the fourth century, the steady

---

47. Congar points out that Thomas formulates a distinction in the teaching magisterium. "He wrote: 'It happens that sacred doctrine is taught in two ways. In the capacity of a prelate . . . The other way is in the capacity of a professor, just as professors of theology teach.' (*Com. In IV Sent.* d. 19 q. 2 a. 2 q a ad 4.) where the word, *magisterium* simply designates the function of the teacher and has not yet acquired its modern meaning of '*the* Magisterium.'" Congar, "Theologians and the Magisterium," 218.

48. "The period was marred by papal corruption (including simony, i.e. the buying and selling of church offices, nepotism, lavish lifestyles, concubinage, brutality, even murder) and the domination of the papacy by German kings and by powerful Roman aristocratic families." McBrien, *Lives of the Popes*, 127.

49. "Although the successive movements from the end of eleventh century onwards were very different from one another, they have in common one demand, often sounding like a protest: *less* of the Church and *more of Christ*." Congar, *Tradition*, 138.

consolidation and transfer of imperial power to the office of the Bishop of Rome effectively transformed the self-understanding of the church.[50]

While the popes themselves most effectively promoted theories supporting claims to Roman primacy, the spiritual character and organizational effectiveness of the popes following the Council of Chalcedon cannot be denied.[51] The consolidation of the papal monarchy during the pontificates of the eleventh and twelfth centuries generated a highly organized papal administration with a system of legates (papal representatives) who rivaled the authority of local bishops. Papal claims of authority in relation to emperors and kings continued to be effectively forwarded.

In the thirteenth century claims of papal authority reached a zenith in the pontificates of Innocent III (1198–1216) and Boniface VIII (1294–1303). Innocent III reframes the papacy, claiming no longer to be simply the vicar of Peter; now, the pope is the vicar of Christ.[52] Boniface VIII, in his bull *Unam Sanctam*, "gives classical expression to the papal concept of the Church as it was understood after eight and half centuries of theoretical and practical development upon foundations laid by Leo I."[53]

> By the words of the Gospel we are taught that the two swords, namely the spiritual authority and the temporal are in the power of

---

50. Augustine's mystical body ecclesiology, significantly adapted over time, is hardly recognized as the *congregatio fidelium*. By the beginning of the eleventh century, the distinction between laity and clergy has taken on a particularly divisive character. With the vast majority of Christians unable to read Latin, the scriptures become the sole domain of the ordained. The church effectively becomes synonymous with the clergy. "On pourrait commencer à cette époque la liste des témoignages faisant consister l'Église principalement dans le clergé." Congar, *L'Église*, 57.

51. Eric Jay points to Gregory I as an example. "He [Gregory] followed his predecessors in maintaining that the see of Rome is 'the Church of the blessed Peter,' and that its bishops were the heirs of the 'prince of the apostles' from whom they had inherited the power to bind and loose. But he saw authority as to be exercised only in humility and service; and the more so, the greater the authority might be. He laboured incessantly to protect Rome from the invading Lombards; he fought plague and famine; he promoted missions for the conversion of the northern barbarians; and in all this displayed a high order of political wisdom, administrative ability, and pastoral concern." Jay, *Church*, 1:99.

52. Jay notes a letter from Innocent III to King John of England in which his understanding of "vicar of Christ" is expressed. "Jesus Christ who is both King of kings and eternal Priest has established both his kingdom and his priesthood in the Church. The Church, therefore, is both a priestly kingdom and a royal priesthood. Christ has set one, the Bishop of Rome, as his vicar on earth over all. As every knee should bow to Jesus, so obedience is required of his vicar. . . . Kingdom and priesthood, for the benefit of each, are to be united in the person of the vicar of Christ." Ibid., 109.

53. Ibid., 110.

the church.... Both swords, therefore, the spiritual and the temporal, are in the power of the church. The former is to be used by the Church, the latter for the church; the one by the hand of the priest, the other by the hand of kings and knights, but at the command and permission of the priest.[54]

In a world ruled by two swords, spiritual and temporal, the potential for abuse steadily increased and set the context within which the synthesis of scripture, church, and tradition would begin to dissolve.[55]

## *William of Ockham*

With the advent of the fourteenth century a chorus of dissenting ecclesial voices came to the fore; among them William of Ockham, to whom Congar attributes the beginning of a new world.[56] Ockham's distinctive epistemology set the stage for a whole new way of thinking and demanded a reassessment of the medieval coinherence of church, scripture, and tradition. Ockham offered a reading of both scripture and tradition that placed the institutional church, particularly in the mode of papal monarchy, under considerable critique.

### "SANE UNDERSTANDING" OF THE SCRIPTURAL TEXTS

With Ockham, the medieval metaphysical synthesis of concept and being began to disintegrate.[57] According to Ockham, universals, as entities, do

54. Ibid., 111.

55. Bernard of Clairvaux cautioned and admonished Pope Eugenius III against an imperial lifestyle that "was likely to present the pope to the world as the successor of Constantine rather than St. Peter." Ibid., 107.

56. "Le grand souci d'Occam est de defendre la liberté des personnes. En ceci jouent à la fois son réflexe d'Anglais, favorable à l'individu, sa philosophie du sujet concret individual et enfin son évangélisme franciscain, qui s'exprime dans une affirmation originale de la liberté évangélique: *libertas evangelicae legis*. Le moins de règles possible! C'est la première fois qu'un théologien de class fait une application ecclésiologique effective de cette grande idée. Les chrétiens ne sont plus sous l'ancienne Loi! Il y a là, chez Occam, un element positif chrétien bien remarquable. Il est initiateur d'un monde nouveau." Congar, *L'Église*, 294.

57. "The assumption that the human mind knows things by intellectually grasping their inherent forms—whether through interior illumination by transcendent Ideas, as in Plato and Augustine, or through the active intellect's abstraction of immanent universals from sense-perceived particulars, as in Aristotle and Aquinas—was now challenged. In the absence of that basic epistemological presupposition, the ambitiously comprehensive systems constructed by the thirteenth-century Scholastics were no longer possible. With the displacement of abstract speculation by empirical evidence as the basis of knowledge, the earlier metaphysical systems seemed increasingly implausible." Tarnas, *Passion*, 208.

not exist. Taking Aristotle's emphasis of concrete particulars to its logical extreme, Ockham asserts that the world consists only of singulars. What is real, and therefore knowable, is the particular.[58] These philosophical commitments underlie Ockham's critical attack on the Avignonese papacy of John XXII.

Ockham approaches questions of catholic faith, including the right reading of scripture, tradition, and papal decrees, from a "sane understanding" of the texts.[59] This interpretative reading presupposes the active involvement of individual Christians as members of the *congregatio fidelium*. Ockham's ecclesiology places great emphasis on how faith acts in constituting the church: the church is the congregation of the faithful, and it is the faith of believers that grounds the church, not vice versa.[60]

According to Ockham, individuals, as rational beings, have a right way of experiencing the world. Christian life, as an interpretative experience, only works on the principle that individuals experience and conceptualize that experience for themselves.[61] Human experience, mediated via concepts, is signed in text or speech to other individuals. Comprehension of the communicated concepts takes place through similar means and is dependent on the experience of the receiver. For Ockham, the principle of Christian faith protects the interpretative enterprise of each Christian. Therefore, the right reading of scripture and tradition is not dependent on a single member, i.e., the pope. Because it is the faith of the believers that grounds the church, the interpretative dimension of Christian life is critical to the faith of the church. Individuals are not bound to institutional authority for its own sake, nor can they be forced to accept papal interpretations that fly in the face of reason and scripture "sanely understood." Papal insistence that Christians suspend judgment on unresolved questions until a final ruling is given represents the gravest of all errors, emptying Christian faith and life of its very essence.[62]

58. "Human concepts possessed no metaphysical foundation beyond concrete particulars, and there existed no necessary correspondence between words and things." Ibid., 202.

59. Brett, introduction, 27.

60. Jay, *Church*, 1:131.

61. Brett, introduction, 27.

62. William of Ockham, *On the Power*, 168. Congar points out that the transition from the medieval synthesis through the conciliar crisis to the Reformation is marked by a significant change in ecclesiological consciousness. The hierarchical leadership of the church de-emphasized the notion of the *congregatio fidelium*, the faithful community continuously sustained by the "ever active *presence of God*" and moved towards a juridical

In *On the Power of Emperors and Popes* (*OPEP*), Ockham pleads for a recovery of a papacy that serves. Only an erroneous reading of scripture and tradition could lead to John XXII's conclusions regarding the nature of papal power: the pope's claim of *plenitudo potestatis* is heretical and threatens to lead the church into heresy.[63] Citing both the apostolic tradition and the writings of the saints, Ockham shows that John XXII's principate of lordship is antithetical with the correct reading of papal power: the principate of service.[64]

> From all this we may draw the conclusion that papal principate was instituted for the utility and advantage of its subjects and not for the honour and glory or the utility and temporal advantage of the holder of the principate, in such a way that such principate deserves to be called "of service" rather than "of lordship."[65]

Using scripture and tradition, Ockham supports his political vision of the relationship between spiritual and temporal power. Christ, the model for spiritual power, did not eliminate the civil authority and the rights of pagan political systems. These temporal systems, whether in the hands of pagans or Christians, serve the purposes of human organization and are inherently limited: prone towards coercion and despotism. On the other hand, the spiritual leadership manifest in the papacy exists in the world not as coercive power-over, but as the principate of service, primarily concerned to secure and enhance the religious and moral freedom of its subjects.[66]

---

self-understanding. In its extreme expression, curial canonists and theologians exalted papal power in an "almost blasphemous" manner. This is the context that shapes Ockham's thinking. Congar, *Tradition*, 94.

63. Ockham, contrary to those who maintain that Christ gave plentitude of power to Peter, contends that Christ set in place "ancient bounds" delimiting apostolic authority. Christ did not give Peter "any such plenitude of power in temporals and in spirituals, that he might regularly do by right anything not contrary to divine or natural law . . . instead, Christ assigned certain limits to his power which ought not to overstep." William of Ockham, *On the Power*, 74–75.

64. Ibid.

65. Ibid., 87.

66. Ockham's law of liberty/law of gospel is a freedom from coercion. The pope does not exercise a political dominion over temporal conditions and, in fact, the pope should avoid all situations that would demand such involvement, except in the cases of extreme necessity. Even then, in such cases, the subjects of papal authority would obey the pope for spiritual reasons, not temporal reason, acknowledging his superior authority in the spiritual realm. Ibid., 99–107.

## The Unraveling of the Synthesis

Thus, in the tumultuous fourteenth century, the medieval notion of the coinherence of scripture, tradition, and church was seriously questioned as major thinkers entertained theoretical questions that queried the possibility of reading the scriptures "outside" the church. At the heart of these questions are the issues of ecclesial identity and purity. Who is the true church? Who can claim the authority to interpret the received apostolic writings? While these questions formed a small counterstream of thought in the Middle Ages, often expressed in sectarian reform movements, in the fourteenth century for the first time these notions made serious inroads into the philosophical, academic, and political theory of the day. The notion of tradition as authoritative papal teaching to which all members of the church are subject to obey was beginning to be undermined by papal excesses and epistemological implausibility.

### *The Reformation: Martin Luther*

The dawn of the fourteenth century saw the controversial transfer of the papal see to Avignon, only to be superseded by even greater scandals: the Great Western Schism and the excesses of the Renaissance popes. During this time, the papal administration developed various methods, including the sale of indulgences, for securing necessary income to maintain itself as well as the curial administration of the church.[67]

By the time of Martin Luther, the practice of indulgences was well established, offering spiritual security to an age desperate for assurance of divine acceptance.[68] The theology pervading this time emphasized a con-

---

67. Clement VI, the fourth Avignonese pope, established the practice of indulgences in the bull *Unigenitus* which taught, "the treasury of merits, a vast reserve of merit built up by Christ and the saints . . . can be applied to individuals, upon recitation of certain prayers and the performance of certain spiritual works, to offset the burden of sin." McBrien, *Lives of the Popes*, 241.

68. This is particularly true in the case of Martin Luther, whose theological training at Erfurt immersed him in the philosophical world of Ockham and Biel. Trained in the *via moderna*, Luther accepted that speculation about God's nature was a useless enterprise. The theological question that mattered was not God's nature, but God's intention for humanity. Particular emphasis was placed on how a righteous God could be turned towards mercy in the light of human failures. While scripture (Matt 22:37, 39) offered the two commandments of love, Luther's teachers emphasized the impossibility of fulfilling this law. Observation of human nature confirmed that even the most loving act of one human being towards another could not escape being at some level self-serving. Human beings were caught in a desperate dilemma. Only the church as mediator of God's grace

tractual relationship between God and humanity. God created both humanity and the means by which salvation could be attained: the church. All that is lacking in human initiative can be made up by the grace of Christ available only through the church.[69]

> People naturally acted on their fear of being lost and condemned, and many pursued holiness through the church as well as through moral self-improvement. They did not do so because some hocus-pocus had been foisted on them by a greedy and power-hungry church. Their actions had a strong theological underpinning that in turn rested on careful observation of human nature, adherence to the teachings of the Scriptures and the traditions of the church, and assiduous exercise of both reason and common sense.[70]

This theological climate precipitated the ecclesial rupture of the Reformation. When Luther, provoked by Leo X's "preachers of indulgences," wrote the ninety-five theses he intended to illustrate, according to Catholic theology, the erroneous nature of the practice of indulgences.[71] Summoned to a hearing,[72] Luther met Cardinal Cajetan in Augsburg where a single theological issue was discussed: how did human beings gain the merits of Christ? Cajetan maintained that the merits of Christ and saints belonged to the church, which dispensed them for the salvation of souls. Luther countered that "while the church may contain the 'treasury of indulgences,' it does not contain the 'treasury of the life-giving grace of God.'"[73] Christ alone, not the church, is the source of this grace.

---

in Jesus Christ could complete partial human efforts to be pleasing in the divine sight. Kittelson, *Luther*, 64–80.

69. "This theology made such good sense and was so pervasive in Luther's day that everyone encountered it. It appeared not only in depictions of God's righteousness and mercy, but also in a slogan that at least university students knew by heart: 'God will not refuse grace to those who do what is within them.' It appeared in sermons for lay people as well. One preacher commonly exhorted his congregation, 'Do what is in you! Use well your natural powers and whatever special gifts God has given you!' Salvation would follow. Christians could earn the grace of God simply by doing their best." Ibid., 73.

70. Ibid.

71. Giles, *People of Anguish*, 34.

72. Giles notes that Luther "took a fateful step" when he requested the intervention of the emperor to have the hearing moved from Rome to Germany. "From that moment on the indulgence controversy became inextricably involved with the political situation in Germany." Ibid., 43.

73. Ibid.

## Sola Scriptura vs. the Traditions of Men

In the protracted conflict that ensued, Luther became convinced that the Roman church had substituted the traditions of men for the Word of God.[74] Indulgences were symptoms of a much larger problem. The church had developed doctrinal notions that effectively undermined biblical faith in God's salvation.

> This error comes from the fact that they suppose the gospel is the teaching of laws. In brief then, let us point out that there are two ministries of preaching; one is the letter, the other is the spirit. The letter is the law, the spirit is grace. The first belongs to the Old Covenant, the second to the New. The glory of the law is the knowledge of sin; the glory of the Spirit is revelation, or knowledge of grace which is faith. Therefore the law did not justify: indeed, since human frailty found it unbearable, grace is veiled by it on Mount Tabor even to the present time. Unless protected by grace, no one can withstand the power of the law.[75]

Because the Roman church had sin wrong, it necessarily had grace wrong. In Luther's view, there was no escaping the just judgment of the law except through the singular grace of faith in Jesus Christ. Any claim to rend the just judgment of God by means of good works or prayer offerings was nothing less than idolatry. Works righteousness was an abomination of the gospel by which the Roman church lulled the faithful into the false belief that their sinfulness could be absolved by means of good works, including charitable donations.[76]

The basis of Luther's doctrinal reform rested on the principle that scripture alone judges the theological soundness of any teaching or ecclesial practice.[77] The sophists had moved away from the text of scripture,

---

74. "Our opponents, having injected their own views into the words of the fathers, rush forward as [would] an ass under the pelt of a lion. These deceitful workers manufacture principle articles of faith for us, not from the opinions of the fathers, but from their own, which they impose on what the fathers say"; and later, "The traditions of men must be abolished from the church." Luther, "Against Latomus," 159.

75. Ibid., 237.

76. "For they (the sophists) attribute to nature what belongs to the grace of God and this is intolerable. Further they lull men into security so that they do not cleanse away sin. They even diminish the knowledge of the mysteries of Christ, and so also the praise and love of God, for they do not consider the goodness spread out over the sinner by the lavishness of grace, but rather make nature innocent." Ibid., 236.

77. "The opinions of the Thomists, whether approved by the pope or by the council, remain only opinions, and would not become articles of faith even if an angel from

undermining "the soundness of Scripture" by "darkening the understanding of its contents."[78] Adding layer upon layer of authoritative glosses onto the scriptural text, the pure, original sense of the scriptures had been lost. Moreover, the technical language of the glosses further separated the people from the "pure grain of the sound and simple Scriptures."[79] Luther's objection to the authoritative claims of ecclesial traditions highlights two significant aspects of his notion of tradition: a deliberate move to recover the pure and simple gospel available within the scriptures; and, echoing Ockham, a unyielding belief in the ability of individual Christians to access the saving meaning of scripture without the intermediary assistance of an authoritative magisterium.

Luther's move to recover the pure gospel of the sacred scriptures *sans* the excess of ecclesial tradition effectively introduced a wedge between scripture and tradition, fostering contempt for any entity posing as substitute for God's Word.

> The sophists have imposed tyranny and bondage upon our freedom to such a point that we must not resist that twice accursed Aristotle, but are compelled to submit. Shall we therefore be perpetually enslaved and never breathe in Christian liberty, nor sigh from out of this Babylon for our Scriptures and our home? . . . What did the fathers do except seek and present the clear and open testimonies of Scripture? Miserable Christians, whose words and faith still depend on the interpretations of men and who expect clarification from them! This is frivolous and ungodly. The Scriptures are common to all, and are clear enough in respect to what is necessary for salvation, and are also obscure enough for inquiring minds. Let everyone search for his portion in the most abundant and universal Word of God, and let us reject the word of man or else read it with discrimination.[80]

Luther's assertion of the primacy of scripture as the singularly privileged source of Christian faith and life represented a new moment in the ecclesial understanding of tradition. The dialogical and dialectical relationship, so defining of scripture-tradition in the early church, was tipped such

---

heaven were to decree otherwise (Gal. 1:8). For what is asserted without the Scriptures or proven revelation may be held as an opinion, but need not be believed." Luther, "Babylonian Captivity," 29.

78. Luther, "Against Latomus," 237.
79. Ibid.
80. Ibid., 216–17.

that the resulting asymmetry (understood as a necessary corrective in the mind of Luther) displaced tradition, particularly in its authoritative structural form. The clear and pure words of scripture needed no further human confirmation or explanation.

### The Boundaries of Interpretation

Yet, for Luther, there are appropriate boundaries within which the right interpretation of scripture occurs. "In Scripture we should let the words retain their natural force, just as they read, and give no other interpretation unless a clear article of faith compels otherwise."[81] When believers are faced with multiple, conflicting interpretations of the sacred texts they should seek out the texts that are "quite unambiguous and plain," having "one, single, definite interpretation," for these alone can be "the basis of a clear and definite article of faith."[82] Luther rejects the multiplication of "new, unknown, obscure, uncertain" interpretations that place older interpretations into question. "In this way no word in Scripture would remain clear, if license were given to every spirit to produce new interpretations and then say the old interpretation is obscure and uncertain."[83] Luther also rejects the claim of "inward witness" as a false use of the scriptures.[84] Those who assert such claims make the scriptures servant to their inward musings rather than subjecting themselves to the authority of God's word, an authority "greater than the capacity of our intellect to grasp."[85]

## *Luther, Scripture, and Tradition*

Luther's *sola scriptura* had an irreversible effect on the question of tradition and the relationship of both to the Christian community. Embracing a notion of church as the *congregatio fidelium* where the gospel is rightly taught

---

81. Luther, "Confession," 270.

82. "For an uncertain text is as bad as no text at all. Now what kind of Supper can that be, in which there is not text or sure world of Scripture? For Christ's words must be sure and clear, otherwise one simply does not have them. We, however, have a text and interpretation that is quite sure, and we take the plain words just as they stand, and we are not at odds with them." Ibid., 163.

83. Ibid., 271.

84. "The devil stalks about boldly and without disguise and teaches us openly to disregard Scripture, just as Munzer and Karlstadt did, who developed their wisdom out of the witness of their 'inwardness', and needed the Holy Scriptures not for themselves but only for the instruction of others, as an external witness to the witness in their inwardness." Ibid., 290.

85 Luther, "Babylonian Captivity," 35.

and the sacraments rightly administered,[86] Luther extended Augustine's idea of the invisible church of the elect. Breaking with the medieval notion of the church as a God-ordained, hierarchically ordered manifestation of the kingdom of God on earth, Luther set the historical church (law) and the spiritual church (gospel) into a dialectical relationship.[87] Thus, the coinherence of scripture, tradition, and church disintegrated into oppositional tensions. Luther's ecclesial distinction between an internal, spiritual church and an external church rended the synthetic interplay between church, scripture, and tradition. The external church was a suspect entity and no longer the privileged seat of right interpretation of God's word.

Questions surrounding right interpretation would continue to shape the Christian communions committed to *sola scriptura*, generating new models of authority, ecclesial communion, and tradition. Protestants must warrant their particular claims of continuity to the original apostolic faith without the external structure of the papacy. Roman Catholicism must manifest how the historical accretions to the Christian faith can be considered authentic expressions of the apostolic witness to Christ.

## Trent and the Counter-Reformation

Congar observes that Luther had what the pre-reformers lacked: the convergence of both a theological framework and a political basis from which to wage reform.[88] The result was a doctrinal battle that fueled and exacerbated political tensions, particularly the aspirations of the German people for national identity. Theologically, the conflict was the single most formative event of the modern question of tradition. *Sola scriptura* questioned the authority of all extra-scriptural texts. Ripped from the context of a divinely instituted church, entrusted with the task of interpretation, the scriptures were freed to stand alone in judgment on that same church. Does scripture judge the church or does the church judge the scriptures? This question shaped the fragmented Christian communions throughout the ensuing period.

---

86. Jay, *Church*, 1:162–63.
87. Whale, *Protestant Tradition*, 110.
88. Congar, *Tradition*, 138–39.

## Martin Chemnitz

A distinctive Protestant Christian identity emerges in the work of Martin Chemnitz, credited as the founder of Lutheran orthodoxy. Chemnitz analyzes the canons and decrees of Trent in his four-book study, *Examination of the Council of Trent*.[89] Using scripture and selected ancient sources, Chemnitz shows how Trent departs from the teaching of scripture. In his sophisticated analysis of the notion of tradition, Chemnitz distinguishes between eight kinds of "traditions," seven of which are acceptable to the reformers.[90] According to Chemnitz, the papalists use the word "tradition" in ways the ancients would not recognize. Chemnitz accuses them of distortion, imposing a notion of tradition that lumps together ancient testimonies without discrimination, thereby "whitewash[ing] all traditions from one pot in order that they may disguise them under the pretext and appearance of antiquity."[91] The significance of Chemnitz's analysis is his clear assertion that traditions with a basis in the scripture are to be held with respect; all other traditions represent a departure from scripture and must be rejected.

> We have shown that we do not simply reject all traditions which are observed under this name and title among the ancients. For what is either contained in Scripture or is in agreement with it we do not disapprove. The question, however, is rather concerning those traditions which (as Andrade says) cannot be proved by any testimony of Scripture. In the case of these the simple assertion that they are apostolic tradition does not suffice. For with respect to this kind of traditions we have shown at great length both the mistakes of some good men and the frauds of evil men.[92]

The debates of the Counter-Reformation centered on the means by which God made revelation known to humanity. Catholics maintained that the scripture alone did not give the full authentic meaning of salvation: saving truth could only be fully realized within the church through

---

89. Chemnitz, *Examination*.

90. Chemnitz documents seven kinds of tradition that the Reformers accept: (1) the oral and then written transmission of the gospel; (2) the handing down of scripture; (3) the primitive form of the creed; (4) the apostolic exegesis of the scripture; (5) dogmas gleaned from the scriptures; (6) "the catholic consensus of the fathers"; (7) ancient rites and customs of apostolic origin. The eighth type of tradition, unacceptable to the reformers, is the ecclesiastical laws, which have no basis in scripture. Ibid., 217–307.

91. Ibid., 220.

92. Ibid., 306.

the gifts of tradition and the magisterium. Protestants rejected this and attributed to scripture "a perfect transparence" such that the words of the text had absolute value in and of themselves.[93] At the Council of Trent, Roman Catholics struggled to reaffirm the church's understanding that its life and guidance were ultimately sourced in the Holy Spirit. "The Fathers who had come together at Trent proceeded with a double preoccupation: to define and affirm the principles which had always governed the life of the Church, and to eliminate the abuses present here as elsewhere."[94]

## *The Council of Trent*

Studies of the Council of Trent agree that the meaning of tradition and the relationship between sacred scripture, apostolic traditions, and ecclesial traditions were among the most important theological concerns addressed.[95] A review of the use of the word "tradition" in the Trent documents reveals a broad and indiscriminate understanding among the Council participants.[96] Seemingly, the notion of tradition, at the time of Trent, presented a question that had yet come to full term. Theologians differed in their views regarding the normativity of ecclesial traditions versus apostolic traditions. The interventions of various bishops and the discussions during the congregations of theologians[97] indicated that the church as a catholic body was not able to affirm a comprehensive principle of tradition.[98] As

---

93. Congar, *Tradition*, 154–55.
94. Ibid., 157.
95. Ibid.
96. Hubert Jedin notes that the discussion of authoritative tradition ranged from distinguishing between apostolic tradition (written and unwritten) and ecclesial traditions to including "ceremonies" in the definition of tradition. While all agreed that the principle of *sola scriptura* was not sufficient, there was no consensus on "the principle of tradition." Jedin, *History*, 52–98.
97. Twenty-seven theologians participated as non-voting members in the discussion on scripture and tradition. "In these congregations the theologians were to be the only speakers, the prelates' role was to be exclusively that of listeners and spectators, in order that they might grasp the trend of their problems. These men were given the title of *theologi minores*, not because they had less knowledge but because they were in a lower rank and were not numbered among the conciliar Fathers entitled to a vote." Ibid., 59–60.
98. A lay theologian present at Trent presented a list of apostolic traditions in support of the argument that a principle of tradition demanded an established catalogue of tradition. The resulting mix of apostolic and ecclesial traditions was not unusual and exemplified much of the available thinking on the topic of tradition because "the frontiers between dogmatic and disciplinary, apostolic and ecclesiastical traditions were not sharply drawn." Ibid., 63.

discussion ensued, distinctions were suggested that differentiated between "ceremonial" traditions and "those traditions involving the faith."[99] Others suggested that the Council limit their discussion to apostolic traditions. Ultimately, confining itself to the written and unwritten apostolic traditions, the Council of Trent defined that both the scriptures *and* the apostolic traditions were to be held with *affectus pietatis*.[100]

## TRENT AND THE GOSPEL

The Council fathers' understanding of "Gospel" provided the context within which Trent engaged the questions of scripture and tradition. The Gospel, expressed in the singular,[101] was that which "had been promised by the prophets, then promulgated by Jesus Christ, the Son of God, who had charged his apostles with the task of preaching it to every creature, as *the source of all saving truth and of all moral discipline*."[102] Scripture and the apostolic traditions flowed from this single source of salvation. Without referring to the manner in which saving revelation comes to all humanity, the Council located the source of salvation in the words and deeds of Jesus, contained in both scripture and the unwritten apostolic traditions: promulgated by Christ, received by the apostles under the influence of the Holy Spirit and handed down "as though passed on from hand to hand."[103]

According to Congar, "Gospel" held specific content for the Council fathers. While "Trent considers the Gospel under its aspects as the revelation of the divine rules of belief and behavior," the Council's notion of Gospel also integrates four significant components: as doctrine, as promise, as vital presence, and as challenge or new law.[104] At the time of the Council of Trent, the predominant notion of Gospel, as evidenced by John Driedo, was as the event of Christ, "the efficacious word of salvation through faith in Christ Jesus," written on human hearts and effecting

---

99. Congar, *Tradition*, 162.

100. Congar describes *pietas* as "the suitable attitude to have towards that which brings or conditions, or serves salvation (cf. I Tim 4.8): a welcoming acceptance full of respect and trust." Ibid., 163.

101. "According to this, 'Gospel', in the singular, meant primarily, not the text of the four gospels, but a certain salvific *content*: essentially the content relating the saving *event* of Christ." Ibid., 159.

102. Ibid., 157.

103. Ibid., 158.

104. Ibid., 158–59.

conversion through the apostolic preaching.[105] The Gospel, a vital presence and a spiritual law, communicates divine commandments to human hearts. The image of the Gospel as the saving source from which flow the means of redemption allowed Trent to affirm the normativity of apostolic traditions without specifically cataloguing these, thus permitting the question to continue to mature. "So the canonical Scriptures and the traditions are for us the two channels by which the water from the source of the one and only Gospel reaches us."[106]

### Scripture and Tradition

One of the most difficult and much-argued questions of the Council of Trent was its description of the relationship between the scriptures and tradition. Reacting against the Protestant principle of *sola scriptura*, the great majority of the Council fathers asserted the parity of scripture and tradition. Yet, dissenters made important interventions. Was not "the whole of the evangelical truth contained in the Scripture, not merely a part"?[107] The notion of scripture and tradition as two equal and independent streams was initially presented in a draft decree.[108] The expression *partim . . . partim* asserted that revelation was partly contained in the scriptures and partly contained in the apostolic traditions. This much-debated expression never made it into the final decree, although it found its way into a number of post-Tridentine theology manuals.[109] Hubert Jedin notes that when Bonuccio, the leader of the Servite Order, spoke against *partim . . . partim*, the majority of the assembly had, up to that moment, accepted the material division of scripture and tradition.[110] Painstaking discussion resulted in the exclusion of *partim . . . partim* and the affirmation that both scripture *and* the apostolic traditions flow from the saving stream of the one gospel.[111]

---

105. Ibid., 159.

106. Ibid., 160.

107. Jedin, *History*, 74.

108. Some Council fathers attempted to express this relationship "as two independent and parallel sources of the rule of truth which is the Gospel." Congar, *Tradition*, 165.

109. "At this time when an exclusively biblicist tendency was threatening the integrity of the principles according to which the Church had always lived, quite a few Catholic apologists presented Scripture and tradition as two complementary principles." Ibid.

110. Jedin, *History*, 75

111. "Faced with two opposing currents of opinion among the Catholic theologians—the one, perhaps the stronger, in favour of *partim . . . partim*; the other in favour of the sufficiency of Scripture—the council, seeing no adequate solution and ever careful

PARTIM . . . PARTIM

Although Trent clearly avoided the assertion that the saving truth is found partly in scripture and partly in tradition, in the years following, the practical understanding of the relationship between tradition and scripture, particularly as described and taught in the post-Tridentine theology manuals, fully espoused a *partim . . . partim* understanding. Effectively, *sola scriptura* remained a partial and insufficient expression of God's saving truth. This inadequate framing in Catholic contention that the one gospel subsists in the church's scripture and tradition persisted well into the twentieth century, as reflected in the debates on revelation at Vatican II.[112]

Catholic theology has historically maintained that all the necessary truths of salvation are found in the scriptures. Simultaneously, Catholic theology asserts that there is a dynamic relationship between scripture and tradition such that it is not possible to single out a Christian doctrine that is solely based in the scriptures. "In actual practice, the Church holds no truth in virtue of Scripture *alone*, and none in virtue of tradition *alone*."[113]

---

to express itself only where Catholics were in agreement, contented itself with affirming, by juxtaposition and with no precision of their interrelation, the *two forms* under which the Gospel of Jesus Christ is communicated, in its plenitude and purity, as the source of all saving truth and of Christian discipline." Congar, *Tradition*, 165.

112. See Aberigo and Komanchak, *History of Vatican II*, 2:385–91. "A paper entitled 'Observations sur le schéma de Constitution *De Divina Revelatione*,' written by Congar, bearing the notation 'confidential,' and dated June 29, 1963, was distributed by the Dutch DO-C Center (no series number). In it the author lists the three possible positions maintained at that time in the Catholic Church: (a) tradition is a source independent of scripture, transmitting truths not contained in scripture (theory of the two sources); (b) tradition is an interpretation and an unfolding of the content of scripture, which is materially sufficient: everything is in the scripture, everything is in tradition (Geiselmann); and (c) in regard to the essentials, the content of scripture and the content of tradition are identical; tradition goes beyond scripture only in a relative and subordinate way (J. Möhler, Scheeben, Newman, Franzelin). In Congar's view, the position that tradition is broader than scripture (*latius patet*) expresses something that is true but not as understood by the promoters of the formula, which needs to be completed: 'For if tradition contains more than scripture in extent, scripture certainly contains more than tradition in depth, being really inexhaustible' (Congar). The whole of the chapter in the mixed commission's text needed basic improvements, especially by defining what is meant by *tradition*, by specifying that tradition includes the development of doctrine in the Church, and by stating that while the deposit of the word is indeed entrusted to the magisterium, it has also been entrusted to the Church as a whole" (2:386n49).

113. Congar, *Tradition*, 168.

### Counter-Reformation and the Notion of Tradition

In the years following Trent, the separate Christian churches continued to define themselves over and against each other, professing communion with the ancient church through contrastive claims of historical succession (papal magisterium) or recovery of pure doctrine (*sola scriptura*). As Protestants became more and more a "people of the Book," Roman Catholics became ever more juridical and ecclesiocentric. Historical events and social conflicts surrounding the Enlightenment further shaped these distinctive identities such that the initial prophetic rupture evolved into a substantial ecclesial chasm. The subsequent ecclesiologies that developed as each communion established its unique claim to the original gospel witness played a pivotal role in the idea of tradition and its authority for the Christian community.

## Enlightenment to Nineteenth Century

### A Contextual Overview

In the years following the Reformation and Counter-Reformation, significant events would prove to test the truth claims of the separated Christian communions, challenging the very notion of an authoritative tradition, whether scriptural or ecclesial. The dawning of the Age of Reason found Catholic apologists engaged in patristic studies, marshalling various ancient texts to support the Catholic claim as undisputed bearer of an immutable tradition.[114] Chief among these, J. B. Bossuet, a Gallican theologian and bishop of Meaux, argued that variation in religious doctrine was a clear sign of error. Bossuet's historical retrieval asserted that the Christian religion came to the church, whole and complete, from Jesus Christ. As an immutable deposit of faith, the true church passed on this treasure without change or diminishment.[115]

---

114. Owen Chadwick points out that in the early seventeenth century, Catholic apologists and Gallican theologians engaged primarily in the study of patristic texts, paying little attention to the immediate Roman Catholic past of scholasticism. Within a polemical context, these theologians maintained that use of the schoolmen (medieval scholastics) would prove fruitless in their attempts to argue against Protestant theologians. Chadwick, *Bossuet to Newman*, 10–11.

115. Ibid., 5–6. In the early seventeenth century the idea of the *development* of doctrine could only be regarded as a denial of the essence of the church as the source of the one, holy, complete gospel. Bossuet's historical studies portrayed Protestant Christianity as the seat of all variation and, therefore, the source of heresy. Conversely, the Roman Church, even in moments of intense theological deliberation, never wavered.

These early quasi-historical studies soon ceded to serious historical scholarship. In the works of Mabillon and other church historians, the pursuit of historical scholarship as an end in itself offered an avenue towards the truth that they confidently believed could not ultimately contradict itself.[116] The advent of historical scholarship "for its own sake" quickly escalated into scholarly controversies that called into question the veracity of previously unquestioned biblical stories such as the circumstances surrounding the birth of Christ, and spilling over into cherished Catholic Marian lore and hagiography.[117] The controversies were magnified by tension between those who applied a critical historical approach and those who found this approach a threat to the faith.[118] The experience of cognitive dissonance precipitated by historical consciousness and the claims of a unique divine revelation within contingent human history had only just begun to work on Western Christianity.

## *The Enlightenment*

With the advent of the Enlightenment, the pressing questions surrounding the authenticity of biblical and ecclesial claims to authority were amplified to a deafening pitch. The religious wars of the most recent past had effectively undermined the truth claims of Protestants and Catholics alike, such that "commonsense was bound to ask where any party actually had any distinctive truth that was worth knowing."[119] The Enlightenment, in

---

116. "But with Mabillon, Montfaucon, Ruinart, Tillemont, we seem to have passed beyond all consciousness, even remote consciousness of the possible theological or controversial effects of their researches. They are confident that truth will prevail: that truth cannot be incompatible with truth: that the problems are to be solved 'for their own sake': that the argument must be followed where it leads. And so they were laying the foundations of modern history." Ibid., 61.

117. Ibid., 62.

118. "You are beginning to find persons for whom the words 'critical approach' represent sanity and the only fruitful avenue to truth or even apologetic. You are beginning to find other persons for whom the noun *critic* is coming to represent a person who is potentially dangerous to the faith and who is possibly arrogant in spirit because he necessarily pretends to be more enlightened than the great Christian thinkers of the past." Ibid., 63.

119. Clement, *Schleiermacher*, 9.

its English, French, and German expressions,[120] fostered a particular spirit: skeptical, coolly rational, formal, conventional and elegant in manners.[121]

Religious belief in this age of rationalism, divorced from the fracas of Christian denominational life, made only modest claims regarding the supernatural. Deism, first given expression by Lord Herbert of Cherbury, ascribed to a Supreme Being who, having set creation into motion, retired from the scene entirely until the final judgment when just rewards and punishments would be meted out. Humans did not need special revelation to know of the existence and requirements of the Supreme Being. Natural reason attested to both, and validated the necessary worship of God in the intentional embrace of a moral life.

Immanuel Kant gives quintessential expression to Enlightenment religious belief in his *Critique of Practical Reason*. Human beings have a constitutive moral element that necessarily demands that they cannot be bound by external authority. As autonomous agents, through the aid of reason, humans can know and act on that which is intrinsically good and true. Human reason, as such, cannot attain to knowledge of the infinite; it is limited to finite reality. Because the human mind can only take in sense data of spatio-temporal reality, metaphysical speculation about God's being and existence is simply impossible; the limits of the human mind prescribe the unknowability of God. This very limit makes way for true faith in God. Humanity, morally constituted by the "categorical imperative," can infer the existence of a universal moral law and Lawgiver.[122]

## Schleiermacher

As an intellectual current, the Enlightenment dominated the Western worldview for the better part of the late seventeenth and early eighteenth centuries. Counterstreams to this worldview, particularly the Pietist move-

---

120. The flavor of the Enlightenment was different in each of these countries. English Enlightenment with its particular focus on physics and mathematics (i.e., Issac Newton, 1642–1727), is credited with the notion of Deism. French Enlightenment, the most critical of authority and vehement in its anti-clerical expression, boasted Voltaire as a prime example of the atheist, material *philosophes* of this age. The German Enlightenment, not unsympathetic to religious concerns, focused on historical studies as seen in the works of H. S. Reimarus (1694–1768), J. S. Semler (1725–91), and G. E. Lessing (1729–81). Ibid., 8–10.

121. "Indeed, everything had its rationally assigned place, even God who was located at a safe distance from the physical world of natural causes and effects, and the realm of human decisions." Ibid., 11.

122. Ibid., 10–11.

ment and Romanticism, eventually gathered density and made significant contributions to thought and life. In Friedrich Schleiermacher these three powerful currents met and found new theological expression. In a time convulsed by the French Revolution, when both romantics and intellectuals rejected biblical and ecclesial claims of tradition and authority, Christianity found itself relegated to the fringes of the intellectual world. Dismissed as antiquated, dogmatic, and unnecessary, Christian theology, Protestant and Catholic, faced its most serious threat. Schleiermacher's genius engaged the core belief of the age, humanism, and explicated how the "discontents," failing to understand religious belief, ultimately failed to understand the full meaning of the human: religious belief constituted the essential core of humanity. By redefining religion in terms of the human, Schleiermacher startled the philosophical and theological worlds of the eighteenth century and set the stage for debates that raged well into the nineteenth and twentieth centuries. His influence on Roman Catholic theology found particular expression in the German Tübingen school.[123]

## ROBERT BELLARMINE

The reigning ecclesiology of the Roman Catholic Church at this time found its classical expression in the words of Robert Bellarmine. Post-Tridentine Catholicism continued to distinguish itself from the invisible church of Protestants by asserting that "the church is a gathering of human beings as visible and palpable as the assembly of the Roman people or the kingdom of France or the republic of Venice."[124] Membership in the church was not conditioned on internal virtue; membership was solely dependent on an external profession of faith and participation in the sacramental life of the church.[125] Bellarmine defined the church as an "assembly of

---

123. With respect to Schleiermacher's view of tradition, Bradford Hinze notes that Schleiermacher's "formal statements about revelation and doctrine should not distract us from recognizing that in practice Schleiermacher always seriously engages with the biblical and confessional heritage of the past as of continuing influence and relevance, even if it is not the only word or the final word in matters of faith, even if this word can be criticized and reformulated for the good of the faith of the church." Hinze, "J.S. Drey's Critique," 20. The entire *Heythrop Journal* issue in which this article is found offers an excellent glimpse into the extent Schleiermacher's influence on the Catholic theologians of Tübingen.

124. Quoted in Congar, *L'Eglise*, 372.

125. Michael Himes notes, "But Bellarmine was far too good a theologian not to recognize that there is more to the church than this. He admitted that he was speaking *ab externis* and tried to right the balance by treating of the church as made up of body and

humans bound together by the profession of the same faith and the communion of the same sacraments under the governance of legitimate pastors especially under the one vicar of Christ on earth, the Roman pontiff."[126] The visible church was a *societas*; moreover, it was a *societas inaequalis*. Mirroring the "absolutism of seventeenth-century politics," the Roman Catholic Church became more visibly monarchical, with the resulting effect that the hierarchy, in particularly the pope, becoming equated with the church. The church was also *societas perfecta*: perfectly complete within itself, the Roman church lacked nothing to accomplish the task entrusted to it. Projecting a notion of the divine not too dissimilar from the Deists, the Roman Catholic Church contended that God had ordained its perfect existence in history to secure necessary certitude in matters of faith. The church had no need of anything outside of its confines to secure the truth of the gospel or the gospel's just demands.[127]

> Divine intervention was required only for the final suppression of the church's enemies and the vindication and public demonstration of what had always been true of it. Since certainty of teaching was seen as an integral aspect of the church's mission, the *societas perfecta* came to be identified with those who possessed all that was required to fulfill that mission, the hierarchy.[128]

Throughout the eighteenth and nineteenth centuries, this dominant ecclesiology stimulated alternative views as Roman Catholics engaged the Enlightenment and its aftermath. The idea of tradition was critical to these theological considerations, particularly given the post-Tridentine distinction between scripture and tradition, which, for all practical purposes, affirmed tradition as a second source of revelation.[129] Two important and distinctive understandings of tradition emerged from the nineteenth-

---

soul. By this analogy he intended the church to be understood as one reality which is both spiritual and corporal, that is, visible." Himes, *Ongoing Incarnation*, 325.

126. Quoted in Sanks, *Salt, Leaven, and Light*, 90.

127 Michael Himes notes that this contention "also succeeded in excluding any eschatological activity of Christ, any decisive act of God, needed for the perfection of the church." Himes, *Ongoing Incarnation*, 326.

128. Ibid.

129. Roman theologians distinguished between *traditio passiva*, the content of tradition, and *traditio activa*, the hierarchy whose role was to pass tradition down. "Since *tradito* was a category under *revelatio*, the hierarchy was now theologically subsumable under revelation itself." Ibid., 325.

century works of Tübingen scholar Johann Adam Möhler and the Anglican convert to Catholicism John Henry Newman.

## *Johann Adam Möhler*

In Catholic Germany, two very different thought worlds dominated the early nineteenth century.[130] Catholic *Aufklärung* (Enlightenment) and Romantic Catholicism, each interested in church reform, offered dissimilar points of departure for theological reflection and subsequently two very different views of church and tradition. Johann Adam Möhler, unquestionably associated with Romantic Catholicism, nevertheless was not untouched by Catholic *Aufklärung*. In fact, Michael Himes' investigation of Möhler's early writings and teaching indicates that Möhler held these two worldviews in a tensive interplay, mirroring the ecclesiological tension of his context.[131]

### The Influence of Catholic *Aufklärung*

Catholic *Aufklärung*, as a reform movement, was rooted in the Enlightenment's concern for historical criticism. Proponents of the movement welcomed historical studies as a means of examining and reclaiming Catholic doctrine, purged from the accretions of a superstitious past. *Aufklärung* ecclesiology emphasized the individual, moral aspect of Christianity and understood the church primarily as a school of morality. Espousing an episcopalist view of church governance, *Aufklärung* proponents placed

---

130. "These two currents differed so completely in their understanding of the meaning of the Gospel, the nature of the Christian life, and the church's mission and structure; in their respective styles of spirituality, attitudes toward communal and private prayer, types of preaching, sacramental celebrations, and pastoral activities that they are best thought of not as competing theologies but contrasted worldviews." Ibid., 2.

131. "Two profoundly opposed ways of understanding the church are found side by side in Möhler's work at the onset of his career. The tension between them may be one important reason why he has exerted such influence on subsequent Catholic theology and especially ecclesiology. For the tension between the ecclesiology of Möhler's canon law lecture notes emphasizing the church as a legal institution, a *societas inaequalis*, divine by virtue of its founder, endowed with full competence for the attainment of its ends, namely, the achievement of moral rectitude in all people by the proclamation of the correct doctrine of Christ, and the ecclesiology of the articles and reviews he published in the *Theologische Quartalschrift* in 1823 and 1824 with stress on the church's pneumatocentric structure, rejection of an essential hierarchical order, emphasis on the common priesthood of believers, and concern with the quality of the individual's experience of the holy within the community formed by the Christian *Gemeingeist*, is a reflection of the ecclesiological tension felt on every level within German Catholicism by the 1820s." Ibid., 71–72.

significant emphasis on the life and practice of the local church.[132] The church, shielded from error by the Holy Spirit, clarified God's universal law, which could be known because God's law was written in the hearts of all human beings. In Catholic *Aufklärung*, a moralistic, individualistic, and law-oriented ecclesiology emerged, similar to deism: "God is not denied, simply removed."[133]

> Thus the point at which the divine activity 'touches' the church is at the moment of institution. Once Christ has delivered his precepts to his disciples, the divine activity in relation to the church is that of preservation from without, much as the divine activity in relation to the universe is now preservation from without.[134]

Various thinkers within Romantic Catholicism challenged this arid, private, rule-driven notion of church, emphasizing communion, personal experience, and the unity between life and thought.

### Möhler and Drey

J. A. Möhler was highly influenced by early Romantic Catholic thinkers,[135] but the most influential was his teacher and mentor, Johann Sebastian Drey. Like Alois Gügler and J. M. Sailer, Drey maintained that theology was "the systematic expression in self-conscious terms of what lies at the very heart of religious living, as expression that furthers religious experience by clarifying it."[136] Convinced that theology cannot be successful

---

132. *Aufklärung* was influenced by a German form of Gallicanism known as Febronianism. Justinus Febronius, bishop of Trier, "summarized and supplied theoretical underpinning for what had long been the German bishops' stance toward papal authority. Papal primacy is one of honor alone, the papal role being that of direction over the whole church to ensure unity and peace." Ibid., 5.

133. Ibid., 11.

134. Ibid., 11–12.

135. Among the thinkers noted by M. Himes are Alois Gügler (1782–1827), Franz von Baader (1765–1841) and Johann Michael Sailer (1751–1832). Gügler's notion of the Holy Spirit as the enlivening soul of the visible community of church impacts Möhler's early work, as does von Baader's social theory in which he moves from a *Gesellschaft* (society) to a *Gemeinschaft* (community) notion of church. Love, not law, is the bond of unity within the church. Sailer, Catholic pietism's most influential representative, almost eclipses the necessity of the church in his emphasis on personal experience (*Erlebnis*). His stress on a church of spiritually awakened members in contrast to those lost in the deadening routine of ancient liturgy and constrictive moral practice, articulates in dramatic fashion the ecclesiological tensions at work in the German Catholic church of Möhler's day. Ibid., 15–32.

136. Ibid., 33.

when thought is separated from life, Drey pursued a scientific study of theology that integrated the life experience of believers, individually and communally. His assessment of the notion of tradition pointed out how a once vibrantly synthetic union "of life and religion, of *Verstand* in service of *Gemüt*, fell apart because of the divorce of reason and life."[137] As a result of this separation, tradition had come to mean "only the inherited weight of decisions and decrees."[138]

> Thus, for example, the mystical spirit vanished from it too, and those who had sought to save it, such as a Fénelon or a Pascal, were oppressed by the opposing party and silenced. The opposing party . . . clung to the letter, the letter of the Bible, the letter of tradition and history, the letter of the fathers and councils. They had so little knowledge of the advantages that the firm, consistent, organic form of Catholicism gave them against their opponents that they had to be made aware of them by Protestants.[139]

Using "contemporary viewpoints on organicism, history consciousness, and development," Drey re-engages the tradition as a dynamic and fluid *locus theologicus*.[140] Drey posits the unfolding of tradition as "a natural process of causation" emanating from the Holy Spirit. His developmental model of tradition is rooted in philosophical commitments to Romantic idealism, particularly as it was expressed in the works of Friedrich Schelling.[141]

> Living tradition, for Drey, develops in both the belief and practice of the Church, as divine truth unfolds from moment to moment in and through the events, experiences, and actions that bring the eternal decrees of God to historical reality. Tradition represents the idea of the Kingdom of God in renewed, and yet renewable,

137. Ibid., 34.
138. Ibid.
139. Drey, "Toward the Revision," 71.
140. Dietrich and Himes, *Legacy*, 12.

141. "Had Drey culled his transcendental orientation from that of Kant or Fichte, this conceptualization of how the idea of the Kingdom of God is realized in experience might very well have been described in a purely formal manner in which a timeless transcendental ego statically fathoms the eternal Transcendental Ego in and perhaps even as itself. But Drey's transcendental perspective was molded not by Kant or Fichte but by Schelling, for whom the ideality of the divine ideas is woven into the reality of time and the events of history. Due to the influence of Schelling, Drey can speak of the necessity of transcendental experience as yet in process and development, and of the idea of the Kingdom of God (and indeed of all theological *Wissenschaft*) as both an eternal truth and a temporal *Verlauf*." Thiel, "Universal," 59.

clarity, as the developing faith and practice of the Church express and re-express the common life of believers in the course of its historical progress.[142]

Theology, as *wissenschaft* (universal science), expresses the fundamental human drive to translate ultimate feeling to conceptual understanding.[143] Drey adopts Schelling's scientific method to develop his understanding of theology as a true science. Fundamental to this method is the commitment to hold life and thought together. Ideas can only be known through an investigation of the phenomena generated by the idea. Science's ability to explain phenomena leads to the elemental idea(s) underlying the embodied ideal. There is an essential mutuality between the ideal and the real. The ideal can only be known in the real; their separation leads to mere abstraction. For Drey the consummate idea of Christianity is the *Reich-Gottes-Idee*, the Kingdom of God. "That this idea is Christianity's supreme idea is clear from the fact that no notion, or doctrine, not even another idea within Christianity can be mentioned which is not included under this idea, ordered toward it, or derived from it."[144] The idea of the Kingdom of God, mediated in each age of the church through its life, teaching, and practices, gradually unfolds and is realized. The eternal will of God expressed in Kingdom motif is never reduced to the tradition of the church, but for Drey the coinherence of the ideal and real makes the historical life of the church "a concrete, revelatory, and progressive manifestation of the divine will."[145] Given this dynamism by which life and thought are intrinsically intertwined, Drey can confidently maintain *extra ecclesia, nulla theologia*.[146] The concrete expression of Christianity, manifest in the church, is never the perfect embodiment of the ideal. Subsequently the life of the church is *sem-*

---

142 Ibid.

143. Drey differs from Schleiermacher, who maintains that theology is a positive science not a universal science (*wissenschaft*). "For Schleiermacher this meant a science whose component fields and disciplines have no intrinsic relation to one another at all; they are brought together because they are useful for the performance of a particular task." Himes, *Ongoing Incarnation*, 36.

144. Drey, *Brief Introduction*, 25.

145. Thiel, "Universal," 58.

146. "It is the church that provides the phenomenal material for the ideal construction of Christianity. It is the church whose history is shown to be the working out of the ideal. It is the church that is the arena of the *praxis* born of ideal knowledge of Christian scientific theology. All scientific theology is in fact ecclesiology, for the church is the concretization of Christianity, the ideal having taken on reality, 'the concrete expression of the science itself.'" Himes, *Ongoing Incarnation*, 39.

*per reformanda*; theologians play a particularly important role in making the living past available to the present Christian community. Theologians must be immersed in the life of the church while simultaneously standing apart "to act as critic and explorer of new alternatives to current doctrinal and disciplinary positions."[147]

## Early Möhler and Tradition

J. A. Möhler, whose ecclesiological perspective becomes representative of the Tübingen school, deploys Drey's scientific method, showing the coinherence of the ideal and the real by construing the church as a living organism. Substituting *life* for Drey's *idea*,[148] Möhler's organic understanding of the church allows him to integrate notions of consciousness, history, and faith, and thus bridging the contrastive dichotomies (personal inward piety vs. hierarchical visible community) that marked the whole of German Catholicism in his day.[149] Moreover, Möhler's organic ecclesiology places new emphasis on the historical life of the church. "Möhler's church can never be ideal, in the sense of an intellectual construct. It is a living organism and must be studied as embodied."[150]

In *Einheit in der Kirche*, the Spirit is the starting point of ecclesiology. The Spirit makes Christ known in the church, and through Christ believers are brought into union with the Father.[151] The Spirit communicates a "spiritual power of life that perpetuates and transmits itself in the Church" which is nothing less than tradition.[152] Tradition is not simply the transmission of artifacts, dogmas, and practices. Tradition is the external expression of the inner Christian consciousness: life in the Spirit of Christ.

---

147. Ibid., 41.

148. "In *Einheit*, Möhler pursues Drey's method but changes its central category. By taking as his principle the notion of the church as a living organism, Möhler shifts the explanatory element, that which renders the data comprehensible, from idea to life." Ibid., 76.

149. Himes notes that the enthusiasm generated by Möhler's *Einheit* endured long after its original publication. Ibid., 74.

150. Ibid., 76.

151. "The Father sent the Son, and the Son sent the Spirit: in this way God came to us. We come to him in the reverse way: the Holy Spirit guides us to the Son, and the Son to the Father. Therefore, I began with what is temporally first in our becoming Christians." Möhler, *Unity in the Church*, preface.

152. Ibid., 86.

> Christianity does not consist in expressions, formulae, or figures of speech; it is an inner life, a holy power, and all doctrinal concepts and dogmas have value only insofar as they express the inner life that is present with them.[153]

Tradition, expressive of Christian consciousness, is the way of life that distinguishes the faith community from its inception. Christianity is fundamentally a life principle, communicated by God's very Spirit and embodied in the believing community. Scriptures result from the experience of Christian consciousness because "the living gospel always preceded the written gospel and went along with it, even after the authors of Holy Scripture had passed away."[154] Fundamentally, there can be no division between scripture, tradition, and church for Möhler; both scripture and tradition express true Christian consciousness and thereby express the one faith of the church.[155]

> The question if tradition is coordinate with or subordinate to Scripture is to be rejected as based on false principles. There is no antithesis between the two. Moreover, this question has at its base the assumption that Scripture and tradition are transmitted together in two parallel lines. As history indicates, this is not so. They proceed in one another and live in one another.[156]

---

153. Himes, *Ongoing Incarnation*, 76.

154. Möhler, *Unity in the Church*, 113.

155. Möhler makes two important ecclesiological shifts. First, he changes the locus of the Spirit from the individual to the community. The life principle, Christian consciousness, resides completely within the community of faith, past and present. Thus, individual Christians come into their faith identity through an awakening to and participation in the Christian consciousness as expressed in the church. Secondly, with the action of the Spirit relocated within the faith community, it becomes necessary to show how the historical church externally manifests the true internal reality that is Christian consciousness. For Möhler, the relationship between the *Gemeingeist* and the institutional church is simple identification. To separate them would betray their organic unity. Here Schelling's influence on Möhler is evidenced; the ideal precedes and seeks expression in the real, and thus, leads the real back to union with the ideal. "If, then, the Church is to be viewed as the external production of an inner forming power, as the body of a spirit creating itself, it is by all means necessarily this institution through which and in which true faith and true love are preserved and perpetuated. *One* common, true, *life* forms itself through the totality of believers as a result of two factors: a spiritual power and its external organic manifestation. Because of this, as has been said, the Christian Spirit and the Church are related as are spirit and body in the human being." Ibid., 211–12.

156. Ibid., 118.

Möhler's notion of tradition in this early pneumato-ecclesiology reflects his initial commitments to a panentheistic understanding of the God-world relationship.[157] Tradition cannot be separated from the life of the church because from the beginning "tradition is also always the name for the word that was first spoken and is continually expounded in a living way in the Church."[158] Living tradition is inherently continuous with the original apostolic teaching because "the word of the divine Spirit moving through all centuries" cannot produce an outward expression that is inconsistent with its ultimate source and identity.[159] Furthermore, it is not the purpose of tradition to serve as prooftext for specific Christian doctrines. Christ did not prove his teaching; he preached the message, making God consciousness available to all who would hear and believe. Thus, the function of tradition is to "set forth its truth of which each person *is to become inwardly conscious. Tradition is only to refute those who establish foreign developments in the territory of the Church and wish to describe these as Christian doctrine.*"[160]

Convinced that this inward consciousness is universally knowable by those who share in it, Möhler asserts that heresy can be communally recognized and rejected as inconsistent with the organic life of the group.[161] The internal dimension of tradition serves "*to demonstrate the identity of the Christian consciousness of each individual member or of a specific generation with the consciousness of the whole Church.*"[162] The divine power "forming itself in the Church from the Church's beginning" is the same through time and binds all believers together into one church, such that Möhler can say that the church knows no past or future, only the eternal present.[163] The divine Spirit, active in every age of the church, brings members into vital consciousness of their truest identity, each an integral part of the ecclesial whole. This consciousness develops within believers, as a seed

157. See Himes, *Ongoing Incarnation*, 82–125.
158. Möhler, *Unity in the Church*, 107.
159. Ibid., 108.
160. Ibid.

161. "The proof from tradition is a call upon the Christian consciousness that always existed and existed among all. To others who do not have it, it is not yet given. Their statements are rightly rejected; no other action is possible against those who do not have this consciousness, who do not possess the faith." Ibid.

162. Ibid.

163. "As a result the belief of one specific generation and of each individual believer is only a new structure and form of this same divine power." Ibid.

comes into full life. Life within the church nurtures faith and gradually makes believers aware "of his or her character as counterpoint and impression of the whole."[164]

> By tradition, then, as soon as the life of the Church has developed in the believer, that believer will be conscious that his or her Christian consciousness agrees with and is the same as the enduring consciousness of the Church, that the Church never lives through a moment in which she has seen herself different from the believer in essential designations, and thus that the believer is the true, same, faithful likeness of that which is the same and unchangeable.[165]

Though there are different external forms and expressions of the Christian consciousness,[166] there remains "*one* consciousness, *one* faith, because *one* divine power forms them."[167] Christianity can never be reduced to a religion of dogmas and formulas; "it is an inner life, a holy power."[168] As an organic life, Christianity "is capable of development and cultivation;"[169] it "unfolds itself ever more, is always more specific, makes itself always clearer."[170] Therefore divine life, as new creation, develops within the church, attaining to the perfection it both completely contains and eschatologically hopes for. "[T]radition contains these successive unfoldings of the higher seed of life by protecting the inner unity of the life itself."[171]

---

164. Ibid., 109.

165. Ibid.

166. External forms, dogmas and practices, are not to be dismissed as non-essential, contingent expressions. As historical manifestations of the Christian consciousness, these forms participate in the divine life and communicate this life to believers, nurturing the growing consciousness of individual Christians, enlivening their faith. "What is given historically [*historich*], the external faith, thus becomes by the power of the Holy Spirit an individual life in the human person. It carries an unmediated certainty in itself and testifies itself how the discoveries proceeding from the association of spirit and body come to consciousness directly from the inner sense. The believer now makes this Christian truth living in himself or herself an object of perception, and *gnosis* is the result of this self-perception which is an acceptance of truth by truth. Faith is not here seen as something existing outside of us which is in us by concepts alone, but as something united with us, rooted in us, living and expanding life. *Gnosis* is thus a reconstruction of the faith of the Church, a scientific development of the content of a believing mind." Ibid., 175.

167. Ibid., 110.

168. Ibid., 111.

169. Ibid.

170. Ibid., 112.

171. Ibid.

## LATER MÖHLER AND TRADITION

There is significant development in Möhler's ecclesiology in his later works, particularly in *Symbolik*, first published in 1830.[172] Michael Himes notes that a central factor influencing Möhler's development was his growing concern over Schleiermacher's construal of the God-world relationship.[173] Initially persuaded to Schleiermacher's view, Möhler became increasingly aware that the "slippery slope" of panentheism led to outright pantheism.[174] Möhler's critique of Schleiermacher's doctrine of the Trinity allowed him to reground his ecclesiology on new categories that reshaped his notion of tradition.[175]

In *Symbolik*, Möhler shifts from a pneumatological ecclesiology to a christological ecclesiology. His dissatisfaction with a panentheistic view of the God-world relationship originates in his concern to safeguard both the transcendence of God and human freedom.[176] Möhler's early theology reacted to a deistic ecclesiology whereby God seemingly initiated the church and then left it in human hands. But Möhler came to see that his initial formulation of the divine-human relationship in *Einheit* threatened the integrity of the human: reducing humanity to the stuff by which the divine realized the divine self.[177] Subsequently, Möhler turned to the classical

---

172. Möhler worked on subsequent editions of this text, five in all, until his death in 1838. Himes, *Ongoing Incarnation*, 209.

173. Ibid., 152–208.

174. Ibid., see esp. chs. 2–5.

175. Ibid., 181.

176. Ibid., 258–95. It is important to understand that for Möhler, the God-world relationship functions a *Grundidee*, much like the kingdom of God functions in Drey's ecclesiology. Möhler's overriding concern is to preserve God's freedom and transcendence (258). Creation is an expression of God's freedom: completely gratuitous, the created world exists when it did not have to be. Thus, maintaining his earlier position whereby the individual comes to truth through participation in the *Gemeinschaft* of the community threatened to reduce the divine self-communication to the community's self-consciousness. Möhler becomes convinced that the individual does not encounter revelation by growing into the group consciousness. On the contrary, revelation is divine self-communication that stands over and against the believers (295).

177. "He had come to see that, for all its brilliance and warmth, that way of establishing the Christian life as an ecclesial life foundered on an unstable God-humankind relation. If the first ecclesiological direction reduced the divine element in the church to its initial founding and then left it to human beings to construct and govern the community, the second was in grave danger of reducing the human component to nothing more than raw material for divine agency and of deifying the church." Ibid., 190.

christological formula of Chalcedon as a guide for positing a divine-human relationship that guarded both God's transcendence and human freedom.

No longer an ecclesial communion born at Pentecost, Möhler relocated the inception of the church at the incarnation. "The visible church is the extension of the Incarnation. The church is implicitly contained in the person of Christ."[178] The predominance of the visible church in *Symbolik* is indicative of Möhler's concern for the God-world relationship. Previously, in *Einheit*, Möhler's focus on the union between the divine and the human threatened to collapse the two, eclipsing their relatedness. In order to establish true relationship and not simple identity, the human has to be posited outside the divine: confronted, not conjoined. This is the condition of the possibility of revelation,[179] and this confrontation must be made in human terms: visible, historical revelation.[180] The revelation of God in Christ requires a visible church.

> Thus, to *a visible society of men*, is this great, important, and mysterious work entrusted. The ultimate reason of the visibility of the Church is to be found in the *incarnation* of the Divine Word. Had the Word descended into the hearts of men, without taking the form of a servant, and accordingly without appearing in a corporeal shape, then only an internal, invisible Church would have been established. But since the Word became flesh, it expressed itself in an outward, perceptible, and human manner . . .[181]

178. "Thus, the visible Church, from the point of view here taken, is the Son of God himself, everlastingly manifesting himself among men in a human form perpetually renovated, and eternally young—the permanent incarnation of the same, as in Holy Writ, even the faithful are called 'the body of Christ.' Hence it is evident that the church, though composed of men, is yet not purely human. Nay, as in Christ the divinity and the humanity are to be clearly distinguished, though both are bound in unity; so is he in his permanent manifestation, is at once divine and human—she is the union of both." Ibid., 259.

179. "For Möhler in 1828, however, revelation is not a matter of union between God and humanity; rather it is precisely because God and humanity stand over against each other that revelation is required. Revelation is required because there is a relationship between God and the human person, not simple identity or even functional identity, which is the danger of panentheism." Ibid., 196.

180. "Man is so much a creature of sense, that the interior world—the world of ideas—must be presented to him in the form of an image, to enable him to obtain a consciousness, or to gain a true and clear apprehension of it, and to hold by it firmly as the truth; and indeed the image must be *permanent*, that being present to every individual through the whole course of the human history, it may constantly renew the prototype. Hence, the authority of the Church is necessary, if Christ be true, determining authority for us." Möhler, *Symbolism*, 265–66.

181. Ibid., 258.

Möhler argues that the logic of the incarnation demands a visible continuation of God's revelation in time and space. The Protestant understanding of an invisible church ultimately undermines the notion of historical revelation confronting humanity with divine authority and purpose.[182] Such an ecclesiology, disconnected from external authority, is doomed to subjectivize revelation, making religion an essentially personal matter. Moreover, an invisible church undermines God's authority in the God-world relationship by disallowing the mediation of the divine authority in history.[183]

> On the other hand, the authority of the Church is the medium of all, which in the Christian religion resteth on authority, and is authority, that is to say, the Christian religion itself; so that Christ himself is only in so far an authority, as the Church is an authority.[184]

Möhler's christocentric ecclesiology refocuses his understanding of tradition, placing renewed emphasis on the formative role of the church in the life of believers. Still convinced of the interpenetration of the ideal and the real in all life, Möhler describes his notion of Christian consciousness in distinctly embodied and historical terms. Christian consciousness is less an immersion in ideal *Gemeingeist* and much more a concrete encounter with communal practices and customs of the Christian community. Speaking of tradition in both its subjective and objective senses, Möhler maintains that subjective tradition grounds the believer in the life of faith. The formative influence of subjective tradition molds the heart of the believer such that "a deep interior sense is formed."[185]

Mohler's understanding of tradition as "a peculiarly Christian tact" is a thoroughly embodied and historical notion. Just as national character

---

182. "If the Church be not the authority representing Christ, then all again relapses into darkness, uncertainty, doubt, distraction, unbelief, and superstition; *revelation becomes null and void, fails of its real purpose, and must henceforth be even called into question, and finally denied.*" Ibid., 266–67.

183. Möhler comes to the understanding "of magisterial authority (however specific expression of that authority may have developed in accord with the dynamics of human societies) as speaking not only *from* the believing community but *to* it, giving voice not only to the present consciousness of the community but the transcendent principle within that consciousness." Himes, *Ongoing Incarnation*, 199.

184. Möhler, *Symbolism*, 266; emphasis original.

185. "By a confiding attachment to the perpetuated Apostleship, by education in the Church, by hearing, learning and living in her pale, by the reception of the higher principle," the hearts of believers are shaped and prepared to receive God's word. Ibid., 277.

marks and distinguishes a people with a "peculiar character, stamped on the deepest, most hidden parts of its being," so Christ, God's true self-communication, transmits a manner of existing in the world, a "fundamental principle," that "retained the spirit of the founder."[186] If the genius of a people can be known and expressed over time, such that members can rightly detect spirits alien to their kin, how much more does Christ, divine founder of the church, transmit "an unerring standard of thought and action for all those who follow such a founder; for the breath of life, which proceeded from him, guides, like a natural impulse, the movements of the whole community."[187] Thus, Christ in the church, and the church in Christ, safeguards the veracity of all ecclesial doctrines and dogmas. These teachings are the objective tradition, the true interpretation of the scriptures.

> Tradition, in the objective sense, is the general faith of the Church through all ages, manifested by outward historical testimonies; in this sense, tradition is usually termed the norma—the standard of Scriptural interpretation—the rule of faith.[188]

The doctrine of the church and the doctrine of scripture are united such that the church cannot err in its interpretation of the scriptures. But the divine truth, expressed in history, necessarily must be found in varying and diverse forms.[189] Thus Möhler asserts that the inherent unity between the scriptures and the church is a unity of substance, not of form.[190] When the Divine Word became human faith it became subject to the laws and limits of history and the human mind.[191] In Möhler's understanding of

---

186. Ibid., 281.

187. Ibid.

188. Ibid., 279.

189. ". . . so this unity applies to the substance only, and not to the form. In respect to the latter, a diversity is found inherent in the very essence and object of the Church, so that, indeed if the divine truth must be preserved and propagated by human organs, the diversity we speak of could not possibly be avoided . . ." Ibid., 288.

190. For Möhler the coinherence of scripture, church, and tradition is so real that "when instruction through the apostleship, and the ecclesiastical education in the way described, takes place in the individual, the Sacred Scriptures are not even necessary for our acquisition of their general contents" This can only be so, if the church is understood as Christ's continuing manifestation in history. "The Church is the body of the Lord: it is, in its universality, his visible form—his permanent, ever-renovated, humanity—his eternal revelation. He dwells in the community; all his promises, all his gifts are bequeathed to the community—but to no individual, as such, since the time of the apostles." Ibid., 278–79.

191. The Divine word "must be constantly received by all the energies of the human

history, this means that divine revelation is simultaneously the original moment of revelation in Christ and the ongoing explication of the original revelation. In history, the unfolding of various disputes serves to clarify and solidify the original self-communication of God in Christ.[192] The "human method" of philosophical reflection, "the peculiar activity of man," advances the original revelation, particularly as false notions attempt to parade as true Christian doctrine.[193]

> The origin of the Nicene formula furnishes the best solution to this question. This form is in itself the human, the temporal, the perishable element, and might be exchanged for a hundred others. Accordingly, tradition often hands down to later generations the original deposit in another form, because that deposit hath been entrusted to the care of men, whose conduct must be guided by the circumstances wherein they are placed.[194]

Tradition, as Christian consciousness, develops as a result of the contest and struggle of history.[195] From the initial struggle, be it with Judaizers, Gnostics, or Manichees, to the Reformation conflict, the living tradition can only assert that which Christ himself would assert.

> The deepest reason for this conduct of the Church lies in the indisputable truth, that she was not found by Holy Writ, but already existed before its several parts appeared. The certainty which she has of the truth of her own doctrines, is an immediate one, for she received her dogmas from the lips of Christ and the apostles; and by the power of the Divine Spirit, they are indelibly stamped on her consciousness or as Irenaeus expresses it, on her heart. If the Church were to endeavor, by learned investigation, to seek her doctrines, she would fall into the most absurd inconsistency, and annihilate her very self. . . . The essential matter of Holy Writ is

---

mind, and imbibed by the same. The preservation and communication of the Word were, in like manner attached to a human method." Ibid., 289.

192. ". . . for various questions of dispute arose, the settlement whereof could not be avoided, and on that account claimed human reflection, and required the formation of notions, judgments and conclusions—things which were not possible to be effected, without tasking the reason and the understanding." Ibid.

193. ". . . the false notions cannot by any means be repelled in a clear, distinct, evident and intelligible manner, unless the Church have regard to the form of the error, and exhibit its thesis in a shape, qualified by the garb, wherein the adverse doctrine is invested, and thus render itself intelligible to all contemporaries." Ibid., 290.

194. Ibid.

195. Ibid., 292.

eternally present in the Church because it is her heart's-blood—her breath—her soul—her all. She exists only by Christ, and yet, she must have to find him out![196]

Although Möhler's notion of tradition clearly shifts with his move from a pneumatological ecclesiology to a christocentric ecclesiology, both represent a locally informed response to the excessively juridical ecclesiologies coming from Rome. The Tübingen blend of Catholic Romanticism, particularly as informed by the philosophical project of Schelling, permeates both the early and later works of Möhler: the interpenetration of the real and the ideal provides the tacit context within which Möhler's understanding of Christian consciousness evolves. But these commitments follow distinctly different trajectories when Möhler reworks his understanding of the God-world relationship. When the mystery of the incarnation replaces the event of Pentecost as focal center of ecclesiological reflection, the result is a move away from tradition as inner power of Divine life (Spirit) to tradition as a distinctly embodied and ongoing historical expression of the Divine Word (Christ).

A markedly different, but equally important view of tradition presents itself in the John Henry Newman's work on the development of doctrine.

## *John Henry Newman*

John Henry Newman responded to the dilemma of historical criticism through an analysis of how living ideas develop in human societies. Unlike liberal philosophies of development, Newman's "hypothesis to account for the difficulty" does not rely on the notion of progress. Newman was a thoroughgoing realist; a conservative who rejected theories that fail to adequately account for the messiness of history. Therefore, Newman approached the Enlightenment split between faith and reason by broadening the notion of reason. "Concerned with the whole mind, not just the narrowly logical faculty, he is also anxious to integrate the intellectual with the moral dimension."[197]

### Antecedent Probabilities

In his early sermons, Newman argues towards an expanded notion of reason. Faith is the reasoning of the religious mind, which acts upon *presump-*

---

196. Ibid., 296.
197. Ker, *Newman on Being a Christian*, 7.

*tions* rather than *evidences*.[198] Faith cannot be reduced to belief based on evidence; nor does faith necessarily follow on the heels of well-reasoned disputations. "Faith follows or not, according to the state of the heart."[199] Biblical evidence indicates that faith is "a novel principle of action," for which a person may or may not be able to give a full account in intellectual terms. The moral element in faith contributes towards a particular cast of mind: an antecedent probability. In the case of Christians, this is the antecedent probability of revelation. Thus, all beliefs, including religious faith, are less dependent on evidence and more determined by "previously entertained principles, views, and wishes."[200] According to Newman, the Enlightenment emphasis on the evidences of Christianity accounts incompletely for the phenomena of faith, which requires a broader notion of rationality, one that takes into account the affections and the function of particular affinities in the process of assent.[201]

> I do but say that it is antecedent probability that gives meaning to those arguments from facts which are commonly called the Evidences of Revelation; that, whereas mere probability proves nothing, mere facts persuade no one; that probability is to fact, as the soul to the body; that mere presumptions may have no force, but that mere facts have no warmth. A mutilated and defective evidence suffices for persuasion where the heart is alive; but dead evidences, however perfect, can but create a dead faith.[202]

Thus, for Newman, there is an essential linkage between mind and heart in human rationality such that belief is not created by facts, but by the convergence of probabilities. Ultimately for Newman, "We believe because we love."[203]

Given the antecedent probability of revelation, how do beliefs and practices, the historical tradition, come into existence and withstand the

---

198. Ibid., 1–8.

199. Ibid., 2.

200. Ibid., 3.

201. "'A good man and bad man will think very different things probable.' This is why 'a man *is* responsible for his faith because he is responsible for his likings and dislikings, his hopes and his opinions, on all of which his faith depends.'" Ibid.

202. Quoted in Ker, *Newman on Being a Christian*, 4. From Newman's sermon "Faith and Reason, Contrasted as Habits of Mind."

203. Quoted in Ker, *Newman on Being a Christian*, 6. From Newman's sermon "Love and the Safeguard of Faith against Superstition."

fortunes of contingency?[204] Newman readily admits that change is inevitable. Moreover, Newman's notion of development of doctrines posits that, given the way living ideas function in human communities, change is to be expected.

### Newman's Notion of Idea

Knowing humans are constantly in the process of making judgments concerning the nature of things.[205] Some judgments are mere opinions that remain with the knowing person temporarily, while other judgments become "firmly fixed in our minds, with or without good reason, and have a hold upon us, whether they relate to matters of fact, or to principles of conduct, or are views of life and the world, or are prejudices, imaginations or convictions."[206] Thus, the human mind is possessed by ideas that may or may not be real, may or may not be true. The human mind, in concert with other minds, explores the reasonableness of the idea and argues for or against its veracity.

Only a living idea can so "arrest" the mind, moving human beings to engage in a thorough examination of all the implications of its claims.[207]

> At first men will not fully realize what it is that moves them, and will express and explain themselves inadequately. There will be a general agitation of thought, and an action of mind upon mind. There will be a time of confusion, when conceptions and misconceptions are in conflict, and it is uncertain whether anything is to come of the idea at all, or which view of it is to get the start of the others. New lights will be brought to bear upon the original statements of the doctrine put forward; judgments and aspects will accumulate. After a while some definite teaching emerges, and, as

---

204. "Here then I concede to the opponents of historical Christianity, that there are to be found, during the 1800 years through which it has lasted, certain apparent inconsistencies and alteration in its doctrine and its worship." Newman, *Essay on Development*, 9.

205. "It is the characteristic of our minds to be ever engaged in passing judgment on the things which come before us. No sooner do we apprehend than we judge: we allow nothing to stand by itself: we compare, contrast, abstract, generalize, connect, adjust, classify: and we view all our knowledge in the associations with which these processes have invested it." Ibid., 33.

206. Ibid.

207. "When an idea, whether real or not, is of a nature to arrest and possess the mind, it may be said to have life, that is, to live in the mind which is its recipient. Thus, mathematical ideas, real as they are, can hardly properly be called living, at least ordinarily." Ibid., 36.

time proceeds, one view will be modified or expanded by another, and then combined with a third; till the idea to which these various aspects belong, will be to each mind separately what at first it was only to all together."[208]

Should the idea endure through the interrogation and criticism inherent in the reception process, it will "in proportion to its native vigour and subtlety, introduce itself into the framework and details of social life, changing public opinion, and strengthening or undermining the foundations of established order."[209] The process by which an implicit idea comes into explicit expression is development.[210]

IDEA AND DEVELOPMENT

A living idea possesses human communities and engages their questions, temperaments, and energies. The idea works on the community as much as the community works on the idea. "[A]n idea not only modifies, but is modified, or at least influenced by the state of things in which it is carried out, and is dependent in various ways on the circumstances that surround it."[211] Time, modification, exchanges of perceptions, disagreements, disputations, and more time: the process by which an idea moves from implicitness to explicitness is not "a pure evolution from a foregoing, but it is carried on through and by means of communities of men and their leaders and guides; and it employs their minds as its instruments, and depends upon them while it uses them."[212] There is obvious risk involved in the interaction between the idea and the community of thinkers; corruption is a real possibility, but this risk is the price of the life of a true idea.[213]

> It is indeed sometimes said that the stream is clearest near the spring. Whatever use may fairly be made of this image, it does not apply to the history of a philosophy or belief, which on the contrary is more

---

208. Ibid., 37.

209. Ibid., 38.

210. "This process, whether it be longer or shorter in point of time, by which the aspects of an idea are brought into consistency and form, I call this development, being the germination and maturation of some truth or apparent truth on a large mental field." Ibid.

211. Ibid., 39.

212. Ibid.

213. "But whatever the risk of corruption from intercourse with the world around, such a risk must be encountered if a great idea is duly to be understood, and much more it is to be fully exhibited." Ibid., 39–40.

equable, and purer, and stronger, when its bed has become deep, and broad, and full. It necessarily arises out of an existing state of things, and for a time savours of the soil. Its vital element needs disengaging from what is foreign and temporary, and is employed in efforts after freedom which become more vigorous and hopeful as its years increase. . . . In time it enters upon strange territory; points of controversy alter their bearing; parties rise and fall around it; dangers and hopes appear in new relations; and old principles reappear under new forms. It changes with them in order to remain the same. In a higher world it is otherwise, but here below to live is to change, and to be perfect is to have changed often.[214]

## Revelation and Apostolic Witness as Implicit Idea

Newman maintains that the original apostolic witness contains the fullness of God's revelation as an implicit idea. The fullness of the Christian idea demands a process by which God's intention can be known. Revelation is God's self-communication. Tradition is the explication of the implicit idea, revelation, over time. Therefore, revelation is not simply subjective. God communicates for a purpose; there is essential doctrine, which becomes explicit in the historical process of development and is utterly necessary for the believer.[215]

> Creeds and dogmas live in the one idea which they are designed to express, and which alone is substantive; and are necessary, because the human mind cannot reflect upon that idea except piecemeal, cannot use it in its oneness and entireness, or without resolving it into a series of aspects and relations.[216]

---

214. Ibid., 40.

215. "People urge that salvation consists, not in believing the propositions that there is a God, that there is a Saviour, that our Lord is God, that there is a Trinity, but in believing in God, in a Saviour, in a Sanctifier; and they object that such propositions are but a formal and human medium destroying all true reception of the Gospel, and making religion a matter of words or of logic, instead of its having its seat in the heart. They are right so far as this, that men can and sometimes do rest in the propositions themselves as expressing intellectual notions; they are wrong when they maintain that men need do so or always do so. The propositions may and must be used, and can easily be used, as the expression of facts, not notions, and they are necessary to the mind in the same way that language is ever necessary for denoting facts, both for ourselves as individuals, and for our intercourse with others . . . A formula, which embodies a dogma for the theologian, readily suggests an object for the worshipper." Newman, *Essay in Aid*, 82–83.

216. Newman, *Essay on Development*, 53.

The movement from implicit to explicit honors both the substantive, complete nature of the original Christian idea and the historically limited expression of this idea in the Christian tradition. Since "there is no one aspect deep enough to exhaust the contents of a real idea"[217] its historical explication serves to draw out the deep truths needed to address questions of particular times and places.[218] New formulations of the original idea do not constitute new or alternative revelation. New expressions signal progress in knowledge of the original revelatory idea. Since it is impossible "to exhaust the contents" of God's revelation in Christ, development in the tradition must be expected as the normal course of things.[219]

### Implicit Ideas, External Forms and True Developments

How does one distinguish true developments of an implicit idea from corruptions, particularly when sameness in external form fails to guarantee an authentic explication of the original idea? Newman acknowledges that "the causes which stimulate the growth of ideas may also disturb them," resulting in corruptions or false developments.[220]

Newman asserts that "revelation is not given, if there be no authority to decide what it is that is given."[221] Since it pleases God to be revealed in the finiteness of creation and history, making specific claims on human minds and hearts, God must provide for "an organ of truth" that will nurture and direct the growth of humanity in its understanding of God's ways.[222] The infallible nature of the original revelation given to the apostles

---

217. Ibid., 35.

218. "If Christianity be a universal religion, suited not simply to one locality or period, but to all times and places, it cannot but vary in its relations and dealings towards the world around it, that is, it will develop." Ibid., 58.

219. "Thus developments of Christianity are proved to have been in the contemplation of its Divine Author, by an argument parallel to that by which we infer intelligence in the system of the physical world. In whatever sense the need and its supply are a proof of design in the visible creation, in the same to the gaps, if the word may be used, which occur in the structure of the original creed of the Church, make it probable that those developments, which grow out of the truths which lie around it, were intended to fill them up." Ibid., 63.

220. Ibid., 170.

221. Ibid., 89.

222. Newman does maintain that all people are capable of receiving and responding to God's revelation because it is available within the heart of every person who listens to their conscience. Christian revelation, while unique, completes and supplements natural religion. Newman, *Essay in Aid*, 250.

cannot be lost to subsequent generations of believers.[223] There must be divine guidance throughout time to judge the forms of Christianity expressive of its original genius.

> Revelation has introduced a new law of divine governance over and above those laws which appear in the natural course of the world; and in consequence we are able to argue for the existence of a standing authority in matters of faith on the analogy of Nature, and from the fact of Christianity.[224]

The reality of human diversity, further exacerbated by contentiousness, can both serve the development of the idea and work towards its corruption. Because progress made in truth requires the engagement of finite minds and hearts, there appears little evidence to support the notion that eternal truths alone can persuade the unanimous allegiance of a group or people. An authoritative body is necessary to command obedience to reveal truths.

> I do not say there are not eternal truths, such as the poet proclaims, which all acknowledge in private, but that there are none sufficiently commanding to be the basis of public union and action. The only general persuasive in matters of conduct is authority; that is, (when truth is the question), a judgment which we feel to be superior to our own. If Christianity is both social and dogmatic, and intended for all ages, it must humanly speaking have an infallible expounder.[225]

The Roman Catholic church shows that it is the "infallible expounder" of Christian faith because ". . . modern Catholicism is nothing else but simply the legitimate growth and complement, that is, the natural and necessary development, of the doctrine of the early church, and . . . its divine authority is included in the divinity of Christianity."[226]

Newman suggests that corrupt developments may be discerned through analysis of the characteristics associated with faithful developments. Towards

---

223. "Supposing the order of nature once broken by the introduction of a revelation, the continuance of that revelation is but a question of degree; and the circumstance that a work has begun makes it more probable than not that it will proceed. We have no reason to suppose that there is so great a distinction of dispensation between ourselves and the first generation of Christians, as that they had a living infallible guidance, and we have not." Newman, *Essay on Development*, 85.

224. Ibid.

225. Ibid., 90.

226. Ibid., 169.

this, he recommends "seven notes of varying cogency, independence and applicability" that correspond to true development.[227]

> There is no corruption if it retains one and the same type, the same principles, the same organization; if its beginnings anticipate its subsequent phases, and its later phenomena protect and subserve its earlier; if it has a power of assimilation and revival, and a vigorous action from first to last.[228]

## Newman and Tradition

Newman's notion of development considers the historical, conditioned relationship between church, scripture, and tradition without engaging the liberal philosophies of progress. Tradition results from the contemplation of the divine idea within the church. The teachings of tradition, dogma, and other definitions of Christian faith further the explication of the divine idea within time and space. Thus, the teachings of the church will run the length of history and are necessary for the complete fruition of the divine revelation. The explication of the divine idea is not a seamless unfolding; it remains a difficult, perilous task, as the Divine Message is risked in new conditions and social times.[229] "No one doctrine can be named which starts complete at first, and gains nothing afterwards from the investigations of faith and the attacks of heresy."[230] Tradition necessarily belongs to the whole church, both the church teaching and the church taught, because growth in tradition can only happen when all members, including the laity, participate thoughtfully and wholeheartedly. Newman remained suspicious of theological schools (in particular the Roman school) that rendered the role of the laity to obedient passivity.[231] Nothing less than the whole church can offer a suitable haven for the living idea of divine revelation.

---

227. Ibid., 171.

228. Ibid.

229. "His Apostles and they alone, possessed, venerated, and protected a Divine Message, as both sacred and sanctifying; and in the collision and conflict of opinions in ancient times or modern, it was that Message, and not any vague or antagonist teaching, that was to succeed in purifying, assimilating, transmuting, and taking into itself the many-coloured beliefs, forms of worship, codes of duty, schools of thought, through which it was ever moving. It was Grace, and it was Truth." Ibid., 356–57.

230. Ibid., 68.

231. "I think certainly that the *Ecclesia docens* is more happy when she has such enthusiastic partisans about her as are here represented, than when she cuts off the faithful from the study of her divine doctrines and the sympathy of her divine contemplations,

> Tradition is "the living voice, the breathing form, the expressive countenance, which preaches, which catechizes." Tradition is more than the sterile repetition of a doctrine, less than rank proliferation; more than logical consequence, less than the random thrusts of the life-force. Tradition is life, moving and developing, governed by laws, sustained by personal forces, penetrated by the Spirit, enlisted by the Spirit, spinning the web of truth untarnished, a vast complexity which is still directed by the one idea.[232]

## Nineteenth-Century Summary

Both Möhler and Newman, though contextually distinctive, responded to an increasingly juridical and centralized Roman Catholic ecclesiology. The reduction of tradition to the teachings of an isolated and entrenched magisterium, hostile to a world no longer subject to its authority, only exacerbated the growing incredulity surrounding claims of infallible papal authority. The ecclesiocentric orientation of the Roman Catholic communion, articulated in the theology of the Roman school, found its consummate advocate in the person of Pius IX, to whom "is attributed the famous declaration: 'La tradizone son' io!'"[233] Architect of Vatican I, Pius IX forwarded the cult of the papacy and realized the hopes of Ultramontane Catholics through successive decisions that effectively undermined episcopal autonomy. Pius IX's *Syllabus of Errors*, cataloging eighty errors associated with modernism, culminated with the final error: "The Roman Pontiff can and ought to reconcile and harmonize himself with progress, with liberalism, and with modern civilization."[234] The convergence of multiple historical, social, and political events provoked a highly defensive response against the perceived threat of modernism. The resulting ecclesiocentrism fostered an isolationist view towards the world, while strongly reinforcing the group's identity as a beleaguered but divinely instituted conduit of eternal life. Roman Catholic attempts to expand on the works of Möhler, Newman, and other theologians seeking to engage modern historical critique were soundly rejected.[235]

and requires from them a *fides implicita* in her word, which in the educated classes will terminate in indifference and in the poorer in superstition." Newman, *Consulting the Faithful*, 106.

232 Biemer, *Newman on Tradition*, 144.
233. Congar, *Tradition*, 206.
234. Sanks, *Salt, Leaven, and Light*, 106.
235. For an excellent review of the Modernist Crisis see O'Connell, *Critics on Trial.*

Underlying this argument is, of course, an ahistorical model of truth and of human knowledge. . . . This clash between the non-historical epistemology, metaphysics and theology of the Roman School and the historical consciousness and historical-critical methods of the nineteenth and twentieth centuries perdured right up to and including the Second Vatican Council.[236]

## Conclusion

Although, the rhetoric of tradition in Roman Catholicism could lead one to believe that tradition is fundamentally about conserving, the evidence indicates that tradition is as much a process of tradition*ing* as it is a product or result, received whole. Conserving energies, often linked with dominant power structures, highlight the received, transcendent quality of divine revelation and foster a notion of tradition as *fidei depositum*, a sacred trust. Forces of innovation, at times associated with the pressing questions of an age, highlight the immanent presence of the revealing Spirit and foster a notion of tradition as prophetic lifestyle: a new vision sourced in an ancient wisdom. These social forces, with all their corresponding complexities, will be further explored from an anthropological perspective in the next chapter: how traditioning processes shape communal identities.

Roman Catholicism, as a social entity, grew in response to varying political and cultural situations as well as intellectual and philosophical currents. Convinced of its divine mission, the church struggled to carry forward God's saving revelation in Jesus the Christ. Integral to this task has been the process by which the community's memory of Jesus is preserved and transmitted, both synchronically and diachronically. Adaptations, shifts in emphases, diversity, and change have undoubtedly marked the historical transmission of Christian revelation. At the same time, from the beginning, Christian communities asserted a specific, *received* story: the life, death, and resurrection of Jesus of Nazareth.

A critical issue evidenced in this review of tradition in Roman Catholicism is the question of right interpretation. The history of Christian tradition is the record of the struggle of interpretation. Caught up in this contest of meanings are all the problems associated with making universal truth claims within contingent history and from cultural particularity. How can a finite, historical, sinful human community make authoritative claims regarding an infinite, eternal, perfectly loving divine revelation?

236. Sanks, *Salt, Leaven, and Light*, 113.

How does the community deal with the distortions, inherent to its historical reality, that threaten to undermine the credibility of its message and mission? What are the enduring connections that authorize and authenticate claims of continuity with the original apostolic revelation? The responses offered to these questions over time reflect the social, political, and cultural structures that ground particular worldviews and underscore the pressing questions and struggles that informed specific contexts. As older forms and expressions of Christian faith grow implausible, new, often initially suspect articulations surface. The dialogical and dialectical process whereby conserving and innovating forces interact, converge, and collide is the condition for the possibility of right interpretation. Attempts to circumvent or abort this process undermine the very process of tradition.

The Christian tradition, a wellspring of sacred symbols, has grounded some of the noblest human movements and, conversely, authorized unspeakable atrocities. As David Tracy has aptly noted, there are no innocent traditions.[237] The symbolic character of the Christian tradition offers the possibility of ever-renewed understanding of the Christian revelation, as well as the risk of failing to "get the message right." In the ambiguity of the religious symbol system is its greatest opportunity and its greatest challenge.

---

237. "At the same time, there is no such thing as an unambiguous tradition; there are no innocent readings of the classics. We are who we are because of the traditions that form us. Our lives are shaped by the preconscious effects of all the traditions whose narratives and ways of envisioning the world have forged our memories and consequently our actions." Tracy, *Plurality and Ambiguity*, 37.

# 3

# Interpretative Anthropology

*Social Identity and Change from the works of Mary Douglas,*
*Victor Turner, and Clifford Geertz*

QUESTIONS AROUND IDENTITY, PARTICULARLY the sources and sustaining energies of social identity, pervade current discourse. In a world made increasingly smaller and more complex by globalization, the processes of identity formation and the cultural/social forces at work in groups, institutions, and societies invites renewed consideration and investigation. Issues surrounding identity have particular significance for theological discourse. As postcolonial, postmodern, and feminist critiques surface and expose underlying, unexamined assumptions, cherished notions of the "order of things" are displaced, pushed off center. In this milieu the notion of tradition and its ability to function authentically in Christian identity formation is suspect. Has the expression of the gospel witness to Jesus the Christ—anthropocentric, hierarchical, and Western—been effectively evacuated of its original promise? Attempts to address this question require further investigation into the complexities of social identity, social change, and how communal traditions function in these processes.

To explore how tradition, as a symbol system, functions in Christian formation and transformation, this chapter investigates social identity and change from a particular perspective and trajectory in cultural anthropology. Interpretative cultural anthropology, with its attention to the function of symbols in culture, offers possible strategies for approaching the specific question of how tradition functions in Roman Catholic identity. The limits of a structural-functionalist approach, particularly its failure to adequately account for the social data surrounding the efficacy of "ritual power," spawned within cultural anthropology a focused investigation into the processes of symbolic communication.[1] This trajectory in cultural anthropology, with its renewed interest in symbol, semiotics, and interpretative anthropology, is well represented in the works of Victor Turner and Clifford Geertz. Turner and Geertz both employ semiotic methodologies that continue to offer rich potential in the study of tradition as a wellspring of religious symbols. Since the mystery of revelation renders all God-talk necessarily symbolic, an interpretative, hermeneutical approach to the Christian symbol system offers a fruitful means towards articulating the surplus of meaning available within the Christian tradition.

Although, strictly speaking, Mary Douglas is more akin to a structuralist perspective than a symbolic perspective, this chapter will also engage her work, particularly her mature reflections. Douglas's lifelong commitment towards describing the relationship between cosmology, cognition, and the variety of social lives that emerge from this relationship offers an important hermeneutical perspective and challenge.

After exploring Douglas, Turner, and Geertz's understanding of social/cultural identity and how change/transformation functions in identity formation, I critically analyze their insights in the light of current cultural anthropology. Building on their critically appropriated works, I explore how their insights might contribute toward a contemporary understanding of Christian tradition and its function in discipleship formation.

## Mary Douglas

Mary Douglas's work has undergone significant transformation, yet always at the service of her initial question: the social character of human cognition. Even more precisely, she has sought to explicate the relationship between social structure and human systems of belief and cosmologies. Douglas employs a structural-functionalist approach to anthropology.[2] She is convinced that there is a causal relationship between social living and social beliefs, reflecting the insights and thinking of Emile Durkheim. In the 1996 introduction to her classic, *Natural Symbols*, Douglas notes two very different intentions simultaneously at work in her research program.

---

1. For an interesting discussion of this, see Bell "Ritual Body," 299–313.

2. Douglas characterizes her method as a "forensic approach to religion" that outlines "a programme for tracing how shifts in organization or in external conditions are accompanied by shifts in the forensic uses of sacred contagion." This methodology has validity for Douglas "since the forensic approach has in its gift the possibility of a Durkheimian analysis of the whole cosmology, with direct implications for theories of cognition, the philosophy of belief and of classification." Douglas, *Natural Symbols*, xvii.

> Looking back on it now with an invitation to write a new introduction I see that my intentions with regard to sociology of religion were subversive and with the times. I wanted to free it from subservience to confessional loyalties embedded in ancient institutions. At the same time my intentions with regard to anthropology were distinctly reactionary. Instead of turning over the old order, the aim was to rehabilitate an old theoretical approach, Durkheimian, and make it available for our understanding of ourselves. In one sense the book was counter-cultural, since I was less interested in attacking forms when they have lost their meanings and suffocate the people involved in them before they die, and much more interested in discovering how they ever get any meaning at all in the first place.[3]

How people think about their experience, the categories they use and those they find implausible, changes and will continue to do so. According to Douglas, these changes are not only the result of growth in science and technological knowledge. Social changes, such as "the dissolution of closed communities and weakening of the coercive control their members exert on each other," have a direct impact on a community's notion of outside danger; the very plausibility of "sacred contagion."[4] The ability to test the idea that social systems inform cosmologies requires a method that can assess several kinds of organizations.

> The model needs to be able to organize a rich store of information, be flexible, and dynamic, so capable of incorporating change. This was my objective in setting up a two-dimensional diagram of cultural bias. On one dimension is variation in constraints on the individual imposed by group membership. On the other the constraints of structure are assessed—that is, rules, classifications, compartments.[5]

Thus was born Douglas's classic assessment model, grid-group.[6] From its inception in 1970 this theory has been a "work in progress."

3. Ibid., xii–xiii.
4. Ibid., xviii.
5. Ibid.
6. Douglas's initial grid-group framework evolved out of her early work in the function of symbols in social life. *Purity and Danger* explored what Douglas believed to be a universal element in human cognitive structures: the human propensity to impose order on experience. In this study, Douglas challenges Durkheim's distinction between the sacred and profane. If both the sacred and the profane are characterized by "contagiousness," what is the qualitative difference between these types of contagion? Douglas insists that dirt is really about disorder. ". . . I believe that ideas about separating, purifying, de-

Douglas sparked a debate that produced numerous studies, both supportive and dismissive. As scholars from a wide variety of fields engaged her model, new permutations were attempted and explored, some (including Douglas) to the point of significantly obscuring the original form. Douglas sees this as part of the dynamism of the idea and welcomes the additions and developments.[7]

## *Douglas's Grid-Group and Social Life*

Social identity and social change are topics that Douglas engages indirectly through her functional analysis of human groups. Douglas wants to explore the differences between types of human societies. Her thesis is that certain types of structures produce certain types of thinking. Thus, in *Natural Symbols*, one of the fallacies she dispels is the myth that secularization is a fundamentally modern phenomenon. Douglas's analysis of different types of primitive cultures reveals that not all primitive cultures are essentially religious. She argues that ritualism, a belief in the efficaciousness of symbolic action, and anti-ritualism, the rejection of this belief, can be found across the board in both primitive and modern cultures. The essential qualities of ritualism are found in both sacramentalism and magic.[8]

Douglas maintains that the possibility to think ritually is dependent on the type of human society that has come to be. She contrasts the life-

---

marcating and punishing transgressions have as their main function to impose system on an inherently untidy experience. It is only by exaggerating the difference between within and without, above and below, male and female, with and against, that a semblance of order is created." *Purity and Danger* pointed out the manifold ways that peoples use classification systems to make sense of their experience. The variety of social strategies for solving the problem of anomaly (avoid it, embrace it, ignore it) raised the question of the possibility of classifying groups by their manner of thinking. This becomes the focus of Douglas's work, resulting in her grid-group model. Douglas, *Purity and Danger*, 4.

7. "With different applications for different fields, it is not surprising that the grid-group diagram never looks exactly the same. It is not necessarily that we have changed our minds . . . or that we are quarreling. Simply, trying to work in two dimensions is extremely difficult, and we are continually moving on, simplifying, shifting axes, or rotating the diagram. . . . There have been great developments. The only thing that matters is the collaborative effort to think about life and human values with a tool that systematically questions the thinker's own starting point. We scout out alternative visions of reality, real alternatives." Douglas, *Natural Symbols*, xxviii.

8. "Both sacramental and magical behaviors are expressions of ritualism. What we learn about the conditions in which magic thrives or declines in primitive cultures should apply to sacramentalism among ourselves and should apply equally to the turning away from magic and ritual which was expressed in the Protestant Reformation." Ibid., 10.

style of Bantu and pygmy peoples, noting that the differences in social structures account for the dramatic difference in religious style. Reflecting on Colin Turnbull's work on the pygmies of the Ituri forest,

> He draws a picture of pygmies, irreverently mocking solemn Bantu rites into which they have been drawn, uncomprehending the magic for hunting and fertility which their Bantu neighbours offer them, overcome with giggling during Bantu attempts to divine for sorcerers, quite unconcerned about incurring pollution of death.[9]

Douglas finds the anti-ritualism of the pygmies parallel to the disdain expressed by Protestants for the empty ritual shows of unthinking "papists." For Douglas, secularization "is an age-old cosmological type, a product of a definable social experience, which need have nothing to do with urban life or modern science."[10]

> I am not merely saying that the people's behavior to their god corresponds to their behavior to each other, though the truism could well be underlined. *I am saying that religious forms as well as social forms are generated by experience in the same dimension.* Pygmies move freely in an uncharted, unsystematized, unbounded social world. I maintain that it would be impossible for them to develop a sacramental religion, as it would be impossible for the neighbouring Bantu farmers, living in their confined villages in forest clearings, to give up magic.[11]

## Grid-Group: The Theory

Mary Douglas proposes that types of human organizations can be classified by assessing how group cohesiveness correlates with group organization. She maintains that both of these factors vary along a continuum from high to low. Her categories, particularly her understanding of restricted codes, are informed by the work of Basil Bernstein in sociolinguistics.[12] There

---

9. Ibid., 14.
10. Ibid., 17.
11. Ibid., 15; emphasis added.

12. Bernstein's analysis of speech patterns among Londoners led him to the conclusion that Londoners employ two different speech codes, depending on their socio-economic position. Restricted codes, used by lower-class Londoners, employ shared understandings of role requirements rather than explanations of inner psychic states to communicate. The latter type of speech pattern, known as elaborated code, is a style of speech used by educated Londoners. As an example, a mother of a poor London family

are a variety of restricted codes used in a wide range of human organizations. Doctors, lawyers, bakers, and soccer teams all use restricted speech codes "which shortens the process of communication by condensing units into pre-arranged coded forms."[13] Most importantly, Douglas perceives *the functional role of restricted code toward enhancing social identity*. "The code enables a given pattern of values to be enforced and allows members to internalize the structure of the group and its norms in the very process of interaction."[14] In this sense the restricted code functions as "a system of control as well as a system of communication."[15]

Douglas's two-dimensional grid-group model allows her to assess how variations in social control (coercive) and social organization (symbol and role clarity) result in social structures with associated, characteristic social thinking patterns.

> We concentrate on the interaction of individuals within two social dimensions. One is order, classification, the symbolic system. The other is pressure, the experience of having no option but to consent to the overwhelming demands of other people.[16]

The vertical axis, *grid*, represents the degree to which peoples share a classification system. Along the vertical axis from zero up, increasingly coherent and ordered classification is mapped. At zero, there is the absence of classification, which Douglas maintains could be utter confusion (no roles, no social boundaries) or the experience of mysticism. Down the vertical axis from zero, increasingly private classification or private thought is mapped. Douglas does not suggest private classification means creating "new conceptual systems from scratch. What is private and innovatory is the way common cultural categories are articulated."[17]

The horizontal axis measures the degree to which *group* pressure is exerted upon the individual. From zero to the right increased pressure to conform to the group is registered. At zero there are no social demands

---

(Bernstein's positional family) is more likely to tell her child to do something because, "In this house good children obey their elders." In contrast to this, Bernstein found that an educated London mother is more likely to assess her child's feelings and appeal to "how good it feels to do something you know is right." Ibid., 54–58.

13. Ibid., 54.
14. Ibid.
15. Ibid., 55.
16. Ibid., 58.
17. Ibid., 61.

made on the individual; the person is alone. From zero to the left the individual has not only escaped group pressure but exerts pressure on the group in increasing measure.[18]

Inspection of the graph created by the two axes allows areas of variance in control and classification to be examined. Above the horizontal line is the area of public classification. Closer to the line are found fringe elements of societies, the marginal sectors. Those found to the lower right tend to be exploited; coercive social forces restrain them. Those to the left of zero have escaped the confines of conformity; here is the realm of innovation.[19]

Douglas identifies four specific social settings from different positions on the grid-group map. (Actually, there are three represented social settings, one of which is a dual structure). These representative types of social structures produce and reinforce specific cosmologies or ways of thinking about the "really real." Although Douglas herself notes that her original thinking on these categories was static, I am going to give an overview of them because her latest work does not radically depart from her original insight. Scholarly exchange has allowed Douglas to refine and modify her thinking on how social institutions and individuals interact. Her lifelong interest remains the study of processes of mutual transformation between individuals and the institutions in which they live.

## Strong Grid-Group

The top right-hand portion of the map represents organizations in which the forces of social cohesion and the discrimination of social roles and norms are both very high. Strong grid-group organizations have extremely well organized cosmological systems where ritual flourishes, purifying the contamination caused by "eruption of the organic into the social domain" and celebrating "the transcendence of the whole over the part."[20] Here the restricted code reinforces the social structure in the classic Durkheimian expression: God is society and society is God.

---

18. Ibid., 59–60.

19. "A musician can innovate, a painter, inventors and writers, too. If his idea be ignored, he is still on the right. . . . If successful, though, the innovator may see the public system of classification change in his own life-time. If he wants to stay original, he will have to keep thinking of something new. . . . To remain free of the public system of classification, the person needs above all not to covet its rewards." Ibid., 61.

20. Ibid., 146.

Strong grid-groups esteem culture over nature, exerting social control over the physical body as well as the social body.[21] The coercive power of this social structure can fail to perceive how the mind is tied to socially generated categories of culture. Alternative views are not welcomed; anomaly is avoided and rejected. "A small shift in definitions is anathema and worth protecting with bloodshed."[22] Misfortunes validate the moral law; diseases and accidents are either moral failures or they are to be nobly endured. In this social system a metaphysical framework elevates human suffering as "part of the order of being."[23] The resulting cosmology of strong grid-groups is highly differentiated and ordered. This universe is ultimately just.

### Small Group

Douglas locates small group organizations in the lower right-hand quadrant of the grid-group map. These societies manifest a high level of social control and at the same time a low level of internal organization: exhibiting strong external boundaries while experiencing internal role confusion, the result of either the lack of clearly defined roles or roles defined such that they are unattainable. Egalitarianism of this type blurs the internal boundaries of roles and offices because the inequality resulting from acquired or ascribed status offsets the goals of the group. Often these organizations arise in response to negative factors within a larger group. Thus, small group organization is well suited to the mission of resistance and protest. But ultimately, the unwillingness to establish clear roles and internal structures creates a level of social ambiguity that increases the competition between members as different people vie for control of the small group. The experience of internal disruption and division only serves to reinforce the members' conviction that status and roles are a hindrance to social life. When the disruption escalates to a point of no return, schism occurs and small group membership is fragmented. Thus, issues surrounding group membership and retention place a particularly strong emphasis on external

---

21. "A complex social system devises for itself ways of behaving that suggest that human intercourse is disembodied compared with that of animal creation. It uses different degrees of disembodiment to express the social hierarchy. The more refinement, the less smacking of the lips when eating, the less mastication, the less the sound of breathing and walking, the more carefully modulated the laughter, the more controlled the signs of anger, the clearer comes the priestly-aristocratic image." Ibid., 77.

22. Ibid., 146.

23. Ibid., 110.

group boundaries.[24] The ongoing struggle to avoid schism and to keep internal discontent at a minimum becomes the central focus of the group, undermining any sustained attempt at an ongoing mission.[25]

## Strong Grid

Douglas locates strong grid along a span of the grid-group diagram from left to right and towards the highest range of grid. This is a dual society in which leaders and followers experience different aspects of this social structure. To the left are located the leaders who, through a series of networked corporate relationships, are able to exert control and influence. To the right of center, Douglas locates the followers, who experience increasing coercive force from leaders as they move towards the right. Members in this coerced state are acted upon and tend towards membership in millenarian groups.[26]

Strong grid describes socially open societies that maintain a strong, competitive atmosphere. Douglas describes this in terms of a "success cosmology,"[27] a social world of shifting alliances and confused social categories. The locus of the social world is each individual person and their networked relationships; the allegiances between persons, familial or economic, shift with the changing fortunes of the individual person.[28]

---

24 Boundary transgression is the act of a traitor: return to the group happens only through ritual cleansing. Boundary integrity must be guarded by a constant awareness of those who could possibly compromise the group, subjecting it to a traitorous unleashing of evil of cosmic proportions; witchcraft is a common accusation in these groups. "Small competitive communities tend to believe themselves in a dangerous universe, threatened by sinister powers operated by fellow human beings. Instead of prayer, fasting and sacrifice to the deity, ritual activity is devoted to witch hunting, witch-cleansing, witch-killing and curing from the effects of witchcraft . . . Ambiguity allows competition within a closed circle of kin and neighbours. In the competition the dangerous powers of the universe are alleged to be under the control of the rival, to whose door all succeeding misfortunes are laid." These beliefs are used in social life of blame and expel those who appear to threaten the group through a lack of conformity. Moreover, since ambiguity feeds role confusion and internal conflict, witch cosmology legitimates schism and expulsion. Ibid., 111.

25. Ibid., 113.

26. "Their options are few. They experience strong grid. Therefore they are susceptible to religious movements which celebrate this experience. Unlike those who have internalized the classifications of society and who accept its pressures as aids to realizing the meanings they afford, these classes are peripheral. They express their spiritual independence in the predicted way, by shaggier, more bizarre appearance, and more ready abandonment of control." Ibid., 93.

27. Ibid., 128, 130, 136.

28. "Where a man is expected to build his own career by transacting with all and sundry as widely as possible to the best of his ability, there is a very different view of human

Although the leaders and followers have distinctly different social experiences, they share the same worldview.[29] In a dual society, postulated on a success cosmology, there is little support for individual development that is not based on personal accomplishment. Since the rules only allow for a limited few to achieve maximum success, the lure of equal opportunity results in extensive competition with the inevitable result of winners and losers.

Strong grid cosmology reflects a highly individualistic, competitive system that asserts a fundamentally optimistic, morally neutral view of the world: the world is meant for human enjoyment and manipulated by straightforward rules. Strong grid societies, fundamentally preoccupied with success, represent an ego-focused social system that purports equal opportunity for all, when in reality the situation is fraught with inequality. Leaders' experience of shifting allegiances places a premium on keeping followers appeased. Competitive forces undermine person-to-person relationships and order the social world according to impersonal rules. There is "limited moral basis" in strong grid structures. Some "moral restraints are generated in the competition itself. Though they inform the concept of the upright man, the honest broker, they do nothing further to relate the individual to any final purposes of the community as such."[30] In the words of Robert Schreiter, Douglas's strong grid society lacks a *telos*.[31]

## *Douglas's More Recent Work*

Those who have studied Douglas's grid-group and followed its development over the years are aware of its limits and its potentials.[32] James Spickard notes that Douglas has changed her unit of analysis from "society"

---

nature. In these competitive conditions, men are not set on either side of a line dividing humanity from inhumanity. They are seen to be unequally endowed with talents, but the inequality is random, unpredictable and unconnected with moral judgement." Ibid., 126.

29. "Their ephemeral social contacts and imperviousness to personal pressures enable them to see the cosmos as a rational order not dominated by people but by manipulable objects. These objects are the impersonal rules which govern their transactions. Their world is not controlled by independent ghosts and witches, or evil men. There is no sin: only stupidity. Human nature is divided between the foolish and the wise, between "those who know," and the others. They feel no need for symbolic action other than triumphal feasts for symbolizing the control of society by the self. Hence, a certain blindness to any symbolic representations of the self being controlled by society which mysteriously transcends it and vests it with greater significance." Ibid., 139.

30. Ibid., 137.

31. Schreiter, *New Catholicity*, 10, 131.

32. Spickard, "Guide," 151–70.

to "institutions," allowing her more freedom in assessing the variety of institutions and social situations that compose present complex societies. Moving away from grid-group as a universal map, Douglas speaks of institutions as tending towards three ideal types of social structures, which are reconsidered versions of earlier grid-group types. Douglas also attends to the manner in which social action is informed by the beliefs held in each social type.[33]

Douglas's "revised functionalism" addresses how beliefs produce structures and structures reinforce beliefs. Beliefs that do not solve problems for people in social situations are implausible. Douglas shows how daily life experience can be used to explain people's belief systems. What is plausible for one group is implausible for another because their social experiences are not comparable. "The exigencies of life in different societies make rational people believe different things about the world."[34]

In *How Institutions Think*, Douglas explores the social factors that create and sustain institutions. Commenting on the factors necessary for institutions to sustain themselves, Douglas notes,

> Any institution that is going to keep its shape needs to gain legitimacy by distinctive grounding in nature and in reason: then it affords to its members a set of analogies with which to explore the world and with which to justify the naturalness and reasonableness of the instituted rules, and it can keep its identifiable continuing form. Any institution then starts to control the memory of its members; it causes them to forget experiences incompatible with its righteous image, and it brings to their minds events which sustain the view of nature that is complementary to itself. It provides the categories of their thought, sets the terms for self-knowledge, and fixes identities. All of this is not enough. It must secure the social edifice by sacralizing the principles of justice.[35]

While there are many different types of institutions, here Douglas focuses on her three ideal types: hierarchical, enclave, and entrepreneurial.

## Egalitarian Enclaves

Egalitarian enclaves (Douglas prefers this term over "sects," which has taken on pejorative connotations) are groups in dispute with the outside world.

---

33. Ibid., 146.
34. Ibid., 154.
35. Douglas, *How Institutions Think*, 112.

As a bounded, egalitarian group, enclaves are characterized by strong group boundaries and weak internal distinctions. According to Douglas three factors mutually inform the social conditions that result in enclave formation. Enclave culture is organized by egalitarian principles, which result from the inability to exert sufficient social pressure to maintain membership. Blurred leadership roles support enclave membership because it expresses the groups "principled opposition to the larger society."[36]

> Trying to be equal, leadership is deliberately and necessarily weak. The result is a fragile organization. The community which has this culture well represented may reap advantages, for it speaks with the voice of conscience. Its opposition to hierarchy makes it a strong spokesman for the underclass, its reproaches against pomp and waste and its suspicion of intellectual pretension raise the normative dialogue to a higher plane.[37]

Douglas describes enclaves as organizations that do not privilege rank. Members are exhorted not to pursue wealth and privilege. Because of their oppositional stance towards "the outside," members lack the patronage of the dominant culture. Enclaves have serious organizational problems to solve because of their weak internal structure. If these problems are not resolved, factions arise within the membership and the enclaves splinter into smaller, more bounded groups primarily focused on the integrity (read purity) of its boundaries. Enclave structure is best suited "for organizing protest and dissent."[38]

### Hierarchical Groups

Douglas's analysis of group life is marked by her premise that people's beliefs serve to justify the structural systems (social relationships) they participate in, which in turn solve the problem of how to deal with collective goods. If egalitarian enclaves (described as "latent groups" in *How Institutions Think*) are best suited as movements of protest, then hierarchical structures provide groups with solutions to the problems of coordination. Hierarchies have diversified, ordered internal structures governed by

---

36. Douglas, *Natural Symbols*, xx.
37. Ibid., xxii.
38. Ibid., xxiii. Douglas notes that some enclaves solve some of their structural problems by organizing hierarchically. Mormons and Roman Catholics are among these types of enclaves. Douglas prefers to call these enclaves "hierarchical groups" and expects that these groups will "show a typically hierarchical culture" (xx).

formal rules. "Its advantages are in its clearly stratified and specialized pattern of roles: it can organize effectively; it is resilient and tenacious in the face of adversity."[39] Because hierarchical structures are able to withstand the contingencies of time and weather conflict within and without, they are able to maintain elaborate doctrines and traditions. Therefore, intellectual achievement is highly valued in hierarchical groups. The disadvantage of this social structure is its exaggeration of regulation and routine. Hierarchical institutions do not respond quickly to new data. Moreover, "there is a pathological tendency to try to control knowledge—for new knowledge is the biggest threat to its ordered rankings. Assimilating new knowledge so that it does not destroy the painstakingly preserved order requires a big output of energy."[40]

ENTREPRENEURIAL INSTITUTIONS

Entrepreneurial institutions are governed by the primacy of the individual. Individuals enter into contractual agreements with others, making and breaking social ties as is required to secure success. "Individualists . . . tend to become more and more uncommitted to each other and more committed to the exciting gamble for big prizes."[41] In this culture, the worshipper is in a singular relationship with God and the universe. Religion is essentially a private affair. The openness that characterizes this social situation affords individuals freedom from social constraint in pursuit of individual ends. In these societies, sin is not a concern, but failure and loss of face are to be avoided at all cost.[42]

While Douglas acknowledges that the perspective afforded by a "revised functionalism" is not among the most popular anthropological lens employed in ethnography today, she (and others as well) maintains that abandoning this view of social life is detrimental to the study of human culture. Douglas's approach offers a nuanced perspective on the causal yet non-deterministic relation between social structures and human cognition

---

39. Ibid.
40. Ibid., xxiv.
41. Douglas, *Essays*, 6.
42. "The freedom of individuals to move out if they are being harassed by neighbours is a freedom to disbelieve the divine punishments that afflict those who defy the community standards. The freedom to say goodbye and walk away does not necessarily imply a loss of religious belief, but it does shake the walls of established religions. Open society leads to private religion." Douglas, *Natural Symbols*, xviii

and belief systems.[43] Douglas insists that anthropologists (and other scholars) must pay attention not only to their unique social location, but also to how their intellectual categories are informed by the social *structures* they live within. How we think and what we believe are informed by the institutions we live in.

## Social Identity and Change

Social identity, as Douglas describes it, is a complex entity, initially emerging from the social activity of classification. Douglas maintains that identity is "conferred" upon objects through a cognitive process of recognition of the "similar." Similarity is not an innate characteristic of objects. Similarity is assigned by human minds in joint agreement. The very notion that similarity is inherent in things results from the experience that "sets of similar things are so well-established within a particular culture that their sameness has the authority of self-evidence. Constructing sameness is an essential intellectual activity that goes unobserved."[44]

The selection process at work in the construction of sameness demands grouping objects into discriminant classes, thus presupposing polarization and exclusion. Classification is a boundary-creating cognitive activity.[45] The social forces at work in the process of identity formation are formative of both the group and the individual. Social, intellectual, and moral processes all work together to inform the task of classification, leading to the creation of a "coherent, workable world."[46]

> Individuals, as they pick and choose among the analogies from nature those they will give credence to, are also picking and choosing at the same time their allies and opponents and the pattern of their future relations. Constituting their version of nature, they are monitoring the constitution of their society. In short, they are constructing a machine for thinking and decision-making on their own behalf.[47]

Douglas's analysis of the relationship between social structure and social belief is based on her conviction that social life (i.e., institutions) is

---

43. Douglas' work remains unapologetically taxonomic. See her "Response to Ninan Smart" in the *Religion* Review Colloquium of her *In the Wilderness*.
44. Douglas, *How Institutions Think*, 60.
45. Ibid.
46. Ibid., 63.
47. Ibid.

legitimated only when it has been successfully embedded in both nature and reason. This entrenchment then allows members to employ a variety of social analogies that order reality according to what is "really real." Furthermore, Douglas maintains that institutions function to control the memory of members by diminishing their practice of remembering experiences that take away from group prestige and calling forward group remembrance of events that enhance group prestige. An institution "provides the categories of . . . thought, sets the terms of self-knowledge, and fixes identities."[48] Moreover, an institution compels individuals towards belief "by sacralizing the principles of justice."[49] Principles of justice appear to be universal precepts that assert a moral authority on all human beings: transgression threatens the moral order of the universe. This corresponds directly to Durkheim's understanding of the sacred. While other elements and their roles in reinforcing social identity may remain unconscious to our awareness, the sacred is most visible and recognizable because it is dangerous. "Entrenched in nature, the sacred flashes out from salient points to defend all the classifications and theories that uphold the institutions."[50]

Social identity is an ongoing dynamic between the individual and the group, where individuals make choices among available analogies to construct a coherent world. Ultimately, the rightness of the social analogy, its "fit" to reality, will depend on its ability to successfully do the work of solving social problems encountered in a contingent world. When the experience of ambiguity or anomaly consistently undermines the constructed social order, adjustments in the social structure must occur. Douglas maintains that, on the whole, social change happens quietly and without much social awareness. Slowly, adjustments are made and shifts in social situations begin to shape the cosmological order.

> We should try to think of cosmology as a set of categories that are in use. It is like lenses which bring into focus and make bearable the manifold challenge of experience. It is not a hard carapace which the tortoise has to carry forever, but something very flexible and easily disjointed. Spare parts can be fitted and adjustments can be made without much trouble. Occasionally a major overhaul is necessary to bring the obsolete set of views into focus with new times and new company. This is conversion. But most of the time

---

48. Ibid., 112.
49. Ibid.
50. Ibid., 113.

adjustments are made so smoothly that one is hardly aware of the shifts of angle until they have developed an obvious disharmony between past and present.[51]

### Conclusion: Douglas and Social Identity/Change

The mutually reinforcing relationship between social structure and cosmology warrants serious attention when considering the nature of social identity and social change. As Douglas maintains, the kinds of institutions we live in greatly shape our values and ideas. The effort to study the institutions that humans tend to create aids our understanding of the experiences that flourish in these social environments. Each of the social structures identified by Douglas has its distinct advantages and disadvantages. Social structures place limits on cognition: certain types of thinking result from certain types of social structure. This is not to say that thought is socially determined or that social structures, as much as they are construed, are the result of "false consciousness." It is to say that cognition is located. Cognition has a social structural location.[52]

In the next section the efficacy of symbols within social groups will be considered in the work of Victor Turner.

## Victor Turner

Victor Turner characterized his work as "comparative symbology," whether he was analyzing Ndembu tribal life or the liminoid phenomena of complex industrial societies.[53] Trained in classical British social anthropology, Turner's study of the social forces at play in the life of the Ndembu people propelled him beyond the confines of structuralist social theory and

---

51. Douglas, *Natural Symbols*, 151.

52. "The two-dimensional diagram presents a set of limits within which the individual can move around. Personally, I believe the limits are real, that it is not possible to stay in two parts of the diagram at once, and that the moral justifications which people give for what they want to do are the hard edges of social change. If they wish for change, they will adopt different justifications, if they wish for continuity, they will call upon those principles which uphold the present order. In a certain sense, the grid/group dimensions are exhaustive of certain possibilities. In another sense, since they are abstractions, suggestions for systematic comparison which can be adapted to whatever level of operations is relevant, they apply to all kinds of social relations, wherever people apply penalties and rewards." Douglas, *Essays*, 4–5.

53. Deflem, "Ritual, Anti-Structure," 15. Turner self-identifies as a comparative symbologist and attributes this to Sigmund Freud in his article "Encounter with Freud," 4.

evolved into "a differentiated methodology for the qualitative analysis of religious symbolic action."[54]

Initially, interested in the role of conflict in social structure, Turner's analysis of the conflicts inherent in Ndembu social structure (matrilineal descent and virilocal marriage) led him to recognize a patterned, four-phased, dynamic process, which he termed *social* drama.[55] Social drama describes the eruption of conflict as phases in the development of possible schism that occur more or less in regular sequence and are processional in form.[56] Conflict is initiated by a *breach* in the norm-governed relationship between persons and groups. There is a period of *mounting crisis* as the effects of the breach, if not resolved quickly, are felt throughout the village. Village leaders initiate *redressive measures* to stem the crisis and restore social equilibrium. Finally, if the adjustments made in the third step are effective, *reintegration* of the troubled parties occurs; if unsuccessful, *schism* results in a split of the village.[57]

From the beginning Turner posited that social structure is a dynamic reality, allowing him to get under the opaqueness of group life to the intrigues of persons and relationships tied up in both structured roles and personal desires.[58] Turner's attentiveness to social process grounds his analysis of Ndembu identity: rather than a contest between insiders/outsiders, Ndembu/not Ndembu, social identity is analyzed for its internal functioning. The social picture is not of a cohesive whole but of contentious

---

54. Boudewijnes, "Ritual Studies," 9.

55. Turner describes his first major work, *Schism and Continuity*, as "dominantly a study of social conflict and of the social mechanisms brought into play to reduce, exclude or resolve the conflict." It is important to note that throughout this study, Turner remains rooted in his structuralist training. "Formal analysis of a social system enables us to locate and isolate critical points and areas in its structure where one might expect, on *a priori* grounds, to find conflicts between occupants of social positions carried into the structure." Turner, *Schism and Continuity*, 78, 90.

56. Ibid., 91.

57. Ibid., 90–94. Turner notes that the new equilibrium is never a return to the old order.

58. Turner, *Ritual Process*, 5. "But beneath the surface conflicts of interests go on and private intrigues provide means whereby individuals seek to realign the social structure in pursuit of their own advantage. Beneath the manifest pattern of daily interactions a reshaping of the social group is taking place—transferences of persons from one faction to another, loss and replenishment of personnel in the followings of leading men—so that in effect a new and at first hidden set of power relations gradually comes into being. There comes a time when this realignment becomes visible in a fresh social drama." Turner, *Schism and Continuity*, 131.

voices structured for competition by the organization of Ndembu social life.[59] In times of crisis, village life is fractured by the departure of seceding members unable to respond to the conciliatory, redressive measures of the village leader(s).[60]

In contrast to ideas of identity that cast the argument in terms of insider/outsider dialectic, Turner discovers "under" the continuity of Ndembu identity ongoing contention within the community, shaping and remaking the social order; in a sense, the shaping and remaking of the Ndembu people.

Turner notes that Ndembu consciousness of being a people results from a common assent of all villages to shared values and laws. "Such a consciousness of national unity obviously depends on the joint recognition by all Ndembu of a common system of values and a common set of norms regulating behavior. Their unity is a moral, rather than a political, unity,"[61] instilled and revitalized most effectively by the community's ritual system.[62] Turner initially viewed Ndembu ritual as one of the available redressive mechanisms employed by the group to maintain social cohesion and unity. However, ongoing fieldwork challenged Turner's initial prejudice towards ritual.

---

59. By making a methodological decision "to take a single village as my universe," Turner explores both synchronically (via spatial, geographical distribution of Ndembu villages) and diachronically (via a series of social dramas over time in a single village) the manner in which social structure constitutes the Ndembu people. Turner's analysis of the social competition between "the unity of the genealogical generation and the unity of the village" reveals that uterine sibling groups (loyalty to brother and sister) prevail over that of the village. Thus, although Ndembu ritual highlights the unity of husband and wife as the most sublime, in reality Ndembu marriage is a very fragile social institution, assailed by the constant pressure of sibling loyalty. Turner, *Schism and Continuity*, 328, 288.

60. In the case of the Ndembu, matrilineal descent and virilocal marriage fuel inherent tensions that constrain village life and force villages to remain small and scattered about geographically. Yet, this very characteristic marks Ndembu identity. For a description of this see in particular *Schism and Continuity*, 288–89.

61. Ibid., 289.

62. "Ndembu society, as we have shown, is torn with perennial disputes, there is little harmony and much conflict between its dominant principles of social organization, and in secular life there is little to bind together more than a small number of people in habitual co-operation. Unity in such a society is maintained by making each outstanding case of personal misfortune the occasion on which the moral norms and values share by all Ndembu are prominently displayed in a number of ways—in prayer, precept, symbol, mimetic action, and in the ritual association of those who have suffered regardless of their kinship or other interlinkages." Ibid., 301.

... I was constantly aware of the thudding of ritual drums in the vicinity of my camp, and the people I knew would often take their leave of me to spend days at a time attending such exotically named rites as Nkula, Wubwang'u and Wubinda. Eventually, I was forced to recognize that if I wanted to know what even a segment of Ndembu culture was really about, I would have to overcome my prejudice against ritual and start to investigate it.[63]

Based on his extensive observations, Turner eventually developed a semiotic theory of ritual efficacy: a method of symbolic analysis in a ritual context that sheds further light on his notion of social identity and social change.

## *Turner and Symbolic Action*

Rituals, symbols, and beliefs are fundamentally connected for Turner and thus play a significant role in his understanding of social identity and change. The study of ritual led him to observe that ritual symbols[64] are always involved in the social process.[65] "I came to see performance of ritual as distinct phases in the social processes whereby groups became adjusted to internal changes and adapted to their external environment."[66] Rituals are filled with polyvalent symbols that function authoritatively and evoke responses from the participants. Symbols encapsulate the norms and values of the group reinforcing social identity. At the same time, ritual symbols exert a transformative power acting upon and changing attitudes and behaviors of the participants.[67]

63. Turner, *Ritual Process*, 7.

64. "The symbols I observed in the field were, empirically objects, activities, relationships, events, gestures, and spatial units in a ritual situation." Turner, *Forest of Symbols*, 19.

65. Turner maintains this position throughout his anthropological studies. In an article recounting Freud's influence on his notion of symbol, Turner lists other thinkers who, with him, maintain that "ritual language is often a language 'about' non-ritual social and cultural processes rather than a direct expression or reflection of them, as the positivist functionalists supposed it to be. It is a metalanguage with its own special grammar and vocabulary for scrutinizing the assumptions and principles which in non-ritual (mundane, secular, everyday, or profane) contexts are apparently axiomatic. This critical function of ritual is still incompletely recognized by investigators who continue to see ritual either as a distorted reflection of 'reality' (that is, 'empirical' or 'pragmatic' reality) or as an obsessional defense mechanism of culture against culturally defined illicit impulses and emotions." Turner, *Blazing the Trail*, 24.

66. Turner, *Forest of Symbols*, 20.

67. Clearly it is difficult to separate the processes of social identity and transformation in Turner's thought. From the beginning, Turner's conception of social structure (tra-

Turner's semiotic approach to ritual exposes the transformative potential residing in the interstices of social structure, which, incidentally, cannot be considered synonymous for the "social." "Field experience and general reading in the arts and humanities convinced me that the 'social' is not identical with the 'social-structural'. There are other modalities of the social relationship."[68]

Perhaps this, then, "the social relationship," is at the heart of social identity for Turner. Human beings who identify themselves as belonging to a people, tribe, nation, or group participate in a dynamic social engagement in which elements of identity and transformation constantly intersect, challenging the notion of a fixed or static identity. While values and norms govern group life, the content of the values and norms are simultaneously being negotiated with each new ritual invocation of their inherent (and inherited) supremacy.

Turner's understanding of ritual as symbolic action in process and his extrapolation of this insight into a theory of social life as a dialectical process between *communitas* and structure hinge on his understanding of ritual symbols and their function.

### Turner's Dominant and Instrumental Symbols

Social identity is caught up in social practice, a dynamic reality where the structural aspects of roles, values, and norms are in constant interplay with the forces of change: contingent events and the dilemmas, dramas, and desires of individuals (and small aggregates of individuals). Focusing on Ndembu ritual process, Turner came to understand that the Ndembu symbol system would not yield to strict structural-functionalist analysis.

> But I was immediately confronted with the difficulty that many of the hundreds, even thousands, of distinguishable symbolic objects and actions I found in ritual performances seemed on the face of it to have little, if anything, directly to do with components of social structure as defined above. And it was no use ignoring this aggre-

---

ditionally the locus of identity) is dynamic. In static models of social structure, conflicts are essentially disruptive of the established order: change threatens structure. Turner's work discloses how conflictual situations among the Ndembu actually create the occasion to call forward the primary elements of Ndembu identity. In and through ritual, the common mind and heart of the people as a people are made symbolically present.

68. "The use of social-structural models has been extremely helpful in clarifying many dark areas of culture and society, but, like other major insights, the structural viewpoint has become in the course of time a fetter and a fetish." Turner, *Ritual Process*, 131.

gate of individual symbols and declaring that at any rate the "implicit aim" or "latent function" of ritual was "to promote or restore social cohesion" and "to reanimate the sentiments of solidarity on which the collective life depends." . . . *The specificity of each symbol and their shifting combinations and permutations in performative ensembles presented a challenge I could scarcely avoid.*[69]

Accordingly, Turner employs methods of structural analysis, cultural anthropology and social dynamics, all of which he believes are necessary to arrive at an adequate interpretation of a living symbol.[70]

Living symbols possess characteristics that allow various aspects of social life to come to expression in a ritual process. Some aspects of social life are consciously expressed and affirmed by indigenous participants, ranging from the pragmatics of the lay perspective to the esoteric interpretations of the ritual specialist. In either case, they most often represent the norm-governed group consciousness. Turner's application of contextual analysis expands indigenous interpretation and, by observing how symbols are used within the total symbol system, other aspects of Ndembu society are made visible: elements that native interpreters may not readily recognize or acknowledge.[71]

---

69. Turner, *Blazing the Trail*, 3–4; emphasis added.

70. "I have suggested in this essay that different aspects of ritual symbolism can be analyzed within the framework of structuralist theory and of cultural anthropology respectively. As I have said, this would be to treat ritual symbols as timeless entities. Many useful conclusions can be arrived at by these methods, the essential nature, both of dominant symbols and of constellations of instrumental symbols, is that they are dynamic factors. Static analysis would here presuppose a corpse, and, as Jung says, 'a symbol is alive.' It is alive only in so far as it is 'pregnant with meaning' for men and women, who interact by observing, transgressing, and manipulating for private ends the norms and values that the symbol expresses." Turner, *Forest of Symbols*, 44.

71. Following the advice of Central Africanist Monica Wilson, Turner uses native exegetical expertise as one of the three fields of meaning explored towards culling the hermeneutical fullness of ritual symbols: exegetical, operational, and positional meaning. Exegesis contains the meanings attributed to the symbol by indigenous informants: received by the anthropologist through interviews with adepts, participants, ritual specialists, and laity. Operational meaning is established by observing how the symbol is handled in ritual. Both what is said about the symbol and how it is used is taken into consideration. Positional meaning is arrived at from observation of the symbol's relationship within the totality of the symbol system. Together these three fields of interpretation reveal how symbols function in a ritual context. Ibid., 50–51.

## Dominant Symbols

Turner distinguishes between *dominant* and *instrumental* symbols. Instrumental symbols are "univocal," generally limited to a single ritual context, and play a role in effecting the specific goal of the ritual. Instrumental symbols can only be understood within the wider context of the total symbol system.[72] Dominant symbols, found throughout various Ndembu rituals, possess three important characteristics: condensation (or multivocality), unification, and polarization.[73]

## Condensation, Unification, Polarization, and Sigmund Freud

Condensation, according to Turner, refers to the symbol's ability to represent many things and actions in a single form. Condensation, also described as "polysemy" or "polyvalency," highlights the flexibility inherent to symbols. Unlike signs, which point towards a single reality and are primarily univocal, symbols are multireferential. In his discussion of condensation and reference, Turner notes Edward Sapir's influence on his understanding of referential symbols and condensation symbols.

> Like Jung's "sign," the referential symbol is predominantly cognitive and refers to known facts. The second class, which includes most ritual symbols, consists of "condensation" symbols, which Sapir defines as "highly condensed forms of substitutive behavior for direct expression, allowing for the ready release of emotional tension in conscious or unconscious form." The condensation symbol is "saturated with emotional quality."[74]

Yet, in an article written only five years before his death, Turner recounts the significant influence played by Sigmund Freud's *The Interpre-*

---

72. Ibid., 32. Turner also describes instrumental symbols as "single-sense vehicles" that are "univocal in representative capacity, having only one meaning, and largely employed to further the ritual action or reinforce of the situationally dominant reference of a dominant symbol." Turner, *Blazing the Trail*, 19.

73. "These vehicles, together with the significations given them by Ndembu, I called 'dominant' symbols. 'Dominance,' however, was a relative quality; a symbol might be dominant in a single episode of complex ritual, in several episodes, in the whole symbolic sequence, in hunters' cults, in gynecological cults, in life-crisis rites, or in the entire field of Ndembu ritual—where it might be considered a 'master' symbol. *Mukula*, the blood tree, was one such master symbol; *mudyi*, the milk tree, was another; *musoli*, the revelatory tree, yet another, as my various writings on Ndembu ritual abundantly document." Turner, *Blazing the Trail*, 19.

74. Turner, *Forest of Symbols*, 29.

*tation of Dreams* in his development of a hermeneutic of ritual symbols. Turner explains that his analysis uses Freudian categories "analogously and metaphorically"[75] such that Freud's "style of thinking" and not his "actual inventory of concepts and hypotheses" helped Turner come to his own "independent theoretical position."[76] While the extent of Freud's influence on Turner continues to be debated[77] (even to the point of suggesting that Turner "socialized" Freudian psychoanalytical concepts),[78] Turner represented himself as ad hoc and creatively selective in his use of Freud.[79]

Confronted with a mass of symbolic data that proved to be intractable to structural-functionalist analysis, Turner discovered in the multi-referential character of Freud's dream symbols a key towards unlocking the cultural meanings available in "each symbol and their shifting combinations and permutations in performance ensemble."[80] Moreover, Turner discovered that, similar to Freud's notion of consonance,[81] the seemingly

75. Turner, *Blazing the Trail*, 21.

76. Ibid., 28.

77. Elliot Oring maintains that Freud's influence on Turner goes far beyond that of mere "style." Turner's hermeneutic of ritual symbols employs two Freudian categories, *condensation* and *unification*, and, although *polarization* reflects much more the influence of Levi-Strauss, Oring asserts that Freudian analysis clearly takes into consideration the positional dimension of symbols. "Each and every aspect of Turner's ritual symbol—its nominal, substantial, and artifactual foundations, its exegetical, operational, and positional dimensions of meaning was well as its sensory and ideological polarization—is easily derived from Freud's theory of dream representations. It is no wonder that Turner emphasized the particular influence of *The Interpretation of Dreams* on his work. What he neglected to reveal was the extent of his indebtedness. He did not borrow a few psychological concepts from Freud but an entire theory of symbol." Oring, "Victor Turner," 285.

78. See Frederick Turner, "'Hyperion to a Satyr.'"

79. "Freud's intellectual cutting tools were better honed to slice up the beast I was intent on carving . . . than those bequeathed to me by the social anthropologists, who were concerned mainly with social and political control mechanisms. . . . I am still Durkheimian enough to think that it is theoretically inadmissible to explain social facts, such as ritual symbols, directly by the concepts of depth psychology. But one can learn a great deal from the way a master thinker and craftsman works with data, especially when he is working in an adjacent field of problems." Turner, *Blazing the Trail*, 21–22.

80. Ibid., 4.

81. "One and only one of these logical relations is very highly favoured by the mechanism of dream-formation; namely, the relation of similarity, consonance or approximation—the relation of 'just as.' This relation, unlike any other, is capable of being represented in dreams in a variety of ways . . . Similarity, consonance, the possession of common attributes—all these are represented in dreams by unification, which may either be present already in the material of the dream-thoughts or may be freshly constructed." Freud, *Interpretation of Dreams*, 354–55.

"disparate significata" of dominant symbols could be organized into contrasting clusters. Even trivial and random associations can be conjoined within a single dominant symbol because of shared common, analogous qualities found over an extensive range of corporate life.[82]

> Their very generality enables them to bracket together the most diverse ideas and phenomena. Thus as we have seen, the milk tree stands for, *inter alia*, women's breasts, motherhood, a novice at Nkang'a, the principle of matriliny, a specific matrilineage, learning, and the unity and persistence of Ndembu society. The themes of nourishment and dependence run through all these diverse *significata*.[83]

From the contrasting clusters of *signata*, Turner construed the notion of two poles functioning within dominant symbols. Polarization refers to a cluster of significata found at both an *ideological* pole and a *sensory* pole within all dominant symbols. The ideological pole refers to all significata related to "components of the moral and social orders of Ndembu society, to principles of social organization, to kinds of corporate grouping, and to the norms and values inherent in structural relationships."[84] The sensory pole of a dominant symbol refers to the outward appearance of the symbol; it is the "'physiological pole' of meaning," conjuring the physical resemblance of a symbol to the bio-physiological world of human life.[85]

A critical dimension of the bipolar characteristic of dominant symbols is the "juxtaposition of the grossly physical and the structurally normative, of the organic and the social."[86] The "coincidence of opposites" encapsulated in dominant symbols has consequences for social action: norms and values deemed obligatory become, via ritual, desirable.[87] Turner's explores

---

82. Turner, *Forest of Symbols*, 28.
83. Ibid.
84. Ibid.
85. Turner refers to the sensory pole as "gross" in two senses: first in the generalized sense of "not taking account of detail," and second in a physiological sense. "Thus, the milk tree has the gross meanings of breast milk, breasts, and the process of breast feeding. These are also gross in the sense that they represent items of universal Ndembu experience. Other Ndembu symbols, at their sensory poles of meaning, represent such themes as blood, male, and female genitalia, semen, urine, and feces. The same symbols, at their ideological poles of meaning, represent the unity and continuity of social groups, primary and association, domestic and political." Ibid., 29.
86. Ibid.
87. Ibid., 30.

## Interpretative Anthropology

how the obligatory becomes desirable with the aid of Freud's notion of sublimation. Noting that "a major difference exists between the sublimation process going on within an individual and this process of sociocultural sublimation,"[88] Turner theorizes that the ritual process creates a social moment where impulses aroused by specific symbols in performative process are deflected towards the normative values of social life.

> These impulses in a culture where ritual was a going concern were regularly aroused by the appearance of the blood tree under the stimulating circumstances of drumming, dancing, singing, wearing unusual dress and body painting, and so on, an appearance which reinforced previous similar experiences in other rituals. The impulses were deflected onto the abstract notions which formed the normative pole of the blood tree's "semantic field," as its total ambience of meaning may be termed. Thus the energy associated with blood images was deflected onto the ordering and maintenance of blood ties.[89]

Turner maintains that the close contact of norms with emotions results in an "interchange of qualities between its poles of meaning."[90]

> Norms and values, on the one hand, become saturated with emotion, while the gross and basic emotions become ennobled through contact with social values. The irksomeness of moral constraint is transformed into the "love of virtue."[91]

Turner's field observations confirm that although anthropologists cannot account for the source of symbols arising from the individual psyche (the domain of psychoanalysis), they must treat symbols and their evocative character as social facts.[92] Turner associates the ritual symbol with Freud's dream symbol and describes it as "a compromise formation between the need for social control and certain innate and universal human drives whose complete gratification would result in a breakdown of that control."[93] There is a contention between the social and individual that dominant symbols bring into the visible arena through ritual process.

---

88. Turner, *Blazing the Trail*, 20–21.
89. Ibid., 20.
90. Turner, *Forest of Symbols*, 30.
91. Ibid.
92. Ibid., 36.
93. Ibid., 37.

Symbols effect action; Turner describes them as "forces" that exert "determinable influences inclining persons and groups to action."[94]

## SYMBOLS AND RITUAL ACTION

Social life is a contest between a variety of forces, voices, and fields of influence, some of which are acknowledged by the participants in a society. There are normative behaviors, verbally affirmed and attested to in native exegesis; there are conflictual behaviors, suppressed in speech, but expressed nonetheless throughout the ritual process.[95]

> Another way of putting it would be to say that not only each kind of ritual but also each phase and episode of a ritual constitutes a discourse or "metasocial commentary" (Geertz 1972:26) on Ndembu culture as viewed from a given sociocultural perspective, a particular corner of observation. Such a commentary may be explicit or implicit, verbal or nonverbal, direct or indirect. In the case of the girls' puberty ritual, its "discourse" reflects upon the full range of consequences of matrilineal organization for Ndembu life. It is a reflection on matriliny itself, the story the Ndembu tell themselves about matriliny. Some consequences are harmonious, others disharmonious. Material objects, such as the milk tree, postulate matriliny as a harmonious frame for social behavior; kinetic and mimetic behaviors (actions) comment upon the struggles between social groups and roles which are the result of dissonance between matriliny and other principles, "commentary" here being in the sense of actions speaking louder than words.[96]

Turner's insight into the depth of meaning expressed in symbolic action helps him to "make visible the invisible" in Ndembu social relationships and offer a dynamic view of the notion of social identity. Ritual as a "system of meanings" within a greater complex of the total symbol system of a group provides a privileged view into the social processes shaping social life. Traditions, as received systems of meaning, possess inherent vital-

---

94. "It is in a field context, moreover, that the properties we have described, namely, polarization of meanings, transference of affectual quality, discrepancy between meanings, and condensations of meanings, become most significant." Ibid., 36.

95. Turner notes that this phenomena of "suppression of speech of what might be termed 'behavioral meaning' is highly relevant." While social life requires the existence of "certain values and norms, imperatives and prohibitions [that] are axiomatic in character, [and] ultimately binding on everyone," in reality equally valid norms can be inconsistent with each other and place individuals and groups into conflict. Ibid., 39–40.

96. Turner, *Blazing the Trail*, 23–24.

ity: submerged, latent, and concealed social meanings may yet emerge.[97] Thus, one of the most important observations Turner makes points out the relationship between symbols and the yet-to-be-known.

> The symbol is the smallest unit of specific structure in Ndembu ritual. The vernacular term for it is *chinjikijilu*, from *ku-jikijila*, "to blaze a trail," by cutting marks on a tree with one's ax or by breaking and bending branches to serve as guides back from the unknown bush to known paths. A symbol, then, is a blaze or landmark, something that connects the unknown with the known.[98]

The indeterminacy of symbols, their ambiguity, allows them to function in a manner that both reveals and conceals. Symbols allow for the contingencies of life; in the not-yet-known there is the possibility of the new.

## *Turner and Social Change*

Turner makes no simple distinction between social identity and social change. While a society may be construed as a "structure of positions,"[99] structural roles and norms, as dynamic realities, are negotiated entities. The forces at play within structural formation are various and often oppositional. In the historical (and therefore contingent) encounter between social norms/values and individual temperament, dispositions, and psyches, what comes to be is unique and *could have been otherwise*. In this way, for Victor Turner, the encounter between the social and the individual is potentially transformative of both.[100]

Social change, understood as change in "place, state, social position, and age," is best analyzed as a process.[101] Arnold Van Gennep's description of three diachronic phases (separation, margin, and aggregation) in *Rites*

---

97. "It is in comparison with other sectors of the total system, and by reference to the dominant articulating principles of the total system, that we often become aware that the overt and ostensible aims and purposes of a given ritual conceal unavowed, and even "unconscious," wishes and goals. We also become aware that a complex relationship exists between the overt and the submerged, the manifest and latent patterns of meaning." Turner, *Forest of Symbols*, 46.

98. Ibid., 48.

99. Ibid., 93.

100. "Turner wanted to bring in the 'human coefficient,' as he called it and show how the social is not something over and above the individual, but how principles of social organization both affect and are manipulated by concrete individuals, i.e., how society and the individual come together." Deflem, "Ritual, Anti-Structure," 19.

101. Turner, *Forest of Symbols*, 94,

*de Passage* provides Turner with a conceptual framework that result in his theory of social life as a dialectical process between social structure and anti-structure.[102] Turner's interpretation of threshold or *limen* is critical to his understanding of social process and change.

### Liminality and Communitas

Turner describes *liminality* as a condition in which social persons slip into the interstices of social structure, caught in a space that is "neither here nor there; they are betwixt and between the positions assigned and arrayed by law, custom, convention, and ceremonial."[103] Liminal persons, deprived of status, position, title, or property, essentially lack social identity, a social persona.[104] As transitional beings, these individuals are in a process of becoming.[105] Their transitional "status," ambiguous and marginal, is yet a recognized source of potency and ritual power.[106] The presence of untapped power in the borderland of liminality is an important dimension of Turner's theory of the social. The experience of liminality, when shared

---

102. In the first phase of passage, *separation*, the focus of the ritual centers on the themes of detachment as ritual subjects embark on the journey of transition from one state of being to another. In the second phase, *margin*, or *limen*, the ritual subjects enter into a time and space of ambiguity. This phase is usually devoid of the cultural and social markers of identity and status associated with the subjects' former state or future state. This phase will become critical to Turner's understanding of the social relationship over time. The third phase, *reaggregation*, celebrates the consummation of the ritual process and the new state of the ritual subjects. Turner, *Ritual Process*, 94–95.

103. Ibid., 95.

104. Moreover, liminal persons in Ndembu initiation rites are "anonymous, sexless, submissive, humble and silent. The neophyte in liminality must be a 'tabula rasa,' a blank slate, on which is inscribed the knowledge and wisdom of the group, in those respects that pertain to the new status." Ibid., 103.

105. ". . . I prefer to regard transition as a process, a becoming, and in the case of *rites de passage* even a transformation—here an apt analogy would be water in process of being heated to boiling point, or a pupa changing from grub to moth. In any case, a transition has different cultural properties from those of a state . . ." Turner, *Forest of Symbols*, 94.

106. Turner observes that the ritual powers of the weak reside in their potential for the new, a potential saturated in the belief that liminal beings possess a sacred character. "One may well ask why it is that liminal situations and roles are almost everywhere attributed with magico-religious properties, or why these should so often be regarded as dangerous, inauspicious, or polluting to persons, objects, events and relationships that have not been ritually incorporated into the liminal context. My view is briefly that from the perspectival viewpoint of those concerned with the maintenance of 'structure', all sustained manifestations of communitas must appear as dangerous and anarchical, and have to be hedged around with prescriptions, prohibitions, and conditions." Turner, *Ritual Process*, 108–9.

by a group of individuals, has the effect of creating a relational moment/phenomenon/event that Turner called *communitas*: a relational space in which all the trappings of structure are suspended.[107] Concrete, historical persons encounter each other beyond the confines of the roles and norms of social personae.[108]

The potency residing in the liminal moment of *communitas* is the critical element in social process. In an apparent contradiction, *communitas*, marked by liminality, marginality, and structural inferiority, animates social action and foment.[109] Prophets and artists are often the manifestation of this energy, offering "glimpses of that unused evolutionary potential in mankind which has not yet been externalized and fixed in structure."[110]

*Communitas* "is often in the subjunctive mood,"[111] and is best expressed in symbolic language.[112] Here, relationships "between total beings

---

107. *Communitas* is a moment of anti-structure. The relationships between individuals are marked by spontaneity, immediacy, and equality. Structure, on the other hand, is characterized by norm-governed, mediated and often hierarchical relationships between social personae. (See Turner, *Ritual Process*, 132.)

Turner emphasizes that the move to *communitas* is not simply the result of biological pressures reacting against the constraints of culture. "Communitas is not solely the product of biologically inherited drives released from cultural constraints. Rather it is the product of peculiarly human faculties, which include rationality, volition, and memory, and which develop with experience of life in society." Ibid., 128. *Communitas* is not a mindless exploding of structure triggered by oppressive outward forces. Choice is a significant element in communitas. "Communitas is not merely instinctual; it involves consciousness and volition." Ibid., 188.

108. "Essentially, communitas is a relationship between concrete, historical, idiosyncratic individuals. These individuals are not segmentalized into roles and statuses but confront one another rather in the manner of Martin Buber's 'I and Thou.' Along with this direct, immediate, and total confrontation of human identities, there tends to go a model of society as a homogeneous, unstructured communitas, whose boundaries are ideally coterminous with those of the human species." Ibid., 132.

109. When discussing a vast array of characters considered liminal (neophytes, mendicants, jesters, small nations) Turner observes, "... all have this common characteristic: they are persons or principles that (1) fall in the interstices of social structure, (2) are on its margins, or (3) occupy its lowest rung." Ibid., 125.

110. Ibid., 128.

111. Ibid.

112. Turner points out that being "forced to have recourse to metaphor and analogy" is not an indication of a lack of scientific precision. "For communitas has an existential quality; it involves the whole man in his relation to other whole men. Structure, on the other hand, has cognitive quality; as Levi-Strauss has perceived, it is essentially a set of classifications, a model for thinking about culture and nature and ordering one's public life." Ibid., 127.

are generative of symbols and metaphors and comparisons; art and religion are their products rather than the legal and political structure."[113] The potency of *communitas* lies in its power "at the edge" where it "transgresses or dissolves the norms that govern structured and institutionalized relationships."[114] Thus, Turner locates the power to change in the liminal, boundary space, the in-between of social structure. On the edge, at the bottom, lie the so-called dangerous, untapped forces: simultaneously a threat to structure and a refuge where "total beings" relate beyond the established, normed existence of social personae.

There is an attractiveness associated with *communitas* that structure does not share: many characteristics of *communitas* resonate with political and moral values of freedom and equality. Structure on the other hand is (all too easily) associated with constraint and oppression. Yet social life without structure is simply impossible; there is a discipline inherent in social life. Norms effect a social order necessary for productive human relationships and ward off social chaos. This is not achieved without negotiation and the give-and-take that is sociopolitical existence.

> Life in "structure" is filled with objective difficulties: decisions have to be made, inclinations sacrificed to the wishes and needs of the group, and physical and social obstacles overcome at some personal cost. Spontaneous communitas has something "magical" about it. Subjectively there is in it the feeling of endless power. But this power untransformed cannot readily be applied to the organizational details of social existence . . . On the other hand, structural action swiftly becomes arid and mechanical if those involved in it are not periodically immersed in the regenerative abyss of communitas.[115]

The nature of social life, according to Turner, involves a dialectical process between moments of structure and moments of *communitas*.[116]

113. Ibid., 128.
114. Ibid.
115. Ibid., 139.

116. Turner distinguishes between three types of *communitas*: existential or spontaneous, normative, and ideological. Of these three, only spontaneous *communitas* is the unstructured manifestation of the liminal social moment. Normative *communitas* results as social control and mobilizing energies are engaged to forward the group's goals and aspirations. Ideological *communitas*, a descriptive expression of the outward features of existential *communitas*, attempts "to spell out the optimal social conditions under which such experiences might be expected to flourish and multiply." Ibid., 132.

Without this dialectic, society does not function appropriately: dominating social structures instigate "pathological manifestations of *communitas*," which in turn generate reactive social structures characterized by "despotism, overbureaucratization, or other modes of structural rigidification."[117] *Communitas* only exists in relation to structure and structure is revitalized only in relation to *communitas*.[118] The periodic, historical manifestation of spontaneous *communitas* among millenarian and "enthusiastic" movements, attempting to make the ecstasy associated with liminality an end in itself, mistakenly ignores an insight into social life expressed in tribal societies.

> In the religion of preindustrial societies, this state is regarded rather as a means to the end of becoming more fully involved in the rich manifold of structural role-playing. In this there is perhaps a greater wisdom, for human beings are responsible to one another in the supplying of humble needs, such as food, drink, clothing, and the careful teaching of material and social techniques. Such responsibilities imply the careful ordering of human relationships and of man's knowledge of nature.[119]

"The careful ordering of human relationships" is as necessary to thriving human social life as the periodic disordering (and ultimately reordering) of those same relationships. Thus, the social is essentially processual.

> Once more we come back to the necessity of seeing man's social life as a process, or rather a multiplicity of processes, in which the character of one type of phase—where communitas is paramount—differs deeply, even abyssally, from that of all others. The great human temptation, found most prominently among utopians, is to resist giving up the good and pleasurable qualities of that one phase to make way for what may be the necessary hardships and dangers of the next.[120]

Ultimately, the multiple processes of social life validate the notion that the structure/antistructure dialectic manifests necessary modalities of the social. In this dynamic, social identity is a constantly evolving entity as

---

117. Ibid., 129.

118. "But the spontaneity and immediacy of communitas—as opposed to the jural-political character of structure—can seldom be maintained for very long. Communitas itself soon develops a structure, in which free relationships between individuals become converted into norm-governed relationships between social personae." Ibid., 132.

119. Ibid., 139.

120. Ibid.

social life moves from structure to *communitas* and back to structure again. The forces that feed this rhythm contribute to social change as energies lodged in the interstices of structure are released and built up into new expressions of ordered social life.

### Conclusion: Turner and Social Identity/Change

Although Turner's notion of culture has been critiqued as a thoroughly modern, integrated understanding of culture, his description of this "integration" is quite nuanced. There is nothing static about Turner's understanding of the social. Moving beyond a strict structural-functionalist view, he approaches the social from the perspective of ritual as symbolic action. Turner maintained throughout his professional life that ritual lends a privileged view into the social identity of a given group. Ritual functions as "a metalanguage with its own special grammar . . . scrutinizing the assumptions and principles which in non-ritual (mundane, secular, everyday, or profane) contexts are apparently axiomatic."[121] Very much like Turner's notion of dominant symbols, rituals, observed in both word and deed, reveal and conceal the social body to itself.[122] The multivocal nature of dominant symbols, with their ability to hold a diversity of meanings in a seemingly dense unity, mirrors the translation of social cacophony into apparent, relative harmony in a ritual context. For Turner, social harmony is always in tensive relationship with social discord. Turner continuously asserts throughout his works the fragile and contingent nature of each negotiation of cultural conflict. Norms and values that govern the social structure of group life are not timeless and static in content; with each new crisis, values and norms are renegotiated and "reintegrated" into the life of the group.

> From the point of view of those enacting a given ritual episode, implicit comment on conflict within supposed harmony may be, if not "unconscious" in the strict Freudian sense, at least temporarily thrust outside the field of individual attention or awareness (is this Freud's pre-conscious?); but from the pansocietal viewpoint its cultural embodiment in symbolic action indicates it to be part

---

121. Turner, *Blazing the Trail*, 24.

122. Rituals, as "metasocial commentaries," both express and suppress common meanings and concerns. Reflecting on the Ndembu, Turner notes that although rituals can only bring into view "one aspect, norm or principle of a cultural or social-structural schema at a time," disharmonious elements find their expression in "kinetic and mimetic behavior," providing additional commentary on the "social group and roles which are the result of dissonance between matriliny and other principles." Ibid., 23–24.

of a collective consciousness, known at least to the ancestors and handed down by tradition—a well from which groups and individuals may draw, if they so need or wish.[123]

Thus, Turner's initial presentation of his notion of *communitas* appears too simplistic to account for the very diversity he describes. The dialectic between *communitas* and structure may be more true to the complexity of social identity when it is examined at the micro level, where life is lived in social relationship: the myriad of normed roles and relationships within the social group. Turner hints at this when he writes of Ndembu women in a later essay:

> Thus women interconnected by matriliny find themselves divided by village affiliation or by loyalty to their husbands or by age group or some other recognized principle. Such division cannot be publicly admitted in ritual which expresses and extols matriliny, or even one of the dyadic relationships (mother's brother/sister's son, mother/daughter, mother's mother's brother/sister's daughter's daughter) composing a matrilineal lineage of restricted span. One might say that communitas based on one principle is constantly endangered by suppressed conflicts engendered by organization on other principles.[124]

The dynamic between structure and antistructure construed as a relational dialectic and contest at the micro level, where individuals constantly negotiate life within a particular symbolic world, may more adequately account for the contrastive data associated with communal life. Communities live out of symbolic worlds, collective consciousnesses, and traditions that contain more than rituals overtly name, yet rarely manage to contain. Social identity is a continuous process simultaneously effected by and formative of individuals, who participate in communal life via an array of possible social-cultural roles where, at any given time, the alliances (particularly between individuals in shared roles) shift according to the opportunities and constraints of a present, contingent reality.

In the next section the role of symbols will be further explored through a study of Clifford Geertz's hermeneutical approach to culture.

---

123. Ibid., 24.
124. Ibid., 23.

## Clifford Geertz

For Clifford Geertz, human cultures are best understood from an interpretative, semiotic approach.[125] Geertz's ethnographic methodology, variously depicted[126] expands "the universe of human discourse"[127] by describing the myriads of ways human beings live their "one wild and precious life."[128] Thus, cultural analysis is "not an experimental science in search of laws but an interpretative one in search of meaning."[129] This hermeneutical shift has significant implications for anthropology: ethnography is less about decoding messages embedded in social artifacts and institutions and more about attending to human behavior and interpreting the social discourse flowing from cultural expressions. As Geertz aptly remarks, "The turn toward meaning however denominated and however expressed changed both the subject pursued and the subject pursuing it.[130]

---

125. Geertz recounts his methodological transition during his years at the University of Chicago. "One thinks that one is setting bravely off in an unprecedented direction and then looks up to find all sorts of people one has never even heard of headed the same way. The linguistic turn, the hermeneutical turn, the cognitive revolution, the aftershocks of the Wittgenstein and Heidegger earthquakes, the constructivism of Thomas Kuhn and Nelson Goodman, Benjamin, Foucault, Goffman, Lévi-Strauss, Suzanne Langer, Kenneth Burke, developments in grammar, semantics, and the theory of narrative, and latterly in neural mapping and the somaticization of emotion all suddenly made a concern with meaning-making an acceptable preoccupation for a scholar to have." Geertz, *Available Light*, 16.

126. "Some . . . called this development, at once theoretical and methodological, 'symbolic anthropology.' But I, regarding the whole thing as an essentially hermeneutic enterprise, a bringing to light and definition, not a metaphrase or a decoding, and uncomfortable with the mysterian, cabalistic overtones of 'symbol,' preferred 'interpretative anthropology.' In any case, 'symbolic' or 'interpretative' (some preferred 'semiotic'), a budget of terms, some mine, some other people's, some reworked from earlier uses, began to merge, around which a revised conception of what I, at least, still called 'culture' could be built: 'thick description, 'model-of/model-for,' 'sign system,' *'epistemé,'* 'ethos,' 'paradigm,' 'criteria,' 'horizon,' 'frame,' 'world,' 'language games,' 'interpretant,' *'sinnzusamenhang,'* 'trope,' *'sjuzet,'* 'experience-near,' 'illocutionary,' 'discurvise formation,' 'defamiliarization,' 'competence/performance,' *'fictiõ,'* 'family resemblance,' 'heteroglossia,' and of course, in several of its innumerable, permutable senses, 'structure.'" Ibid., 17.

127. Geertz, *Interpretation of Cultures*, 14.

128. Oliver, "Summer Day," 94.

129. Geertz, *Interpretation of Cultures*, 5.

130. Geertz, *Available Light*, 17.

## Interpretative Anthropology 151

Well aware that "culture" ("the *mot* not the *chose*—there is no *chose*")[131] is a highly contested notion,[132] Geertz suggests,

> As interworked systems of construable signs (what ignoring provincial usages, I would call symbols), culture is not a power, something to which social events, behaviors, institutions, or processes can be causally attributed; it is a context, something within which they can be intelligibly—that is thickly—described.[133]

Thick description, as a method of ethnographic analysis, focuses on "densely textured facts" manifest in cultural acts, in order to limn "the structures of signification."[134] This requires skills more akin to literary analysis than to sciences traditionally associated with ethnography.[135]

> To discover who people think they are, what they think they are doing, and to what end they think they are doing it, it is necessary to gain a working familiarity with the frames of meaning within which they enact their lives. This does not involve feeling anyone else's feelings, or thinking anyone else's thoughts, simple impossibilities. Nor does it involve going native, an impractical idea, inevitably bogus. It involves learning how, as a being from elsewhere with a world of one's own, to live with them.[136]

Thick description, as a second- and third-order interpretation of a participant observer, is a fashioned, therefore fictive, account of the flow of social discourse emanating from symbolic action; constructed, made, and not untrue descriptions of what people may have been up to. [137] In order to fashion a *fictiō* that construes the informants' cultures in their own terms, Geertz attempts to stay as close as possible to empirical events, in-

---

131. Ibid., 12.

132. "Everyone knows what cultural anthropology is about: it's about culture. The trouble is that no one is quite sure what culture is. Not only is it an essentially contested concept, like democracy, religion, simplicity, or social justice; it is a multiply defined one, multiply employed, ineradicably imprecise. It is fugitive, unsteady, encyclopedic, and normatively charged, and there are those, especially those for whom only the really real is really real, who think it vacuous altogether, or even dangerous, and would ban it from the serious discourse of serious persons. An unlikely idea, it would seem, around which to try and build a science. Almost as bad as matter." Ibid., 11.

133. Geertz, *Interpretation of Cultures*, 14.

134. Geertz borrows this phrase from Gilbert Ryle. Ibid., 7.

135. Geertz, Ibid., 9.

136. Geertz, *Available Light*, 16.

137. Geertz, *Interpretation of Cultures*, 10.

specting them for the light they lend towards understanding "the informal logic of actual life."[138] Employing a "microscopic" method, Geertz immerses himself in the local, the concrete, and the particular.[139] "Behavior must be attended to, and with some exactness, because it is through the flow of behavior—or, more precisely, social action—that cultural forms find articulation."[140]

However, the inscribed accounts do not so much capture events as portray meanings.

> A good interpretation of anything—a poem, a person, a history, a ritual, an institution, a society—takes us into the heart of which it is the interpretation. When it does not do that, but leads us instead somewhere else . . . it may have its intrinsic charms; but it is something else than what the task at hand . . . calls for.[141]

Cultural analysis does not distill particular behaviors, separating out and clarifying its constitutive human properties; it does not extract the "truly human" from the dross of social life. Cultural analysis requires both guessing at meanings[142] and deciding which of the possible hermeneutical hunches will find their way to print. Reflecting on ethnographic accounts ("glancing experiences and half-witnessed events" transcribed into "formed, written, recounted fact")[143] Geertz asserts,

> What recommends them, or disrecommends them if they are ill-constructed, is the further figures that issue from them: their capacity to lead on to extended accounts which, intersecting other accounts of other matters, widen their implications and deepen their hold. We can always count on something else happening, another glancing experience, another half-witnessed event. What we can't count on is that we will have something useful to say about it when it does. We are in no danger of running out of reality; we are in constant danger of running out of signs, or at least of having the old ones die on us.[144]

---

138. Ibid., 17.
139. Ibid., 20.
140. Ibid., 17.
141. Ibid., 18.
142. Ibid., 19.
143. Geertz, *After the Fact*, 18.
144. Ibid., 19.

Geertz's practice of ethnography in the micro dimension is not without its pitfalls. The move from particular to universal is fraught with difficulties, not the least being the ultimate erasure of the distinctive particular in an effort to arrive at "bloodless universals."[145] Both uniformitarianism and cultural relativism lead to impasses. Universals, failing to say anything of depth or import, make the move to relativism quick and easy, leaving only "a lowest common-denominator view of humanity."[146]

Geertz believes that these pitfalls can be avoided by recognizing that the analysis of local knowledge is more a comment on human nature than a prescriptive universal generalization about humanity. "Ethnographic findings are not privileged, just particular."[147]

> The methodological problem that the microscopic nature of ethnography presents is both real and critical. But it is not to be resolved by regarding a remote locality as the world in a teacup or as the sociological equivalent of a cloud chamber. It is to be resolved—or, anyway, decently kept at bay—by realizing that social actions are comments on more than themselves; that where an interpretation comes from does not determine where it can be impelled to go. Small facts speak to large issues . . . because they are made to.[148]

## Geertz on Social Identity

Geertz's semiotic analysis of human behavior is rooted in the conviction that "humanity is as various in its essence as it is in its expression."[149] The diversity of human cultural experience is significant not only because of its scope.[150] More recent anthropological study has shown that human social life is no mere additive ingredient. The human nervous system, most particularly the neocortex, developed only as a result of an intricate and essential relationship with social life.

---

145. Geertz, *Interpretation*, 43.
146. Ibid.
147. Ibid., 23.
148. Ibid.
149. Ibid., 37.
150. "In fact, as the *Homo sapiens* brain is about three times as large as that of the Australopithecines, the greater part of human cortical expansion has followed, not preceded, the 'beginning' of culture, a rather inexplicable circumstance if the capacity for culture is considered to have been the unitary outcome of a quantitatively slight but qualitatively metastatic change of the freezing-of-water sort." Ibid., 64.

> The Ice Age appears [to be] . . . a time in which were forged nearly all those characteristics of man's existence which are most graphically human: his thoroughly encephelated nervous system, his incest-taboo-based social structure, and his capacity to create and use symbols. The fact that these distinctive features of humanity emerged together in complex interaction with one another rather than serially as for so long supposed is of exceptional importance in the interpretation of human mentality, because it suggests that man's nervous system does not merely enable him to acquire culture, it positively demands that he do so if it is going to function at all. Rather than culture acting only to supplement, develop and extend organically based capacities logically and genetically prior to it, it would seem to be ingredient to those capacities themselves. A cultureless human being would probably turn out to be not an intrinsically talented though unfulfilled ape, but a wholly mindless and consequently unworkable monstrosity."[151]

This has profound significance for the understanding of what it means to be human. If human nature is not biologically possible without the presence of culture, if the neocortex is dependent upon "the accessibility of public symbolic structures to build up its own autonomous, ongoing pattern of activity,"[152] then symbolic expression among human beings can never be "just a symbol." The "guidance provided by systems of significant symbols" is utterly essential for human life; symbols are the condition for the possibility of the species *Homo sapiens*. "Without men, no culture, certainly; but equally, and more significantly, without culture, no men."[153]

### Symbols and Religious Meaning

Geertz defines culture as "a historically transmitted pattern of meanings embodied in symbols, a system of inherited conceptions expressed in symbolic forms by means of which men communicate, perpetuate, and develop their knowledge about and attitudes toward life."[154] The interpretation of culture is about the interpretation of a people's symbol system.[155]

---

151. Ibid., 67–68.
152. Ibid., 83.
153. Ibid., 49.
154. Ibid., 89.
155. Geertz defines symbol as "any object, act, event, quality or relation which serves as a vehicle for a conception—the conception is the symbol's meaning." Ibid., 91.

Symbols are the conveyors of meaning; religious symbols are about ultimate meanings.

> A religion is: (1) a system of symbols which acts to (2) establish powerful, pervasive, and long-lasting moods and motivations in men by (3) formulating conceptions of a general order of existence and (4) clothing these conceptions with such an aura of factuality that (5) the moods and motivations seem uniquely realistic.[156]

Religious symbols function by creating a compelling vision of the 'really real" while simultaneously authenticating a people's way of life, thereby offering a particular perspective on social identity. Symbol systems and social life inform each other. Symbols are extrinsic entities shaped into existence by human minds, a social cognitive process. If symbols are successful in communicating meaning, they in turn shape the social life: commitments are made, relationships are fostered, agreements are negotiated, cosmologies are authorized. The social life perpetuated will reflect the order of the universe affirmed in a group's symbol system.

Ritual engagement of the symbol system reinforces the sentiments and beliefs of the group. "Moods and motivations" induced in the members reflect the symbol system's ability to shape individual and communal life. These dispositions, termed "religious" when oriented towards the transcendent, validate the "really real," thus holding at bay the ambiguous and the inexplicable.

> It is this sense of the "really real" upon which the religious perspective rests and which the symbolic activities of religion as a cultural system are devoted to producing, intensifying, and, so far as possible, rendering inviolable by the discordant revelations of secular experience. It is, again, the imbuing of a certain specific complex of symbols—of the metaphysic they formulate and the style of life they recommend—with a persuasive authority which, from an analytic point of view, is the essence of religious action.[157]

A fundamental aspect of human beings is the quest for making meaning. When the "basic congruence" of life is disrupted, the belief system is challenged to make sense of the disruption. Because religious symbol systems deal in ultimate meanings, their explanations of the ambiguous and anomalous must be able to deal with the greatest threats to the established

---

156. Ibid., 90.
157. Ibid., 112.

order. Geertz notes that human beings, when confronted with the chaos of disruption, turn to their symbol system to make sense of the nonsensical.

> The thing we seem least able to tolerate is a threat to our powers of conception, a suggestion that our ability to create, grasp, and use symbols may fail us, for were this to happen, we would be more helpless, as I have already pointed out, than the beavers.[158]

Symbol systems are the means by which humans make sense of life in all its dimensions and struggles. In the end, a human being can endure almost anything if the experience can be made meaningful. Once meaning is lost, once a symbol system fails to guide an individual or group from chaos to interpretation and reintegration, anxiety sets in.

> Any chronic failure of one's explanatory apparatus, the complex of received culture patterns (common sense, science, philosophical speculation, myth) one has for mapping the empirical world, to explain things which cry out for explanation tends to lead to a deep disquiet—tendency rather more widespread and a disquiet rather deeper than we have sometimes supposed since the pseudo-science view of religious belief was, quite rightfully, deposed.[159]

### Ethos and World View

The move from troubling disquiet to a sense that "things are as they should be" is a distinctive characteristic of a religious perspective. This move is only possible when people invest their symbol system with a prior authority: the authority of faith. "The basic axiom underlying what we may perhaps call, 'the religious perspective' is everywhere the same: he who would know must first believe."[160] Geertz maintains that the authority of faith emanates from cultural performances of a religious nature: ritual or "consecrated behavior." In ritual, ethos (moods and motivations) and worldview (general conceptions of order) meet and reinforce each other.[161]

The fusion of ethos and worldview that occurs in religious belief has major implications for social identity. Ethos expresses the tone and character of a people; it is the quality of their life, including its moral and aesthetic dimensions. Ethos manifests the fundamental sentiments and notions

158. Ibid., 99.
159. Ibid., 100.
160. Ibid., 110.
161. Ibid., 112.

that a people hold about themselves and how they inhabit that world; it speaks to ontology.[162] Worldview includes all the notions a people hold to be true about the general order of reality; it is their cosmology. In religious belief, ethos and worldview merge to mutually reinforce each other: ethos validates a people's way of life as reasonable, attuned to the order of the universe; worldview affirms the vision of life it limns through tangible expression in an actual way of life.[163] All of this vital social communication is located in the symbolic action of religious belief.

> [R]eligious symbols, dramatized in rituals or related in myths, are felt somehow to sum up, for those for whom they are resonant, what is known about the way the world is, the quality of the emotional life it supports, and the way one ought to behave while in it. Sacred symbols thus relate an ontology and a cosmology to an aesthetics and a morality: their peculiar power comes from their presumed ability to identify fact with value at the most fundamental level, to give to what is otherwise merely actual, a comprehensive normative import.[164]

Geertz makes a strong case for the dual aspects of the moral imperative experienced within a social group: the relationship between the actual (is) and the normative (ought). There is a meaningful and potent relationship between what a people value and the general order they construe upon existence.

> Religion is never merely metaphysics. For all peoples the forms, vehicles, and objects of worship are suffused with an aura of deep moral seriousness. The holy bears within it everywhere a sense of intrinsic obligation: it not only encourages devotion, it demands it.... Never merely metaphysics, religion is never merely ethics either. The source of its moral vitality is conceived to lie in the fidelity with which it expresses the fundamental nature of reality. The powerfully coercive "ought" is felt to grow out of a comprehensive factual "is," and in such a way religion grounds the most specific requirements of human action in the most general contexts of human existence.[165]

---

162. Ibid., 127.
163. Ibid.
164. Ibid.
165. Ibid., 126.

If the result of the fusion of ethos and worldview is that a "powerfully coercive 'ought' is felt to grow out of a comprehensive factual 'is,'" then as much attention must be paid to the ontological (actual) as to the ethical/moral (normative).[166]

> An approach to a theory of value which looks toward the behavior of actual people in actual societies living in terms of actual cultures for both its stimulus and its validation will turn us away from abstract and rather scholastic arguments in which a limited number of classical positions are stated again and again with little that is new to recommend them, to a process of ever-increasing insight into both what values are and how they work.[167]

Here, Geertz locates the great interest that religion should have for cultural anthropologists. Religion is interesting not because it describes the social order, but because of its power to shape the social.[168]

## Geertz and Social Change

From ritual to internal conversion to an examination of how the social forces of epochalism and essentialism function in nationalism, Geertz grounds his understanding of social change in a heuristic methodological distinction between the cultural and social aspects of human life. Pointing out the inadequacies of a functionalist approach to social change, particularly the functionalist tendency to associate religious rituals with social cohesion, Geertz explores ways in which religion may be disruptive of the social order. His assessment of this possibility leads him to construe cultural and social structural processes as "*independently variable* and *mutually interdependent*."[169] While phenomenologically inseparable, Geertz's conceptual abstraction of culture and social structure[170] allows him to explore these systems and the patterns of integration associated with them.

166. Ibid., 127.
167. Ibid., 141.
168. Ibid., 119.
169. Ibid., 143–44.
170. "On the one level there is the framework of beliefs, expressive symbols, and values in terms of which individuals define their world, express their feelings, and make their judgements; on the other level there is the ongoing process of interactive behavior, whose persistent form we call social structure. Culture is the fabric of meaning in terms of which human beings interpret their experience and guide their action; social structure is the form that action takes, the actually existing network of social relations. Culture and social structure are then but different abstractions from the same phenomenon. The one considers

Geertz uses Pitirim Sorokin's distinctions to highlight how cultural systems and social systems are organized differently. Cultural systems, described as having a "logical-meaningful integration," exhibit an orchestrated integration as found "in a Bach fugue, in Catholic dogma, or in the general theory of relativity; it is a unity of style, of logical implication, of meaning and value."[171] Social systems, described as having "causal-functional integration," manifest the type of systems integration similar to dynamic equilibrium in biological systems. It is "the kind of integration one finds in an organism, where all the parts are united in a single causal web; each part is an element in a reverberating causal ring which 'keeps the system going.'"[172]

The heuristic distinction between cultural and social structural systems allows Geertz to examine in greater detail the intricacies and complexities of a Javanese funeral and its failure to effect the kinds of social and psychological support and reintegration associated with religious belief and expression. Using thick description, Geertz interprets the prevailing disquiet that characterized this particular religious ceremony.[173]

> I shall try to show how an approach which does not distinguish the "logico-meaningful" cultural aspects of the ritual pattern from the "causal-functional" social structure aspects is unable to account adequately for this ritual failure, and how an approach which does so distinguish them is able to analyze more explicitly the cause of the trouble. It will further be argued that such an approach is able to avoid the simplistic view of the functional role of religion in society which sees that role merely as structure-conserving, and to substitute for it a more complex conception of the relations between religious belief and practice and secular social life.[174]

---

social action in respect to its meaning for those who carry it out, the other considers it in terms of its contribution to the functioning of some social system." Ibid., 145.

171. Ibid.

172. Ibid., 145. Because of the difference in the modes of integration in cultural and social systems there is a fundamental tension between them. Tension exists also between cultural-social systems and a third factor, motivational or personality structures. Quoting Talbot Parsons, Geertz highlights the fact that these three factors, cultural, social and motivational, are indispensable, irreducible and, simultaneously, interdependent and interpenetrating. Each of the three elements needs the others to exist and at the same time none of the three can be derived from either of the other two. Ibid., 145–46.

173. For Geertz's "thick description" of this event please see his *Interpretation of Cultures*, 146–62.

174. Ibid., 146.

By analyzing the cultural and social aspects of the situation, Geertz shows how the participants, all members of a Javanese *kampong*, are caught in a cultural and social conflict. [175]

### Social and Cultural Conflict, a Javanese Example

While *kampong* social life is largely informed by an urban context, *kampong* cultural life remains very much connected to the traditional village. As urban-dwellers, *kampong* people no longer inhabit the social structures associated with village life. Outside the village, where each person makes their living independently from their geographical neighbor, there is less need for interdependence and connectedness. Village structure reinforced social cohesiveness because each person's survival depended on the group surviving together. Geertz contends that urban *kampong* living "is not so much a destruction of traditional ways of life, as a construction of a new one."[176] As new social structures evolve, *kampong* people remain culturally tied to their village life. This is the heart of the trouble experienced as urbanized *kampong* people gathered to carry out a traditional cultural ritual, the *slametan* (funeral ceremony). Religious symbols take on political meaning in the social context of the *kampong*. Ideological and political differences that mark Javanese urban life engage religious differences such that "the rituals themselves become matters of political conflict."[177] "The people who came into Karman's yard, including Karman himself, were not sure whether they were engaged in a sacralized consideration of first and last things or in a secular struggle for power."[178]

Moreover, since ritual is a form of social interaction as well as a pattern of meaning, social conflict is highly probable when a village pattern of social interaction is imposed on an urban social context.

> As emphasized earlier, the slametan is essentially a territorially based ritual; it assumes the primary tie between families to be that of residential propinquity. . . . In the town this pattern has in large part changed. . . . The new urban form of organization consists of a careful balance of conflicting forces arising out of diverse contexts:

---

175. *Kampongs* are "the off-the-street neighborhoods in which the common Javanese townsmen live crowded together in a helter-skelter profusion of little bamboo houses [where] one finds a traditional society in which the traditional forms of rural living are being steadily dissolved and new forms steadily reconstructed." Ibid., 150.

176. Ibid.

177. Ibid., 176.

178. Ibid., 165.

> class differences are softened by ideological similarities; ethnic conflicts by common economic interests; political opposition . . . by residential intimacy. But in the midst of all this pluralistic checking and balancing, the slametan remains unchanged, blind to the major lines of social and cultural demarcation of urban life. For it, the primary classifying characteristic of an individual is where he lives.[179]

There is a lack of fit, an incongruence that, though uncomfortable, does not mean that there is a lack of social cohesion. From the storehouse of the symbolic, the *slametan* conjures a vision of social life that the participants recognize no longer fits their urban experience. Ritual failure occurs not because people are alienated, but because the type of social cohesion found in village social structure and captured meaningfully in the religious symbolism of the *slametan* is not the cohesion of urban social life.

> In sum, the disruption of Paidjan's funeral may be traced to a single source: an incongruity between the cultural framework of meaning and the patterning of social interaction, an incongruity due to the persistence in an urban environment of a religious symbol system adjusted to peasant social structure.[180]

Geertz points out in this analysis the complexity that needs to be attended to when considering the effects of change in a society. By bringing into relief dimensions of social life and their interrelatedness, Geertz challenges theories that effectively reduce the cultural and social structural to mirror images of each other.[181] Social conflict is not necessarily symptomatic of social decay. The human quest to create both meaning and a livable space is a negotiated journey.

> The driving forces in social change can be clearly formulated only by a more dynamic form of functionalist theory, one which takes

179. Ibid., 168.
180. Ibid., 169.

181. "Either culture is regarded as wholly derivative from the forms of social organization—the approach characteristic of the British structuralists as well as many American sociologists; or the forms of social organization are regarded as behavioral embodiments of cultural patterns—the approach of Malinowski and many American anthropologists. In either case the lesser term tends to drop out as a dynamic factor, and we are left either with an omnibus concept of culture ('that complex whole . . .') or else with a completely comprehensive concept of social structure ('social structure is not an aspect of culture but the entire culture of a given people handled in a special frame of theory'). In such a situation, the dynamic elements in social change that arise from the failure of cultural patterns to be perfectly congruent with the forms of social organization are largely incapable of formulation." Ibid., 143–44. Geertz is citing Leach, *Political Systems of Highland Burma*, 282, in this passage.

> into account the fact that man's need to live in a world to which he can attribute some significance, whose essential import he feels he can grasp, often diverges from his concurrent need to maintain a functioning social organism.[182]

## *Conclusion: Geertz and Social Identity/Change*

Geertz's interpretative anthropology relocates the idea of culture in a semiotic context. He challenges anthropological assertions that fail to recognize that the logic of cultural organization lies in the use of symbols. Anthropology as a hermeneutical science cannot inspect cultural forms and assign intrinsic properties. Anthropologists observe, question, and interpret how cultural forms interact. Things, objects, and events do not bear intrinsic meaning; meaning is conferred by human beings. All experience is construed, interpreted.[183]

Cultural systems are complexes of interdependencies that vary in their degree of connectedness. The notion of cultural integration and cultural disorganization are better understood in this context. At any time in a cohesive culture there exist the underlying elements of its disruption.[184] Social identity is never completely defined, expressed, or finished. In coming to understand the complexity of human social identity, it is important to attend to its consistently partial and negotiated nature. Therefore, in any cultural system the rifts and cracks are as interesting and important as the connections and links.

> And as there are some rather compelling theoretical reasons for believing that a system which is both complex, as any culture is, and fully joined cannot function, the problem of cultural analysis is as much a matter of determining independencies as interconnections, gulfs as well as bridges.[185]

---

182. Ibid., 169.

183. ". . . the nature of cultural integration, cultural change, or cultural conflict is to be probed for there [i.e. the social world]: in the experiences of individuals and groups of individuals as, under the guidance of symbols, they perceive, feel, reason, judge, and act." Ibid., 405.

184. ". . . patterns counteractive to the primary ones exist as subdominant but nonetheless important themes in, so far as we can tell, any culture. In an ordinary, quite unHegelian way, the elements of a culture's own negation are, with greater or lesser force, included within it." Ibid., 406.

185. Ibid., 407.

Geertz's interpretive anthropology is truly anthropology "from below." His analysis of culture is grounded in thick description of symbols and clusters of symbols, moving from the observation of symbols towards an account "of the underlying regularities of human experience implicit in their formation."[186]

> A workable theory of culture is to be achieved, if it is to be achieved, by building up from directly observable modes of thought, first to determinate families of them and then to more variable, less tightly coherent, but nonetheless ordered "octopoid" systems of them, confluences of partial integrations, partial incongruencies and partial interdependencies.[187]

Cultural change is "rather like an octopus too." Cultures change in fits and starts, instigated by "impulses" that register and move rather unpredictably through the system. Geertz maintains, however, that it is not "too unreasonable" to suppose that "if such impulses appear within some rather closely interconnected and socially consequential part of the system, their driving force will most likely be high."[188]

Geertz's semiotic approach to the study of culture engages the local and particular, encountering there other voices, other strategies, other symbols, other uses, other answers to perennial questions and challenges to human societies. By examining human behavior from a symbolic perspective, Geertz attends to human diversity as an essential aspect of existence. By immersion into the particular, he hopes to arrive at a more comprehensive image of the human.

> To look at the symbolic dimensions of social action—art, religion, ideology, science, law, morality, common sense—is not to turn away from the existential dilemmas of life for some empyrean realm of de-emotionalized forms; it is to plunge into the midst of them. The essential vocation of interpretive anthropology is not to answer our deepest questions, but to make available to us answers that others, guarding other sheep in other valleys, have given, and thus to include them in the consultable record of what man has said.[189]

---

186. Ibid., 408.
187. Ibid.
188. Ibid.
189. Ibid., 30.

## Critical Assessment of Douglas, Turner, and Geertz

Turner, Douglas, and Geertz represent modern views of culture, each contributing to a notion of culture that remains relatively innocent of the power dimensions involved in the praxis of ethnography. The absence of this dimension requires that their contributions be reconsidered in the light of the underlying assumptions that inform their method, analysis, and conclusions.

### *Gender Critique*

The work of all three thinkers assumes that male and female experiences of culture are fundamentally similar. If and when women's experiences are described, it is in the light of unexamined assumptions regarding gender. Carolyn Walker Bynum observes in her analysis of Turner's notion of liminality that when the stories of medieval women are considered, very different conclusions regarding *communitas* come into focus. Bynum contends that status reversal, liminality, is primarily a male experience; *communitas* as antistructure is release for men. For women, the conditions associated with antistructure are not liminal; they are the conditions of their everyday life.

> To medieval women, at any rate, Christ on the cross was not victory or humility but "humanity." And in eating and loving that "humanness" one became more fully oneself. What women's images and stories expressed most fundamentally was neither reversal nor elevation but continuity.[190]

Bynum's critique of Turner reflects the ongoing work of gender studies and analysis, a discourse that only began to take form in the late 1970s when women's studies literature began to distinguish between gender and sex.[191] Gender, conceptualized, also contextualizes; sexual differences are no longer seen as inherently biological. Cultural and historical representations of roled relationships, the focus of numerous case studies, are analyzed to show how "gender relations and representations [are] produced, legitimated, changed and perpetuated."[192] Through these methodologies, feminist and postcolonial critiques have furthered the theoretical basis for undermining the dominance of certain cultures and histories, raised to the level

---

190. Bynum, *Fragmentation and Redemption*, 50.
191. Kratz, *Affecting Performance*, 45.
192. Ibid., 47.

of "natural universals."[193] These discourses, emphasizing relation, context, power, and difference, offer very different views of social identities.

## *Postcolonial Critique*

While Turner, Douglas, and Geertz reject a static notion of social identity and attempt to account for the dynamic between social stability and social change, their analyses, particularly Turner's and Douglas's, tend to assume identity as a social fact, a more or less congealed substantial entity originating from norms and values expressed in the social structure. From this foundation they proceed to probe and describe identity's activity in the social order. Conversely, the deconstruction of identity, particularly the work of postcolonial theorists, attempts to underscore how power and interest saturate the constructed notions of ethnicity. *Primordialism*, an essentialist view of ethnicity, and *instrumentalism*, ethnicity as imagined community, form the extremes of the debate's continuum.

> The most extreme view is to treat ethnicity as another form of resource mobilization. Ethnic groups are then a form of interest groups. An advantage of this view is that it distances itself from the essentializing claims of identity politics; the limitation of the rational choice approach is that it underrates or ignores the cultural character of ethnicity and the importance of symbolic resources, which are all flattened to economic choices.[194]

John Comaroff asserts "that ethnic—indeed all—identities are not things but relations; that their content is wrought in the particularization of their ongoing historical construction."[195] He outlines four points regarding the "empowered production of difference and identity":

1. Ethnicity originates in "relations of inequality," particularly in the social domains of politics, economics and cultural symbols.
2. Ethnic identity is forged in the particular of the daily, "in the routine encounters of the ethnicizing and the ethnicized."
3. Ethnic identities, after they are constituted become objectified "appearing to be natural, essential and primordial."

---

193. Ibid.
194. Pieterse, "Varieties of Ethnic Politics," 27.
195. Comaroff, "Ethnicity, Nationalism," 165.

4. Social identity is forged under a set of conditions that may not be the optimum conditions for sustaining identity.[196]

Comaroff contends that social scientists need to "establish how the reality of any identity is realized, how its essence is essentialized, how its objective qualities come to be objectified."[197] In the context of the politics of identity, these questions help focus study on "how collective attachments take root in the histories people imagine they share."[198]

## *Crisis of Representation and Ethnographic Method*

The crisis of representation within cultural anthropology, referred to earlier in chapter 1, has generated intense debate around the nature of ethnography and its supposed complicity in forwarding the hegemonic improvisations of the West. Talal Asad extends the depth and scope of postcolonial analysis by offering a critical genealogy of "religion," exposing the universalizing conceptual commitments that inform this anthropological category. Convinced that all conceptual formulations are embedded in social practices, Asad explores how the notion of religion has changed from ancient, medieval, and modern Christianity. Asserting that Augustine would not recognize the entity moderns designate as "religion," Asad demonstrates how the notion of religion emerged as a universal category following the Reformation.[199]

His critique asks important questions for those who practice interpretive anthropology. How does power, understood as "the effect of an entire network of motivated practices," function in religion?[200] Is it the mind that responds to religious truth in a moment of transcendent encounter, or is truth experienced because of the conditions afforded by certain socially validated practices? Although practitioners of symbolic anthropology do not negate the fact that symbols communicate within a context, the authorizing effect of disciplined practices are, for the most part, eclipsed by the emphasis given to interpretation. In this sense, Asad pushes the logic of thick description, extending its epistemological implications.

---

196. Ibid.
197. Ibid., 166.
198. Ibid., 180.
199. Asad, *Genealogies of Religion*, 34–54.
200. Ibid., 35.

My argument, I must stress, is not just that religious symbols are intimately linked to social life (and so change it), or that they usually support dominant political power (and occasionally oppose it). It is that different kinds of practice and discourse are intrinsic to the field in which religious representations (like any representation) acquire their identity and their truthfulness. From this it does not follow that meanings of religious practices and utterances are to be sought in social phenomena, but only that their possibility and their authoritative status are to be explained as products of historically distinctive disciplines and forces. The anthropological student of *particular* religions should therefore begin from this point, in a sense unpacking the comprehensive concept which he or she translates as "religion" into heterogeneous elements according to its historical character.[201]

By paying more concerted attention to the interplay between symbols and authorizing disciplines, a more adequate picture of social identity emerges. Practices expand the locus of interpretation. Rarely free-floating within a tradition, symbols are social products, never simply the interior construction of lone souls. Symbols, as social/cultural products, have a functional lineage, a history of use, within a group. Symbols necessarily participate in the authorizing practices that contribute towards a sense of group identity. Thus, distinguishing practices, abounding in symbolic content, are received by (perhaps even imposed upon) members of social groups. To paraphrase Asad, membership resides as much in those who adjust themselves accordingly to particular social practices as to those who articulate an acceptable interpretation of the symbol system.[202] Thus, as Comaroff maintains, the relational character of social identity is forged in the day-to-day encounters between "the ethncizing and the ethncized."[203]

Paying attention to the cultural matrix in which symbols arise, are validated, and flourish (and in some cases, die), only affirms Geertz's contention that culture is a context, not a thing. If, as Geertz eloquently notes, "One of the most significant facts about us may finally be that we all begin with the natural equipment to live a thousand kinds of life but end in the

201. Ibid., 54.

202. I believe that Asad's emphasis on practice eclipses the place of meaning in social life. My use of his critique attempts to uncover the forces that inform and limit the hermeneutical process, not to reduce hermeneutics to a function of social practice. The relationship between construed meanings and disciplined practices is an area of ongoing debate and research.

203. Comaroff, "Ethnicity, Nationalism," 165.

end having lived only one," then thick description still offers a relatively adequate method towards expanding the discourse on the meaning of the one human life we all live, rather briefly, on this planet.[204] The descent into the particular, albeit a more self-conscious descent, still offers a fruitful course for ethnography.

Corinne Kratz's work with Okiek women's initiation is an example of dense method, incorporating a broad spectrum of theory, adapted and revised by the ethnographer to address the specific tasks of ritual observation and interpretation. Kratz's work results in a thick description that is particular, gendered, and treated both synchronically and diachronically. Kratz notes the current critique of identity and points to two problems.

> First, precipitate generalization disguises important distinctions and divergent interests within groups that share some identity. Conversely, such heightened attention to ever more particularized divisions can be so balkanizing that little sense of shared identity remains, common interests seem elusive, and any generalization becomes a sign of insensitivity. Critical reformulations suggest not that a balance be struck between these poles but that identity be reconceptualized in multiple terms, emphasizing the simultaneity and interplay of intersecting identities and perspectives.[205]

As Kratz describes above, the current intellectual climate informing identity mirrors Jan Nederveen Pieterse's insight that social belonging is caught on the horns of the ethnicity dilemma: primordialism vs. instrumentalism. The seeming either/or of this debate, the tensions inherent in safeguarding particularity while simultaneously avoiding the complete delegitimation of shared social identity and the traditions associated with them, requires a new way of thinking about identity: multiple, convergent, interactive, simultaneous, asymmetrical, and potentially conflictive perspectives. Identity, understood as a set of relational repertoires, both received and construed, may more adequately account for the way in which groups draw upon the available traditions to forge the practical (and necessary) social relations that constitute a viable social life. What, then, can a study of Turner, Douglas, and Geertz contribute towards a reconceptualization of Christian identity, construed as discipleship, and the role of tradition in this reconsidered view of identity?

---

204. Geertz, *Interpretation of Cultures*, 45.
205. Kratz, *Affecting Performance*, 48.

## Mary Douglas Revisited

What others have termed Douglas's "modern" (read outmoded) commitment to a taxonomic methodology may actually fare better if viewed as a genealogical approach to a basic question confronting symbolic anthropology: How do symbols become invested with meaning in the first place? Douglas asserts that symbols acquire meaning through a socially negotiated process whereby individuals come to agreement on the *meaning of sameness* by practices of differentiation and exclusion/inclusion. These decisions have profound implications; far more than mere theoretical categorization, this selection process distinguishes social relations. Since sameness is not inherent in reality, but constructed/construed and conferred by those who come to agreement, the process of coming to agreement is itself a means of distinguishing "me and mine" from "those others." Thus, the social negotiations constituent of shared classifications and meanings are constituent of the relationships that result in social organizations. Yet, it is important to note that Douglas may imbue the selection process with more freedom than may actually be the case. Douglas's scenario assumes a non-coercive space, affording conversation, disagreement, and argument among equals. Here Asad's concern for the authorization of space may offer a helpful corrective. The social affirmation of sameness may result less from cognitive agreement ("I truly see it your way") and more from survival strategies ("The only way I can make a life in this context is to agree with you").

Given this, a critical appropriation of Douglas's geological exploration into the life of institutions and the beliefs that sustain them may lend light to how traditions are used to reinforce the "really real-ness" of socially structured relations and undermine the plausibility of others. Douglas maintains that one of the primary functions of institutions is to confer identity and to foster the social conditions that emphasize group greatness while diminishing group blunders. The social control of memory, cultivating remembrances of prestige while fostering social amnesia around disastrous events, operates as a selective traditioning process.

> When we look closely at the construction of past time, we find the process has very little to do with the past at all and everything to do with the present. Institutions create shadowed places in which nothing can be seen and no questions asked. They make other areas show finely discriminated detail, which is closely scrutinized and ordered. History emerges in an unintended shape as a result of practices directed to immediate, practical ends. To watch these

practices establish selective principles that highlight some kinds of events and obscure others is to inspect the social order operating on individual minds.[206]

The use of the past for the purposes of the present presupposes traditioning processes whereby social groups create and sustain identity via selected practices of remembrances. An investigation of a group's *constructed practices of remembrance* offers a potentially fruitful avenue for exploring the relationship between identities and traditions. More specifically, how do the constructed practices of remembrance within Christianity function towards the formation and transformation of Christian discipleship?

## *Victor Turner Revisited*

Both Turner and Geertz, through a semiotic, interpretative approach to anthropology, contribute towards an understanding of identity as multiple, and even conflictual. Turner's work in rituals, particularly his notion of the dominant symbol, exposed the vast number of possible social referents held within a single ritual symbol. Moreover, Turner's field experience led him to re-evaluate anthropology's prejudice against ritual and to consider ritual practice as a significant lens from which to view the intricacies of social life. Given the symbolic character of traditions, a hermeneutical approach continues to have much to offer the investigation into social identity. Certainly, the move towards primordialism provides ample evidence of the role of symbol systems in the effective constitution of new communities. Whether understood as received, constructed, or both, traditions as privileged reservoirs of symbolic content continue to function within human communities, providing the basis for both continuity and change. Thus, a critical appropriation of Turner's notion of symbol as multivocal can be helpful when considering the contested character of social belonging.

Corrine Kratz points out that Turner's dominant symbol, with its polar, tensive, conceptual hold of sensory aspects and ideological values, presupposes certain universals regarding embodiment that Marcel Mauss's notion of *habitus* renders implausible since "understandings of the body

---

206. Douglas, *How Institutions Think*, 69–70. See also Corinne Kratz's discussion of tradition and innovation in Okiek ceremonies. She notes that one of the five rhetorical techniques employed in the traditioning process is "canonization through silence." Silence "is an effective and versatile way to deemphasize and eventually erase ceremonial change. As alternatives drop from memory, silence canonizes change as enduring tradition." Kratz, "'We've Always,'" 54.

and body experiences are cultural categories that are literally embodied and taken on in social interaction."[207] Furthermore, Kratz points out that Turner's notion of dominant symbols appears to neglect how the symbolic context, the actual ceremonial performance, contributes toward symbolic efficacy.

> His image of isolated, powerful, dominant symbols popping up at the center of ritual episodes is a most unsatisfactory depiction of ceremonies and ritual efficacy. An adequate explanation must consider the efficacy of symbols and the efficacy of ceremonies together. It must also consider the way a ceremony's performative nature, its structure over time, both draws out that potential and contributes to its force.[208]

Kratz suggests C. S. Peirce's sign theory as a helpful corrective of Turner's dominant symbol, thus shifting emphasis from representational interpretation towards associational communication: the focus on sign relations allows the multiple associations of symbols, as sign modes, to come more clearly into view. Pivotal to Kratz's critique is her contention that "the symbolic associations of signs are fundamental in cultural analysis."[209] Thus, by reconsidering and refining Turner's notion of the dominant symbol, Kratz expands the understanding of the polyvalent character of all symbols. Symbols are both *multivalent* and *multifunctional*. The associations that symbols accrue (and shed) over time, the multiple layers of significance and their webbed connections as well as the contrasting sense of contextual embeddedness and fluid crossover, contribute towards an overall sense of the complex communicative character of symbols as sign carriers of sociocultural meaning.[210]

Building on this, Kratz explores the virtues and limits of Turner's notion of polyvalency. While Turner consistently holds that one symbol can (and often does) represent different, conflicting meanings, he does not allow for the possibility that conflictual messages simultaneously reside within a single form.[211] "Turner's multivocality shows one voice saying different things in different media—not multiple voices saying different

---

207. Kratz, *Affecting Performance*, 19. See also Mauss, "Body Techniques."
208. Kratz, *Affecting Performance*, 19.
209. Ibid., 21.
210. Ibid.
211. Ibid., 23.

things simultaneously, at times in the same medium."[212] The notion that diversity exists not simply in multiple social forms, but that divergent, multiple, conflictual meanings can be expressed in the same communicative form (Bakhtin's heteroglossia) highlights the need to pay attention to the multiple associations and relations informing a particular symbol at a particular existential moment, as well as the history that informs these associations and relations. [213]

With regard to the study of traditions and their relationships to social identities, this revised consideration of Turner's symbol theory contributes towards a more nuanced understanding of the synchronic and diachronic social forces at play in corporate identity. Social processes, variously construed as repetitive cycles, linear trajectories, and the interruptive crises of historical contingencies, constitute the interactive ground where social life is negotiated and cultural meanings are contested. Social identity, more specifically Christian social identity, construed as a community of disciples, happens within an ever-changing historical and cultural matrix and therefore has always and everywhere been *diverse*. The multivalent, multifunctional character of the various symbols forming the repository of Christian tradition affords the tradition both elements of continuity and seeds of change. As a symbol system, the Christian tradition is subject to all the opportunities and hazards of the interpretative process. And therefore, as Kathryn Tanner wisely notes, the diverse character of Christianity makes Christian identity necessarily provocative.

> Differences in theological judgment can suggest therefore the possibility of genuinely conflicting understandings of discipleship among equally "good" Christians. If the requirements of Christian culture are loose enough not to enforce uniformity, they may be loose enough to give rise to a genuine fight about what they imply.

---

212. Ibid., 24.

213. "Bakhtin's sense of multiple voices (heteroglossia) is radically different. His voices have speakers who are communicating in particular contexts and who have particular interests. Bakhtin's implicit social theory is akin to that of Giddens, a theory that 'power is integral to the constitution of social practices' (Giddens 1979: 54). Bakhtin's special concern is with multiple voices and purposes carried simultaneously by the same communicative forms and exchanges, not simply multiple associative meanings. He is concerned with contradictions and tensions that arise when different perspectives and different interests meet (sometimes within a single person) and with tensions between 'official' and 'unofficial' understandings of culture carried simultaneously in the same cultural forms." Ibid. Kratz here quotes from Giddens, *Central Problems in Social Theory*.

One cannot rule out the possibility then, that Christian discipleship is an essentially contested notion.[214]

Exploring Christian identity through an analysis of its symbol system's *provocative polyvalency* will help to underline how "the simultaneity and interplay of intersecting identities and perspectives" informs a renewed understanding of tradition's role in Christian identity and transformation.

## Clifford Geertz Revisited

Geertz's methodology of thick description, limning the contours of human behavior in search of that which people say they are about (i.e., meaning), works to expand anthropological discourse and shifts the ethnographer's gaze from cultural facts locked in artifacts towards the behaviors of human subjects engaged in making sense within a common life. The result is a crafted, second-hand (possibly third-hand) description circumscribed by all the limits of a single interpretative perspective. As such, this stance parallels that of a trained microbiologist's attempts to account for the observations of microbial behaviors. Clearly, observing people and observing amoebae require a host of different skills, but in both cases the written results of such observations are attempts to describe what the observed may be about. The phenomenon of scientific writing, popularly accepted as fact and not interpretation, is receiving much more academic scrutiny.[215] As Geertz notes, "The flat presentation of bankable findings does indeed seem simpler and more straightforward, comforting, knowledge as it is supposed to look. The only trouble is that it is, itself, a bit of a romance, and not altogether the most artless one."[216]

The point remains that a certain "Cartesian anxiety" pervades much of what is written about culture, and that anxiety is as much reflected in those who would deny any hope of shared sources of knowledge as in those who, in quixotic fashion, defend the existence of some Archimedean point. The shifting ground that characterizes epistemology today, the awareness of how power-knowledge and interest saturate cognition, both how and what we know, makes all human claims for knowledge suspect. These are the conditions under which all human cognition operates. Given

---

214. Tanner, *Theories of Culture*, 159.

215. For an excellent analysis of how scientific epistemology is changing see Van Huyssteen, *Shaping of Rationality*.

216. Geertz, *After the Fact*, 62.

this, partial, limited, contested knowledge is not necessarily false; it may simply be incomplete: not the whole story. Thus, however criticized the concept of culture (and its ethnographic methods) may be, culture and its students persist. Clearly, there is no point of arrival. The proverbial quest for meaning in human existence has only become more complex, resisting "bloodless universals" for a more intricate, expansive, "true" account of the range and depth of the potentials, realized and unrealized, that constitute human life.

In recounting cultures studied and the study of cultures, Geertz's ethnographic career affords a conjunctive view, a nuanced perspective into the particular intricacies of two social worlds: Java and Morocco.[217] The result of this juxtaposition does not reduce these cultural lives into "a collection of abstractable easily stateable themes (sex, status, boldness, modesty . . .) differently tied into local bundles, the same notes set into different melodies."[218] Geertz readily admits that these cultures express "complex and contradictory fields of significative action."[219] There is no easy congruence between them, yet when "juxtaposed, these fields can shed a certain amount of light on one another."[220] Thus, "the comparing of incomparables . . . however illogical," can be informative about human life without making the fields of comparison "variants of one another nor expressions of some superfield that transcends them both."[221]

Geertz's perspective, crafted into constructed interpretation, does not attempt to say something descriptive of all humanity, but it does spark interest and attention for a particular way of being human.

> To describe a culture, or as I have here, selected bits, purposely arranged and cut to fit, is not to set out some odd sort of object, a knot in hyperspace. It is to try to induce somebody somewhere to look at some things as I have been induced, by journeys, books, witnessings, and conversations, to look at them: to take an interest.[222]

Thick description, seriously attended to, enlarges the discourse concerning the nature of human existence and therefore offers a particularly fruitful methodology for an ecclesial community in the throes of transition

217. See ibid., particularly chs. 1–2.
218. Geertz, *After the Fact*, 49.
219. Ibid.
220. Ibid.
221. Ibid.
222. Ibid., 61–62.

from a Western church identity to a world church identity. The practice of *juxtaposed thick descriptions*, the effort to "elaborate a language of significative contrast," offers a method for approaching cultural incomparables Western Christianity has blatantly ignored, without falling into the chasm of utter incommensurability ordained by radical historicists.[223] The sometimes all-to-easy unity represented in Western formulations of ecclesial membership has both masked significant conflict and denied new, potentially legitimate and harmonious expressions of Christian life. An approach to Christian social identity through a practice of juxtaposed thick descriptions may more effectively attend to the strands of sameness and difference, symmetry and asymmetry, accord and discord, compatibility and incommensurability, that form the fabric of Christian life and traditions, and thus help to shape a truly catholic notion of discipleship.

## Conclusion

An investigation of social identity and change from an interpretative cultural anthropological view exposes the breadth and depth of issues associated with social identity. Initial intuitions regarding the fruitfulness of symbols as bearers of sociocultural meaning remain viable and cogent, even as the shortcomings of earlier methodologies are disclosed. While a modern, integrative view of culture can no longer account adequately for the data of social life, neither can a view of culture as terminally fragmented and disintegrated. Monolithic notions of culture will not do. If culture is less a thing and more a field of contested relationships, then multiple strategies are needed to draw out the multifaceted phenomena of social identity. Corporate belonging, group solidarity, social identity, however construed, happens within a relational matrix, at once product and producer. Thus, traditions, understood as symbol systems embedded in distinctive disciplined practices, contribute towards a sense of shared history and destiny, *and* simultaneously contain the elements of their own dissolution.

In this chapter I have suggested three strategies, gleaned from a critical reappropriation of Douglas, Turner, and Geertz, toward an interpretative view of Christian tradition and its role in Christian discipleship. Examining the Christian tradition's *constructed practices of remembrance* sets the context for exploring the *provocative polyvalency* of its symbol system: the condition for the possibility of multiple, potentially harmonious expressions of Christian discipleship. From this follows the need for

---

223. Ibid., 20.

a world church to develop a *practice of juxtaposed thick description* of its various expressions of Christian discipleship, extending and expanding the cultures contributing to the theological discourse on Christian revelation.

In chapter 5 these three strategies will be critically correlated with the theological understanding of Christian discipleship found in the writings of Yves Congar (surveyed in chapter 4) in order to ascertain the fruitfulness of an interpretative anthropological view of Christian tradition.

# 4

# Yves Congar on Christian Discipleship

*A Thick Description of Christian Identity*

SOCIAL IDENTITY AND TRADITION represent highly contested notions in a postmodern world. Multiple, compelling ideological critiques of modernity question the possibility of shared resources of identity. Are these resources and traditions truly wellsprings of hallowed pasts, ordering and orienting self and community in a chaotic present toward a better future? Or, are these symbolic sources and social practices the not-so-recent inventions of "imagined communities": functionally significant, but hardly continuous with an authoritative past. In the previous chapter, the contested character of social belonging was examined from a particular trajectory within cultural anthropology. Interpretative anthropology, with its concern for meaning and how cultures construe it, offers a variety of useful methodologies for approaching the possible meanings articulated from polyvalent symbols. Ricoeur's oft-quoted phrase regarding symbols and their "surplus of meaning" comes to mind: "Symbols give rise to thought."[1] Mary Douglas would say that these symbol-inspired thoughts had better solve problems or adequately address the pressing questions of the group; otherwise, the shared cognitive dissonance of the group will render the symbolic construals a fatal blow.

Indeed, since all God-talk is symbolic, the historical overview of chapter 2 glimpses one such view of the Christian community's struggle to make sense of the world in the light of God's revelation in Jesus. This is the task of ongoing theological reflection: to interpret the meaning of divine revelation such that it is intelligible, prophetic, and faithful. New historical circumstances offer fresh opportunities for interpreting the church's faith experience of God in Jesus. Although the notion of tradition has changed as the self-understanding of the church has changed, the understanding of *tradere* (literally, to hand on), the handing down of the faith to succeeding

1. Ricoeur, *Symbolism of Evil*, 348.

generations, remains intimately connected to the notion of revelation. The gift of divine revelation is, in the words of Sandra Schneiders, *not* like a radio signal that, once emanated in history, is now only weakly detected from so great a distance of time and space.[2] However dwarfed or reduced by ideological and political concerns, the enduring ecclesial understanding of tradition in Roman Catholicism, affirmed in Vatican II, is its function as a revelatory source of God's living Presence. This sacramental sense of tradition, although variously interpreted and at times, eclipsed by magisterial propositionalism, is the interpretative basis by which the Roman Catholic Christian community negotiates its historical journey in faith.

The more recent history of Roman Catholicism documents the church's struggle to come to terms with the "modern world," now gone postmodern. The challenge facing the church's tradition is no longer simply a matter of abandoning ahistorical propositionalism in the embrace of historical criticism. In *"tiempos mixtos"* the very notion of history and the possibility of a diachronic tradition must be warranted. The preceding chapters have addressed these questions. Clearly, while nostalgic claims associated with an antimodern retrieval of the past must be ideologically critiqued and exposed as illusory false consciousness, the fact that traditions are not innocent does not negate the powerful social forces that symbolic sources nurture and sustain. If Christianity is to effectively witness to the revelation of God in Jesus, it must critically assess its ecclesial practices of remembrance, exposing the ways in which Christian traditions have and continue to legitimate social practices and power structures at odds with the gospel itself. Moreover, Christianity must create spaces for new, potentially harmonious expressions of its ancient faith.

Multiple theological voices have been raised in the last thirty years in an attempt to draw attention to the present predicament. Liberation theologies, as well as political theologies, from diverse contexts have pointed out the manner in which tradition, reified and uncritiqued, threatens to remove Catholic theology from any meaningful engagement of the critical issues of the time. In some cases, the Christian tradition is believed to be so compromised by its entrenchment in the status quo (i.e., patriarchy) it can no longer function as a locus of the Divine Presence.

In the light of these deeply serious claims and concerns, renewed interest in both tradition and Christian identity has sparked a recovery of *discipleship* as a theological category. For many liberation theologians this

---

2. Schneiders, *Revelatory Text*, 76.

category forms a significant locus for uncovering the meaning of Christian life, particularly in the daily practices of faith.[3] There is renewed interest in how popular religious devotions and practices authorize religious and social identity particularly among oppressed peoples, thereby solidifying social resistance via a vital undercurrent of alternative interpretations.

While there are many diverse (and potentially conflictual) notions of what makes a disciple of Jesus of Nazareth, this study focuses on the notion of discipleship that informs the theology of Yves Congar. Since the relationship between tradition and ecclesial identity is the question this work engages, Congar's notion of discipleship offers one particular view into the social dimension of discipleship. Congar's own monumental contribution to the renewal of the Roman Catholic Church through detailed study of the church's past highlights the transitional and conflictual context within which Vatican II came to be. Convinced that "hierarchology"[4] was distorting the ecclesial identity of the church, Congar pursued a tireless retrieval of the sources of Christian life and his work helped to catapult Roman Catholicism into a recovery of local church, laity, liturgy, ecumenism, and tradition. Although Congar never wrote a major work on discipleship, it is a category that saturates his writings. His ecclesiology recaptured for Roman Catholics a renewed understanding of the fullness of ecclesial membership at a critical moment in Catholic self-understanding. Yet, this fullness, which reclaimed the baptismal dignity of the laity, blurred the rigid boundaries of roles and responsibilities within Roman Catholicism, while transforming the Church's relationship to the modern world.

Wanting to know how the requirements of discipleship should be applied to the church as a social institution, Congar wrote,

> I should like one day to devote a whole work to this question: to what extent should and can the Church herself, the Church as such, apply to herself the Gospel requirements that tend to be restricted to individual Christians—forgiveness of enemies, turning the other

---

3. See in particular Aquino, *Our Cry for Life*; Gutierrez, *We Drink*; Sobrino, *Principle of Mercy*.

4. Congar coined this phrase to describe the overemphasis of the hierarchical function within the church. Hierarchology resulted in a laity that was more the object than a subject of the church's mission. While Congar states clearly that this overemphasis was never a denial or an exclusion of lay membership, ultimately, "forgetfulness of the true role of lay people leads to both clericalism in the Church and laicism in the world." Congar, *Lay People*, 42–47.

cheek, choosing the ways of poverty, meeting the temptations of the spirit.[5]

This chapter offers a possible answer to Congar's question by exploring the distinctive features of ecclesial membership, individual and communal, described throughout his corpus. After a review of the context and commitments that informed Congar as a theologian, this chapter explores Congar's notion of discipleship by examining the elements he identifies throughout his major works as significant markers of Christian identity. This chapter concludes with a thick description of what the requirements of the gospel might demand of the Roman Catholic Church as social institution today.

## Congar: Context and Influences

At the time of his death, Yves Congar was eulogized as one of the greatest ecclesiologists of the twentieth century.[6] A scholar, theologian, and ardent believer, Congar's historical retrieval of Roman Catholic tradition helped to give birth to the Second Vatican Council and nurtured its long-term effects on the Catholic Church's self-understanding, particularly in the area of ecumenism. Congar's lifelong passion for the unity of the Christian churches can be traced to his preparation for ordination to the priesthood. In his own words,

> Ma vocation ecclésiologique et unionique m'est apparue en 1929 et 1930, durant cette année de ma preparation au sacerdoce. Autant que je puisse préciser maintenant, dès 1929. C'est en lisant l'Évagile de saint Jean, dans la perspective de ma preparation au sacerdoce, que j'ai conçu un grand amor pour l'unité de l'Église et celle des chrétiens. C'est en méditant le chapitre XVII de saint Jean que j'ai conçu ou reçu cette vocation à ne consacrer à l'unité et à la reunion.[7]

This sense of call, of being at the service of the Word of God for the unity of the church, pervaded Congar's life and work. Described as "indefatigable," Congar was well known for working ten-hour days into his eighties, until a debilitating neuromuscular disease refused to be ignored any longer.[8] Even in the dark period when his work and that of other scholars

---

5. Congar, *Power and Poverty*, 13.
6. Dulles, "Yves Congar," 6–7.
7. Congar, *Journal d'un théologien*, 20.
8. Komonchak, "Return of Yves Congar," 402.

linked to the *nouvelle théologie*[9] were suspect and ultimately silenced for a period of time, Congar responded to the dispute with characteristic passion for the truth and respectful yet tenacious engagement of ecclesial authority.[10] Yves Congar's vocation evolved during one of the most constricted times in Roman Catholic ecclesiological history. Coming of age as a theologian on the heels of the modernist crisis, Congar inherited an ecclesial legacy fraught with all the tensions and unresolved questions surrounding the meaning of revelation in the light of historical criticism. The Roman Church's unyielding ahistorical stance threatened to reduce the Church's rich tradition to the propositional teachings of the magisterium. In response to this critical situation, Congar, inspired by the historical retrieval forwarded by mentor and colleague Marie-Dominic Chenu, OP, pursued a return to the living source of the tradition: *ressourcement*.[11]

Congar's particular genius, historical theology, allows him to approach the task of the theology from the ground of history, which he believes offers a privileged view of the Spirit's work over the centuries.

> History is a great teacher of truth. . . . Through familiarity with historical forms we can distinguish more clearly the permanence of the essential and the variation of forms; we can locate the absolute and the relative more exactly, and so better remain true to the absolute when we shape the relative to the needs of the time.[12]

For Congar history not only matters; by God's design history is the means by which "the Alpha of God's intention" reaches its culminating fruition in the Omega when and where God shall be all in all.[13] "Everything is human, everything is historical. Everything moves towards the goal aimed at by God, and He makes sure that everything arrives there."[14] This eschatological perspective pervades Congar's theology. Through it, he is able to synthesize the major theological sources of his thought: biblical revelation,

---

9. See Fergus Kerr's discussion of *nouvelle théologie* and *ressourcement* in Ford, *Modern Theologians*, 105–8.

10. O'Meara, "'Raid on the Dominicans.'"

11. "The movement of thought that prepared the way for the Council can be described as a *re-sourcement* in the sense meant by Péguy, who coined the word—a rising up of vitality from the source into the present, rather than a simple return to the sources of Christian faith, although this also certainly took place." Congar, *I Believe*, 2:150.

12. Congar, *Power and Poverty*, 13–14.

13. Congar, *I Believe*, 2:39.

14. Congar, *This Church*, 93.

tradition, Thomism (of the early twentieth century at Le Saulchoir), and the call the engage in dialogue with the modern world.

Yet, the primary influence on Congar's theology is undeniably his passion for the church.

> Do not man's words flow out of what fills his heart? The subjects dealt with here constitute the passion of my life. Saint Louis had engraved inside the ring he carried on his finger: God, France, Marguerite. His three loves. May I be permitted to engrave in the front of this work on dogma and spirituality: Church, Laity, Priesthood, linking these three loves by a common relation to the Missions.[15]

Ecclesiology is the particular focus of "faith seeking understanding" in Congar's life. His ecclesiology is fundamentally christological and pneumatological. In his trinitarian view of the mystery of revelation, the complementary missions of the Son and the Spirit create and sustain the church for God's purposes in time and space.

> If I were to draw but one conclusion from the whole of my work on the Holy Spirit, I would express it in these words: no Christology without pneumatology and no pneumatology without Christology.[16]

Thus, rooted in history and guided by an eschatological hope in trinitarian life, Congar examines the ecclesial practices of the People of God. Convinced that the "Church's own life is an indispensable 'locus theologicus,'" Congar tracks the divine purposes that guide and preserve the apostolic witness to the present.[17] The church, in his view, is a living historical communion, animated by the Spirit of Christ, in dynamic unity with the original witnesses.

## *Theological Underpinnings: Eschatology, Trinity, Sacramental Worldview*

An analysis of a fair amount of Congar's corpus leads me to posit that three important theological categories are woven throughout: eschatology, Trinity, and sacramentality. Each of these elements contributes significantly to Congar's complete theological project and, in a particular manner, to his notion of Christian life and discipleship.

15. Ibid., 7.
16. Congar, *Word and the Spirit*, 1.
17. Congar, *Mystery of the Church*, 145.

## Eschatology

Congar draws from biblical eschatology the profound insight that the truth of reality, of any being, is only known in its term, its completion. "In the Bible, 'truth' is an eschatological reality. It is, in other words, the end towards which all things are destined by God."[18] The intention of God guides the cosmos from the Alpha of its inception to the Omega when all shall be caught up into the completion of the kingdom of God. History is the place where God accomplishes salvation; it remains God's doing, yet God invites humanity into relationship and to join in the divine initiative by making that initiative their own. "[T]he economy of salvation is historical. It is punctuated by facts and divine initiatives, which, as soon as they take place, change what comes after them."[19] History is not dismissed as empty and useless, nor is creation so fraught with limits and errors that the coming kingdom will result in an annihilation of matter in order to give birth to the reign of God.[20]

> It is not in spite of time and its unfolding, but in them that the Church carries the gifts of God and puts them into practice. History and the action of men in time and through the means usually employed by them, are not, for the work that God pursues in and through the Church, an extrinsic element, or even a hostile one, which should be reduced as much as possible, forgotten or even eliminated; nor is it an external framework within which a non-terrestrial scenario will develop. It is rather that in which and through which a divine enterprise is realized.[21]

In his early thought, Congar, in agreement with other scholars, maintained that history expressed a pattern in the covenantal mystery of God's self-gift to humanity. Accordingly, there was a *progressive* movement from all people to a single people, the Hebrew people, and finally to a single man, Jesus Christ. From Jesus Christ, the movement extended once again to a faith community that was commissioned to invite all people into the alliance.[22] In his later writings Congar retains the notion of progress

---

18. Congar, *I Believe*, 2:34.
19. Ibid., 2:77.
20. Congar, *Lay People*, 86.
21. Congar, *This Church*, 89.
22. "It has been shown how sacred history was marked by a sort of progressive concentration from mankind into one people, from one people into a remnant, and from this remnant into one person, Jesus Christ; and how there followed from him an inverse

but speaks instead of the forward movement of salvation towards ever-increasing degrees of interiority: the realization of God's saving work when all shall be all in God.

> The "economy" or God's plan, to which Scripture bears witness, moves forward in the direction of greater and deeper interiority. Eschatology will be the realization of absolute interiority: "God all in all." This progress is clear in the Old Testament. It reaches its conclusion in the New Testament, where it is connected with a more perfect revelation and experience of the Spirit. It is possible to establish a progressive commitment and at the same time a more complete revelation of God himself, as Father, Son and Holy Spirit.[23]

It is God's design and intention that effects saving revelation in the midst of human history. Only through the limits and partiality of the human condition is God's revelation encountered and human life approaches its fullest realization. Eschatological hope affirms that the "regenerating power that will finally operate is already at work in our world, transiently, precariously, fragmentarily and generally unperceived."[24]

The Christian mystery unfolds in a dynamic, dialectical tension of "already" and "not yet." We are in the "order of the new alliance" and we possess the full gift of the "final and definitive realities," but only in a "restricted and precarious" manner.[25] The Christian mystery holds this tension, acknowledging simultaneously completion and partiality. In terms of discipleship, the Christian receives the world as both gift and task.[26]

This notion of things moving towards their completion, their full truth, allows Congar to distinguish between the divine gift of life in Christ through the indwelling Spirit and the historical and cultural forms that attempt to express the divine reality in time and space. Though we have the assurance of the guidance of the Spirit, all attempts to articulate the

---

movement, the mission of the ecclesial apostleship being to carry salvation in Jesus Christ to the ends of the earth." Congar, *Lay People*, 55.

23. Congar, *I Believe*, 1:12.
24. Congar, *Lay People*, 86.
25. Congar, *Mystery of the Church*, 63.
26. "Nous avons déjà exprimé brièvement cette loi caractéristique de l'oeuvre de Dieu et de l'Église, que nous avons appelée la dialectique du donné et de l'agi. L'Église est le résultat de la synergie d'un don fait gratuitement et qui, étant de Dieu, est parfaitement pur, et d'une activité de l'homme dans laquelle jouent sa liberté, ses limites, sa faillibilité naturelle." Congar, *Vraie et Fausse*, 97.

mystery remain limited. The "Absolute of the gospel" expresses itself in "partial and precarious translations."²⁷

> In the concrete, this means that, however, true and venerable they may be, the forms that we know are not the last word about the ultimate realities that they express. Dogmas are not yet perfect. The Church is, in its structures, an open system. The Word is the form and the Spirit is the breath.²⁸

## Trinity

The God who creates and calls all humanity into relationship is profound mystery, forever beyond human comprehension or approach.

> [I]f he (God) speaks to us, if he communicates his Spirit to us, this is because between him and ourselves there exists a radical resemblance. . . . And yet the moment we have said this, we have to contradict it . . . [for] the "state of divine perfection" signifies a positively infinite distance, a radical and unalterable disparity.²⁹

It is God who approaches us and invites us into a relationship that fundamentally changes us. We are given access to the Divine Life and to new energies that, through the power of the Spirit, allow us to participate in the plan of God. Congar's theology is centered on this affirmation. "From the infinite diversity of mankind and the many different peoples, God, who is three times holy, gathers for himself and unites a people who form his people."³⁰ Congar approaches the reality of human diversity and the work of human unity from a divine perspective. In the divine economy, unity is never uniformity or a blurring of identity. The Trinitarian persons remain eternally distinct in their tri-unity. This mystery challenges human notions of unity that threaten diversity and seek to eliminate difference. In the divine economy unity stimulates diversity. "Nothing less than the Spirit of God is needed to bring all these different elements to unity, and to do so by respecting and even stimulating their diversity."³¹

A particular aspect of the Trinitarian life to which Congar devotes extensive thought throughout his corpus is the mission of Christ and the

27. Congar, *Faith and the Spiritual Life*, 44.
28. Congar, *I Believe*, 2:34.
29. Congar, *Revelation of God*, 83–84.
30. Congar, *I Believe*, 2:8.
31. Ibid., 17.

Spirit. In his first work, *Mystery of the Church*, Congar attempts to explicate the missions of Christ and the Spirit in their creation of the church. In this text he established a dualism between the church's structure and its life. This construct was an attempt to show how Christ in his mission provided the church with its essential structure of apostles, divinely instituted and commissioned. Once established, this structure was animated by the Spirit, whom Christ sent. The Spirit's mission was to quicken to life the structures established by Christ and, later, the apostles.[32] In his mature thought, Congar completely retracts the dualistic construct of structure and life, rejecting its subordination of the Spirit to Christ.[33]

> It is a mistake to think, as I did in 1953 (in the *Mystery of the Church*) that a kind of "free sector" reserved for the Holy Spirit exists alongside the operation of the instituted structures and means of grace. The whole of Christian history bears witness to the fact that this freedom really exists, but it is the freedom of the living and glorified Lord Jesus together with his Spirit. They are what Irenaeus called in a very fine image the "the hands of God."[34]

Throughout his mature theology, Congar's understanding of the workings of Christ and the Spirit are rooted in the affirmation, ". . . no Christology without pneumatology and no pneumatology without Christology."[35] The dual missions of Christ and the Spirit are central to Congar's theology. The activity of God outside of Godself in creating and drawing humanity (and all creation) back to God is expressed in the mission of the Son and Spirit. The Father, the source of all life in the Godhead, who cannot be sent, is the author of the missions of the Son and Spirit. The act of mission presumes two relationships: first, a relationship between the sender and the one sent; and secondly, between the one sent and those receiving. The act of sending is not about motion or movement; it is nothing less than the creation of a new relationship between God and creature.

> The fact that the Word and the Spirit come does not mean that they move. *It means that they make a creature exist in a new relationship with them.* This means that the procession that situates them

---

32. Congar, *Mystery of the Church*, 147.
33. Congar, *I Believe*, 2:11; and Congar, *Word and the Spirit*, 61.
34. Congar, *Word and the Spirit*, 61.
35. Ibid., 1.

in the eternity of the Uni-Trinity culminates freely and effectively in a created effect.[36]

The church exists only by virtue of the complimentary missions of Christ and the Spirit. The Spirit remains ever the Spirit and Christ remains ever the Christ, not confused or mixed, yet united in effecting the same work. Their unity is a functional unity. They are "functionally so united that we experience them together and are able to accept the one for the other: 'Christ in us', 'the Spirit in our hearts', '(we) in Christ', 'in the Spirit'—all of these are interchangeable."[37]

Sacramental Worldview

How is the union of the divine with the human possible? How does the infinite and absolute communicate to and through the finite and relative? Congar approaches these questions regarding the possibility of relationship with the divine through a sacramental worldview, rooted in the thoughts and insights of Thomas Aquinas. Congar's Thomism is not of the scholastic manual variety, but reflects his intimate knowledge of this thirteenth-century doctor of the church, formed in the light of renewed studies of Thomas at Le Saulchoir. In the company of Chenu and other historical theologians, Congar retrieves Thomas, particularly his notion of grace, from the extrinsicism of Counter-Reformation manual theology.

> We are too prone to be satisfied with a dogma in itself, which has not to be worked out but is all laid down in the catechism or the theological manuals. We retail it, we are purveyors of orthodox theology, and that is all. *We are in the process of finding out that the dogma must be someone's dogma or someone's living thought, otherwise it will not bear its fruit.*[38]

Congar's theology constantly seeks to hold the inherent tension that exists between theology "from below" and theology "from above." All divine-human contact is mediated contact: material reality that is the stuff of history and culture.

> But it must not be overlooked that between God and us there is mediation through the order of things in which he has put us, and this mediation, if it be authentic, partakes of the absolute character

36. Congar, *I Believe*, 2:8; emphasis added.
37. Congar, ibid., 2:12.
38. Congar, *Priest and Layman*, 209; emphasis added.

of his authority. That is why it is not ridiculous to hold oneself responsible before Society, the World, Mankind, History, or to write those words with capital initials—they designate so many faces of God, since they represent so many orders of his will.[39]

A sacramental worldview acknowledges both the integrity of the material world in its own facticity and its capacity to hold and communicate the Divine Life, however partial or incomplete. The limits of the material do not fundamentally frustrate or negate the divine initiative and intention to bring all creation to its ultimate fruition in knowledge and love. "We hold that the historical stages punctuated by events pointing to God's work are true qualitative moments in his communication of himself to and in Jesus Christ."[40]

Between the Alpha of God's intention and the Omega of consummation, there is the journey of creation through history; a history that is not empty or without fruit.[41] God joins us; Christ and the Spirit are intimately involved. Creation matters: it is the only means by which we can come to know God in the Spirit. Life in the Spirit is fundamentally incarnational life: the Word continuously made flesh by the activity of the Spirit in the minds and hearts of believers. Furthermore, the life of the Spirit is not circumscribed by the limits of the community of believers. God's Spirit remains forever at work in creation, and because of this it is imperative for believers to be alert to the presence of Spirit in the new, the challenging, and the unresolved. "The Spirit takes the realization of the Christian mystery forward in the history of mankind."[42]

Congar's sacramental notion reflects his profound rootedness in Thomism. Congar understands the operations of grace in creation to occur in two stages. God brings creation, humans, and all living things into being, giving them everything they need to exist in themselves. Then God "calls them [human beings] to a goal which surpasses the possibilities of their powers, but which responds to the profound aspiration of things or man."[43]

> The supernatural is something different from the powers by which things are constituted; it implies a new intervention, entirely gra-

---

39. Congar, *Lay People*, 415.
40. Congar, *I Believe*, 3:166.
41. Congar, *Priest and Layman*, 279.
42. Congar, *I Believe*, 1:58.
43. Congar, *This Church*, 70.

tuitous, of God. It responds, however, to the needs of nature, if the latter must not only exist, but exist in its fullness and truth, which can be realized only in the perfect communion with God. It is *nature* that grace heals, lifts up, transforms, and makes it tend toward its perfection, beyond its own possibilities, although not beyond that which it desires in an ineffective way.[44]

Whether articulated in the philosophical notion of higher and lower principles or in the biblically informed categories that mark his later writings, Congar remains committed to this anthropology.

> This is not a Platonic, but a biblical concept. God is not the "eternal celibate of the centuries," but love and goodness. He places beings outside himself in order to bring them back to himself, so that they can participate in what he is in his sovereign existence, in other words, in the beginning and the end of their existence. He places outside himself beings who are similar to himself. Because they are like him, those beings are capable of knowing and loving freely, capable of giving themselves freely and returning to him equally freely. He animates them with a movement and therefore with a desire that is an echo in them of his own desire that he has revealed to us as his Spirit. . . . The Spirit is the principle of love and realizes our lives as children of God in the form of a Gift, fulfilling that quality in us.[45]

In summary, three theological "givens" significantly inform Congar's project. Eschatological fulfillment, the diversity-in-unity of God, and a sacramental worldview each represent significant threads that are woven into the fabric of Congar's work, from his earliest articles to his latest and greatest tome on the Holy Spirit. Each of the topics that Congar considers is situated in a context that:

1. acknowledges the real presence of truth in reality and at the same time its partial character until the consummation of God's reign;
2. asserts that the condition for the possibility of diversity-in-unity can only be found in and received from the life of God; and
3. affirms an ontology of grace by which God offers God's own self to us for our completion and God's own delight.

---

44. Ibid.
45. Congar, *I Believe*, 2:67.

## The "Christian Mystery": Ecclesial Fellowship, Witness, Service

> It is a question of combining the Alpha of God's intention with the Omega in such a way that his intention and his gift are identical throughout history, throughout the development and hazards of which it has been, is and will be the place. It is a question of preserving the messianic and eschatological way of living in community that was received from the Lord until he comes again. At the level of individual life, the first generations of Christians called this "keeping the seal of baptism shining." It is, however, also a question of the Church as such.[46]

This quote captures essential dimensions that limn Christian discipleship in Congar's thought. This next section will explore Christian discipleship as a "messianic and eschatological way of living in community . . . [as] received from the Lord" and expressed in ecclesial fellowship, witness, and service.

### *The Christian Mystery*

Congar speaks of the "the Christian mystery," an important phrase that highlights the fundamental truth of Christian life as initiated and fulfilled only in God.

> I have used the words "Christian mystery." Christ is the principle and the center of that mystery, but he came "for us men and for our salvation" and he does not operate without Christians, not even without all who are called (see Rom 8: 28-30). . . . The Christian mystery is God's revelation and communication of himself through his Son, Jesus Christ, in the Holy Spirit, who is undoubtedly, in the words of Irenaeus of Lyons, the *communicatio Christi*—"communion with Christ."[47]

Life in Christ is realized in the Holy Spirit who effects the character of filial belonging to God. In the Spirit, believers belong to God in the very way that Christ belongs to God. "Now, a very positive element is stressed in this use of the idea of assimilation or similarity. It is that grace makes us resemble, not the Father, or the Spirit, but the Son, or possibly the divine nature insofar as that is hypostasized in the Son."[48] We are

---

46. Ibid., 2:39.
47. Ibid., 2:28.
48. Ibid., 2:91.

brought into a filial relationship that makes us nothing less than sons and daughters of God.[49]

> In the communication of covenant and grace, God gives himself in a new way to the creatures made in his image, through the gifts that enable them to reach him in a very real way as the reality towards which their knowledge and love are directed.[50]

Christians respond to the God who invites humanity into the divine life by calling on "Abba, Father" as Jesus taught and by focusing the totality of their life Godward. Christians look to Jesus whose complete attention towards the desire of God opens the way for all who seek to know and love God in like manner. Christian life is not simply a matter of following in the way of Jesus as one would follow a good example or fulfill rules and regulations; it is more than living a moral life or fulfilling laws.

> Christianity is not a law, although it contains one, and it is not a morality, although it contains one. By the gift of the Spirit of Christ, it is an ontology of grace which involves, as its fruit or product, certain attitudes that are called for and even demanded by what we are. This is both extremely strong and at the same time terribly fragile.[51]

The Christian mystery, strong and fragile, is centered in the affirmation, "his mystery becomes our mystery."[52] By a gracious gift of God, the disciple shares in the life of God as son and daughter. Christian life is "not just a moral life on the human plane inspired by Christ but actually a life of Christ in mankind."[53] The gift is eschatological and its fulfillment is nothing less than deification.

> ... God himself communicates himself to us, makes himself active in us and thus enables us to perform actions of "Christ in us," which are the actions of sons.... This is not a case of God replacing us.... God's substance does not take the place of our substance. There is communication of dynamism or of an active faculty and

---

49. Congar consistently uses male imaginary in his discussion of God's relationship with human beings. While he does not intentionally exclude women, neither does he make any attempt to speak of "daughters" of God. Congar has a complementary notion of *imago Dei* and understands women to be included in the notion of sonship.

50. Congar, *I Believe*, 3:151.

51. Ibid., 2:126.

52. Congar, *Lay People*, 57.

53. Congar, *Mystery of the Church*, 120.

> we continue to act.... This fine distinction is important, because this is a question of what the Fathers of the Church called "deification."... It has to be recognized that we are and will be the subjects of a quality of existence and activities which go back to God's sphere of existence and activity. This is the ultimate context of the promise and the real fruit of the Spirit and the principle of our eschatological life.[54]

This return to the Father is the source of deification; it is the return of all creation that is the ultimate purpose of the incarnation:

> ... the formation of a new man which we too have to become through our incorporation in Christ. It is commonplace that the Fathers are never tired of repeating: "The Son of God becomes man in order that men might become God."[55]

The Christian mystery is the lifelong process by which the Spirit creates within each believer the condition of filial belonging. "The whole of our filial life is animated by the Spirit."[56]

### Critical Markers: Ecclesial Fellowship, Witness, Service

Congar describes the Christian way of life as both messianic and eschatological. As a means of organizing this section I will first explore the topic of "the Christian way of life" under the descriptor "*ecclesial fellowship*," clearly a central marker of Christian discipleship for Congar. Following this discussion, I will relate how the descriptors "messianic" and "eschatological" function to highlight two other primary markers of discipleship for Congar: *witness* and *service*.

### Ecclesial

> Our life in Christ—or his life in us—is ecclesial.... Whoever is united to the glorious body of Christ and is permeated with the Spirit through faith, baptism and the bread and wine of the Last Supper is spiritually—and therefore really—a member of Christ and forms a body with him at the level of the life of a son which promises God's inheritance.[57]

---

54. Congar, *I Believe*, 1:31–32.
55. Congar, *Revelation of God*, 73.
56. Congar, *I Believe*, 3:171.
57. Ibid., 1:32.

The church is the fruit of the complimentary missions of Christ and the Spirit. As such the church is the result of the overflow of the Divine Life outside of itself. Because the church originates from both the Christ, who *expresses and makes God known*, and the Holy Spirit, who *stirs love for God and the things of God*, Congar can assert that the church is "an organism of *knowledge* and *love* co-instituted by the missions of the Word and Spirit."[58] The sending of Christ and the Spirit effects a new relationship between God and world. Congar often refers to this as a new dynamism, released and active in time and space. The heart of this new energy is relational; God enters our world and invites humanity to build a world that God desires.

> [I]t is not simply the fact of a transcendent act of God, of an operation of Christ invisible in Heaven or of his Spirit: it is the fact of realities or energies which originate in God but which have entered into the world and man's history with the incarnation of the Word. God's design is not to do his work by purely heavenly means used in the setting of mankind; it is to do it by a *humanization of his action*, communicating to an institution of human form the exercise, with him, of activities by which men can enter into communion with him on a basis of faith.[59]

The indwelling of the Spirit in believers, communally and individually, effects a communion that is a sheer gift of God. The Spirit penetrates all without violence or confusion.[60] The Spirit vivifies, refreshes, supports, upholds, enlivens, and breaches distances while stimulating diversity and giving birth to the new moment. The Spirit is fully God in transcendent power and autonomy and inwardly intimate in the depths of persons and creation. The Holy Spirit "is the extreme communication of God himself, God as grace, God in us and, in this sense, God outside himself."[61] By the grace of this indwelling, the church is both a communication of the holy things of God and a communion of the holy ones of God. As members, we participate "in the good things of the community of salvation together with other members of that community."[62]

> The rich and profound theme of the indwelling of the Holy Spirit in our bodies and the community that we form is the other side of

58. Ibid., 2:8; emphasis added.
59. Congar, *Lay People*, 26.
60. Congar, *I Believe*, 2:17.
61. Ibid., 2:17–18.
62. Ibid., 2:59. See also Congar, *Un Peuple Messianique*, 76.

the balance in a theology affirming God's immanence whilst avoiding confusion. The Spirit can be the principle of communication and communion between God and us and between us and our fellow-men, because of what he is as Spirit—sovereign and subtle, unique in all men and uniting persons without encroaching on their freedom or their inner lives.[63]

The indwelling Spirit creates a people of God and exists in each individually and the whole together as their life principle. The Spirit is "not a mere force or a mere activating principle";[64] the Spirit is the very "co-instituting principle" of God's people.[65] Israel, under the old alliance, was truly the People of God. In Jesus, the old passes over to the "new and final dispensation that can be followed by nothing newer or more perfect."[66]

Following Jesus can only happen within the community of faith, formed and fostered by the Spirit's own life. This life is the sacred possession of the People of God who follow the Spirit's lead towards the fulfillment that is God's promise and culminating word. The People of God exist in the world for God's purposes. They are the messianic people of God, "chosen, instituted and consecrated by God to be His servant and witness" as "a sacrament of salvation offered to the world."[67]

> Thus, He has placed Jesus Christ in the world and depending on Him and originating in Him, the Church, the messianic people, gathered according to the new and final disposition of the alliance, living by the benefits of this alliance through the means established by the Lord for that purpose. The people of God is established by revelation, by the institutions and the sacraments of the new and the final disposition of the alliance, is in the midst of the world, and is for the world the sign and the sacrament of salvation offered to all men. A people marching toward a consummation, a people which is servant and witness . . .[68]

A foundational theme in Congar's ecclesiology is the notion of the church made from above and below. Because the essential identity of the church abides in the missions of Christ and the Spirit, the church's tradi-

---

63. Congar, *I Believe*, 1:33.
64. Congar, *Revelation of God*, 151.
65. Congar, *I Believe*, 1:9.
66. Congar, *Revelation of God*, 171.
67. Congar, *This Church*, 19.
68. Ibid.

tion has faithfully taught that the *ecclesia* is more than a human communion. There is a "divine element united to the human" in the form of an alliance originating from God.[69] The church is evidence that God is doing something new in the world: something distinct from, yet within, material existence and history. For at the same time the church remains both human and historical.

> [O]nce, again, she is made from above and from below. From above, as from a source of holiness given by God as a positive principle, not included in the world's possibilities, which thus constitutes a special sacred and saving order. That is why the Church is a different thing from the world or history attaining a perfect maturity through their own development (which moreover is impossible since, as we have seen, their perfection must be given them from above). At the same time the Church is formed also from below, from history and the world, whose contributions, redeemed, restored, cleansed, have to return to God in Christ, their royal first-fruits.[70]

As a human community, the church has an organized social structure; as a faith community, the church possesses an ecclesial structure organized by the charisms received from the Holy Spirit. Disciples within the community of faith contribute their unique Spirit-gifts to the upbuilding of the Christian life in fellowship, witness, and service. The presence of diverse gifts creates a differentiated community, equal in the bonds of faith and charity and diverse in the expression of this same faith and love. In Roman Catholic ecclesiology this diversity has historically expressed itself in hierarchical distinctions, distinguishing disciples ordained for the service of leadership from the rest of the disciples. Congar's understanding of the hierarchical distinction within the community of faith develops over the course of his theological project. Initially, Congar differentiates between the *structure* and *life* of the church. In this early construct, he associated apostolicity with the *structure* of the church and, reflecting the theological milieu of the time, maintained that the hierarchical gifts preceded and created the community of faith. Congar asserted that the *life* of the church (the laity) could only authentically grow and flourish from within the framework of her God-ordained structure;[71] like Ezekiel's dry

---

69. Ibid., 89.
70. Congar, *Lay People*, 110.
71. Ibid., xxxiv.

bones, the Spirit must gather and structure the skeleton before enfleshing the being with life.[72]

The shift in Congar's thought happens when he corrects his notion of structure and life. Congar consistently maintains that apostolicity is a gift that necessarily imposes a hierarchical character upon the institutional structures of the community of faith. But he reverses the order of their prominence, asserting that "the Church is an institution, but it is also and even primarily the 'we' of Christians."[73] Christian discipleship flows from the Spirit-diversified community of faith whose life in fellowship is a sacramental expression of God's saving presence in the world. Christian discipleship is both a gift received from God in the communion of Divine Life and a task, a mission, a sending forth as witness and servant.

When the ecclesial dimension of individual discipleship is considered from this perspective, what issues of Christian life and faith present themselves?

### Ecclesial Fellowship and the Full Subjecthood of the Baptized

In Congar's discussion of the ecclesial nature of discipleship, the recovery of the subjecthood of the laity plays a significant role and dominates his work during the 1950s and 1960s. While never failing to affirm the foundational role of the hierarchy in the divine gift of the church, Congar consistently challenges the aberration of "hierarchology" and the Christendom mentality that replaced the original ecclesia-world tension with a lay-cleric tension.[74]

> Thus, whilst in the Church of the Martyrs there was a tension, not inside the Church between the various categories of Christians, but between the "ecclesia" and the world, henceforth within a society entirely Christian, tension grew inside the Church or within

---

72. "By *structure* we understand the principles which, because they come from Christ, representing with him and in his name the generative causes of the Church, are the things in her, as her *pars formalis*, that constitute men as Christ's Church. These are essentially the deposit of faith, the deposits of the sacraments of faith and apostolic powers whereby the one and the other are transmitted. Therein resides the Church's essence. By life we understand the activity which men, made Church by the said principles, exercise in order that the Church may fulfill her mission and attain her end, which is, throughout time and space, to make of men and a reconciled world the community—temple of God." Ibid., 249.

73. Congar, *I Believe*, 2:130.

74. Congar, *Lay People*, 45.

> Christian society, between monks or priests on the one hand and laymen on the other.⁷⁵

Recovering the church-world relationship is integral to Congar's understanding of the full witness of the baptized community of Christ. The whole People of God is necessary for the completion of the mission of Christ and Spirit in the world.

> Everywhere the pastoral position demands, and doubtless will demand more and more, that the work of the Gospel be considered as belonging not to the clergy alone but to the clergy and laity together; . . . It is not simply because of the shortage of clergy, or of any clerical inadequacy; it is because there is a qualitative insufficiency in the pastoral field, an intrinsic ineffectiveness in the apostolic set-up, if the laity is not organically associated in the work of the Gospel—not just a few of the laity, "safe people," but the Christian laity taken as a whole.⁷⁶

Engaging the subjecthood of the laity required a new perspective and a significant task of re-education and socialization into active membership within the Body of Christ. Clericalism effectively undermined the development of the laity. Spiritual books and movements for lay Christians were often "stamped with an unhealthy romanticism . . . [and] with that exuberant enthusiasm of children which is generous, but somewhat unreal."⁷⁷ The extreme emphasis on external perfection in a church dominated by juridical norms left lay people inappropriately dependent upon the clergy.⁷⁸ Congar, in contrast to this, ascribes to a state of Christian adulthood marked by self-possession and self-donation. The Christian adult "passes from an attitude which is ego-centric" to a self-possession only fully realized in the gift of self to others.⁷⁹

> There is no law in the whole of the New Testament and the Christian Tradition that is more strongly affirmed than this law of mutual service and mutual building up. There are many gifts of the Spirit—a multiplicity of gifts—and Paul's list is neither systematic

75. Congar, *Power and Poverty*, 57.
76. Congar, *Lay People*, 358.
77. Congar, *Faith and the Spiritual Life*, 146.
78. Congar bemoans the laity's "mania for looking for directions that dispense them from thinking out their problems" and the clergy's "habit of deciding and prescribing for everything." Congar, *Lay People*, 417.
79. Congar, *Faith and the Spiritual Life*, 144.

> nor exhaustive. They are gifts made to persons, but those persons are not monads with individual autonomy. They belong to a people, a tradition, a culture and a sociological group, to which their gifts are in a sense appropriated. The Church's catholicity calls for these gifts to be gathered together and exchanged, and for the different parties contributing them to be aware of the whole and of its unity.[80]

The ecclesial dimension of Christian discipleship places the individual in a dynamic, creative tension between the personal and social; a tension which is absolutely necessary for both the full realization of the individual and the community. According to Congar's anthropology, humanity mirrors the divine in its form of life; mature persons are only realized through acts of self-donation. Self-donation is the very life of the Trinity. *Perichoresis*, or the interpenetration of the persons of the Trinity, does not violate the distinctness of persons in the one God. So, too, with humanity; a realized individual emerges only when the self has been given as gift. This perichoretic interplay between the individual and the community witnesses to the graced possibility of human unity: not superficial uniformity, but catholic diversity.[81]

## *Witness*

> The gift and the activity of the Spirit cannot be limited to a single aspect in the development of faith. . . . Indeed, this anointing of faith is so much the work of the Spirit that it is an extension and a communication to believers of the prophetic and messianic anointing that Jesus received from the Spirit at his baptism. This anointing is active in the whole life of faith of the one who is baptized and who bears witness, whether he be personally inspired or officially commissioned. The Spirit deepens the faith of the disciples and strengthens it. He is essentially the Spirit of truth.[82]

Witness is the second characteristic that marks Christian discipleship in Congar's theology. Christian witness is fundamentally rooted in Jesus Christ, the faithful Witness to God's promises to the world. As we have seen, the Spirit is the Gift of God who creates within us the filial relation-

---

80. Congar, *I Believe*, 2:26.

81. "The unity of mankind—still more, the spiritual unity of men in Christ—has to be established, not by physical fusion and loss of personality, but by that love in which, by uniting himself to others, each becomes most truly himself." Congar, *Mystery of the Church*, 27.

82. Congar, *I Believe*, 2:102.

ship making us God's very own. Congar understands the baptism of Jesus to be that moment when Jesus is declared in a unique way "the Son of God." Congar affirms that the incarnation is the activity of the Spirit, effecting the hypostatic union of the Word, Jesus of Nazareth, within the womb of Mary; but it is not until Jesus' baptism in the Jordan by John that Jesus is recognized as one filled with the Spirit.[83] Christ's anointing by the Spirit at his baptism is a new declaration of his sonship because in it he becomes the Son-for-us. "[H]is baptism is a new act in which his divine sonship was made present—the act that made him and declared him to be 'Christ.'"[84]

As Jesus' baptism anointed him for his messianic mission of proclamation, so each believer receives at baptism a share in Christ's own anointing and mission. Baptism, as the principle sacrament of initiation into Christian life, communicates to the believer Christ's own life and a share in Christ's saving work. The disciple of Christ bears witness to the paschal event and its power, even now at work, bringing all to salvation.

Christian witness is both a recollection of a past event and an assertion in the here and now that the power of the resurrection is real and present.[85] In his etymological study of the word "witness," Congar shows how both Hebrew and Greek influences provide a hermeneutic for the meaning of Christian witness.[86] The Hebrew verb *udh* means "to bear witness" and "expresses the idea of repetition and this involves the idea of affirmation and a commitment of the will."[87] The places where God reveals his will (the ark of the covenant and the tabernacle), as well as the Law, are God's "testimonies," and, like God's Word, they are *vorwärtgerichtet*, "'directed forward,' and not *zurückschauend*, "backward-looking." This forward-directed testimony is contrasted with the Greek word *marturein, martur*, which comes from Indo-European words meaning "to remember."[88] New

---

83. Congar is following the work of Heribert Mühlen who challenges the highly christocentric theology of the Roman school. This overemphasis contributed to an ecclesiology in the Roman Church that envisioned the church as an ongoing expression of the incarnation, characterized as "ecclesiological monophysitism" (see Malanowski, "Pneumatology"). Congar discusses Mühlen's contribution to his own pneumatology in *I Believe*, 1:22–25.

84. Congar, *Word and the Spirit*, 88.

85. Congar, *I Believe*, 2:41.

86. Congar notes that he "derived great help here from the posthumous work by Ragnar Asting published in 1939. Ibid.

87. Ibid.

88. Ibid.

Testament testimony derives its meaning by holding both the notions of memory and advancement. Christian witness is simultaneous a movement backwards to the original saving event and a projection forward from that event into its present salvific expression.

> In the messianic and eschatological age which began with the mission and gift of Jesus Christ and the Holy Spirit, both values of "witness" are to be combined. The first is the recollection and attestation of what has already taken place; the second is a dynamic affirmation of the present effectiveness of those realities and their fulfillment in the apostolic mission brought about by the facts themselves, until they are eschatologically consummated.[89]

There is an essential continuity between these moments that only the Spirit of God guarantees. "The Spirit is . . . given to the Church as its transcendent principle of faithfulness."[90] This is the critical point Congar stresses regarding the apostolic witness of the church. First and foremost, it is the church that is apostolic, and she is made so by the gift of the Holy Spirit. Congar notes that the inspiration of the Spirit within the church

> . . . was frequently represented as automatic and occurring as a matter of course in the predominantly juridical ecclesiology that resulted from the Church's conflict with secular power, the Counter-Reformation and the reaction to the French Revolution.[91]

This unfortunate emphasis clouded the centrality of the church's apostolicity as "a communion with the apostles, and with and through them a communion with the Father and his Son Jesus Christ."[92] While the historical expression of the transmission of the faith has been connected to the role of the bishops, this succession needs to be viewed within its larger context of "universal apostolicity."

> This universal apostolicity is fundamentally an apostolicity of faith, but it is also an apostolicity of service, witness, suffering and struggle. The "apostolic succession" in the technical sense of this term, has to be placed within the context of this apostolicity, that is, of this communion extended in time. It is, after all, possible to speak of an apostolic succession in the case of all believers, but only in the wider context of the faithful transmission of the faith.

89. Ibid., 2:42.
90. Ibid., 2:43.
91. Ibid., 2:44.
92. Ibid., 2:45.

It is only in this communion that the "apostolic succession" in the strict sense of the term, in other words, the succession of the bishops, can take place.[93]

As a community of apostolic faith, the pilgrim People of God give witness to the inbreaking of God's saving Presence in the world. The messianic task of disciples is evangelization, bringing the message of God's mercy to the world. Christian disciples also work to influence the world towards conformity with God's design.[94] The Christian disciple must both speak God's Word and build God's world. This task belongs to the entire community and its goal is conversion.[95] The call to conversion has its consequences, as the Christian story bears out. Rejection and the threat of violence are painfully familiar in the history of Christian discipleship; in fact, it is often a sign of an authentic witness. If discipleship is truly a sharing in the life of Christ, then the Christian disciple, as witness, risks suffering, setbacks, misunderstanding, betrayal, and death.

> Biblically speaking, a witness is not simply someone who speaks or exhibits a sign; he is someone who acts and who makes God's purpose and will a reality in this world. To witness . . . is to testify to the same thing a number of times, just as a nail is driven home by repeated blows; it is to proclaim God's will in the world and this inevitably provokes the world's hostility. And this is the reason why one gets killed.[96]

Disciples do not become witnesses simply because they speak, nor do their violent deaths make them martyrs. They are killed because of their provocative, disturbing witness.[97]

Conversion, the heart of Christian witness, must also provoke the ongoing development of the seed of faith and love within the faith community. The anointing of the Holy Spirit "gives us a clear consciousness of our own wretchedness and of the untruth and selfishness that fills our lives." The awareness of God's judgment is "forestalled by grace, with the

---

93. Ibid.

94. Congar, *Priest and Layman*, 255–56.

95. ". . . the apostolate is always a call to conversion, to repentance, and the first act of the Holy Ghost is to convince the world of its wrong, its sin. That, too, is why the apostle suffers from those afflictions inseparable from his messianic calling, inherent in the furtherance of the Kingdom of God . . ." Congar, *Mystery of the Church*, 50–51.

96. Congar, *Faith and the Spiritual Life*, 177.

97. Ibid.

result that our false excuses, our self-justifying mechanisms and the selfish structure of our lives breaks down."[98]

> Something of this kind happened to Zacchaeus. Grace came into his home, forestalling him, and at once he knew that he was a sinner. It is worth noting the boldness and at the same time the depth of understanding on the part of the Church in using this passage in Scripture (Lk 19:1–10) in the liturgy of the dedication of a church. The Church itself is a sinner forestalled by free forgiveness and is converted when the Lord comes and takes up residence in it. The Church is and always will be the coming of salvation to a house where the Lord comes to dwell, and this process begins with a conviction of injustice and sin.[99]

Christian witness finds the ground of its authenticity in its bold affirmation that the Christian community stands in continuous need of the support of the Spirit on its historical journey from Alpha to Omega. Though the community possesses the first-fruits of the salvation effected by Jesus' death and resurrection, its grasp of this gift is partial, incomplete, and even, at times, a source of grief to the Holy Spirit.[100] Christian witness "is always conditioned by the historical nature of knowledge, language and expression."[101] The Spirit indwells the church on its pilgrim journey, recalling the People of God from ill-fated detours to their original grace and final home.

How does the notion of witness as a marker of Christian discipleship express itself in the lives of individual Christians?

### Witness as Vocation

The individual Christian in the world witnesses to God as the ultimate source and fulfillment of creation. For the early fathers of the church, baptism, the means by which one comes into the *ecclesia*, is synonymous with "the state of witness for the world."[102] The disciple witnesses not to "a supreme being, an everlasting celibate detached from the world, but a God who is alive, whose existence involves our own, a God actively concerned

---

98. Congar, *I Believe*, 2:123.
99. Ibid.
100. Ibid., 57–58.
101. Ibid., 46.
102. Congar, *Priest and Layman*, 261.

with human beings."[103] In this sense, God is God-in-the-world through the faithful witness of Christian disciples.[104] "Each form of life has its own conditions, duties and resources, and the *vita in Christo* is influenced accordingly."[105] Christian life expresses itself in diverse vocations, states and conditions of life sourced in "the holy and hallowing will of God."[106] According to Congar's notion of vocation, each person exists to effect some aspect of God's design. Within the unique inclinations, preferences and opportunities of each life, a gift of God to the world emerges.[107]

> [A]ll vocations have their place within the total purpose that embraces the whole destiny of the created universe, so that God's will for each one always involves imperatives having in view the actualizing of his mercy for the whole world and for all men.[108]

Disciples "keep the seal of baptism shining" through a dual commitment to God and the world. World building is not optional; it is a central part of the Christian vocation. Believers live a "two-fold loyalty, towards God and towards the world" in all the complexities of human life and relationships.[109] The unfolding of life offers each disciple the raw materials by which they make a human life in the Spirit. The particularity of each person's existence is the sacred space where Christ is made present. "Only God, in other words, can make us act divinely. It is, however, we who act."[110]

Christian discipleship is always a work in progress, as the disciple actualizes the gift and task of baptism.[111]

> The baptismal gift is a gift of fullness because, through faith and the anointing of the Holy Spirit, it is a communion in the mystery of Christ with eschatological salvation in mind. It is what Irenaeus called, in a well-known text, the *communicatio Christi*. This fullness must be made present and developed, according to the good

---

103. Congar, *Faith and the Spiritual Life*, 168.

104. "The criterion of a Christian life might well be this: in all life's circumstances, in the choices we make of greater or lesser significance, we should always say, 'Thou art my God.'" Ibid., 179.

105. Congar, *Lay People*, 379.

106. Ibid., 403.

107. Ibid., 407.

108. Ibid., 405.

109. Ibid., 228.

110. Congar, *I Believe*, 2:135.

111. Congar, *Lay People*, 312.

pleasure of the Lord indeed, as Irenaeus said, but also according to the degree of development of our conscious understanding and our entry into human society and the history of the world.[112]

The attempt to witness and forward God's vision of the world presumes that the disciple makes every attempt "to learn what God wants for the world in general, [and] for us in particular."[113] Discerning God's ways is a communal task. History confirms that those who claim to know unambiguously God's will often bare fruits of violence and corruption. Therefore, in the company of fellow seekers, disciples search together for God within an all-pervasive milieu of itinerancy. Disciples are sojourners and pilgrims, not tourists.[114]

The particularity of each believer's concrete circumstances evokes a variety of responses to the challenges of life. From the vast diversity of human cultures to the fundamental uniqueness that makes even blood relatives a mystery to each other, human beings live amidst relational complexities that inherently place individuals into conflict. Choice, decision, strife, and division all characterize the historical conditions under which Christians strive to live the vocation entrusted to them by the Spirit.[115]

> In this world we suffer—and in some way all creatures suffer with us—through our being external to one another and not forming a fellowship which makes of all one whole, each thing being nevertheless respected for its own sake. Made in God's image, which is perfectly one in many and many in one, we long to overcome the exteriorities and sometimes intense oppositions from which we suffer. I am not thinking only of the numberless disagreements of daily life, but of those deeper oppositions, grounded in otherness (*extériorité*), ontological, which are a kind of disintegration for us beings who thirst for unity: otherness of man and of nature, of one man and of another, of man and woman, of power in relation to life, of public duties and of authority in relation to persons and their life, the supreme otherness of man and God.[116]

---

112. Congar, *I Believe*, 3:221.

113. Congar, *Faith and the Spiritual Life*, 140.

114. ". . . we are pilgrims, travellers, in the world. . . . Ours is the position of one who delivered from bond-service, is given a new task, or simply the same one, as a vocation and labour of love." Congar, *Lay People*, 411.

115. Ibid., 392.

116. Ibid., 87.

Only the Spirit actualizes the unity we desire, yet we have a "duty of unity." Reflecting particularly on Roman Catholic Christianity, Congar acknowledges that the expanding boundaries of the present world offer increasing opportunities for legitimate disagreement among the baptized. The duty of unity demands that believers hold to that which unites with as much tenacity as that which represents authentic difference.

> As one comes down the scale the range of possible choices and opinions gets larger, and in consequence the opportunities for Catholics to disagree increase.... Amidst their legitimate differences of choice and commitment, Catholics still have a duty of unity; and this is the more difficult because that unity is not to be imposed (as some people would still like) by uniformity in everything...[117]

The witness to Christ in its multiple, authentic expressions will provoke hostility, even within the church, where certain perspectives are, at times, privileged over others, sacrificing the full catholicity of the communities' witness. The effort to engage in the task of faithful witness requires the full gift of the disciple to the mission. "It will become more and more evident and this is our profound and rational conviction, that Christian life requires such a major effort."[118]

## Service

The witness of the messianic community in word and deed is both a received gift and an entrusted task. "God indeed will give all from on high, and all will be new, but he purposes that we should have nothing in which we have not been enabled to co-operate."[119]

In this light, service is that quality of discipleship that places the believer in the world to influence or "christofinalize" the world.[120] It is not enough that disciples call the world from evil and sin to Christ. Christians are disciples to the extent that they embrace the task of Godward action in the world. "The biblical way is wholly theological and theonomic: it does not involve any deprecation of man, who, being placed in a relation of faith to God, is invited, on the contrary, to action in the world."[121] The

---

117. Congar, *Lay People*, 331.
118. Congar, *This Church*, 100.
119. Congar, *Lay People*, 97.
120. Ibid., 110.
121. Congar, *Priest and Layman*, 253.

Christian disciple receives the world in a new way from God and participates in the world's transformation. Congar describes Christian life as paradoxical: a consequence "of a twofold loyalty" to be in the world, but not of the world.

All Christian life is based on the fundamental notion that in Christ the disciple has died to the world.

> In every authentic Christian life, therefore, there is a kind of devaluation and dismissal of the things of this world: husband or wife, money, health, bodily strength and beauty, influence or fame, the intellectual life and its resources, social life, and even culture itself. No Christianity and no holiness without death to all that.[122]

But this is not the end of the story. Even as Christians deny the world, the world is restored to them in a new and Spirit-imbued manner. The world is restored to us

> . . . not in an earthly and carnal way . . . as we received them originally when we were born from the flesh—but from above, as duty and grace: for every duty, every mission implies a task to be done that is assisted by corresponding resources of grace.[123]

The history of the relationship between the Christian community and the world is marked by polar tensions. The dilemma re-presents itself to the disciple as a question of how to remain thoroughly engaged in the task of world building without succumbing to the allurements of power and wealth? At times, the dynamic between the dual poles of church and world collapses, resulting either in a world without a church or a church without a world.[124] Neither of these conditions honors the incarnational wisdom of God in Jesus Christ who came that all might "have life and life in its fullness" (John 10:10).[125]

---

122. Congar, *Faith and the Spiritual Life*, 138.

123. Ibid., 138–39.

124. "In the presence of a religion without a world, men formulated the ideal of a world without religion." Congar, *This Church*, 18.

125. "Within its historical and cultural context, the self-understanding of the Christian community has always affirmed that the church is something other than the world." Congar, *Lay People*, 400. When this distinction was absorbed in Christendom, roles within the faith community, particularly the relationship between the laity and clergy, became problematic. "History shows that the apostolate of the laity is only taken seriously when a real "world" exists to confront the Church, and the Church is aware of it. Then the tension is felt for what it is, a tension between the Church, seed and sacrament of the Kingdom of God, and the world. In those conditions priests and laity feel

Communities of disciples serve the world by their very distinctiveness. Maintaining a presence in the world, while working to be less of the world, places the disciple in a gospel tension that attempts to honor both loyalties.

> What we need to develop is a cultivation of faith, of biblical faith, of faith in the living God, of faith regarded as a human activity projected by God into the world and endowed with a motivation towards him. A modern Christian is called to live with an intense loyalty a life that is a complete acceptance of both the world and God. . . . No ready-made formula exists; we simply have to lead our lives in a twofold and equally intense loyalty to God and to the world.[126]

The heart of a Christian's loyalty to the world is rooted in the belief that the Spirit is effecting the reign of God in all creation. The world, by God's design, is more than a means "subordinate to the absolute end."[127] The world is the place where the "signs of the times" are to be read and interpreted. In the light of the insights and questions of each generation, disciples are called to mission.

> However useful and indeed necessary the work of sociologists may be, these indications [signs of the times] should not be interpreted purely sociologically, but rather in the light of the gospel, inspired by faith and led by the Holy Spirit. At the least, these broad facts point to developments in the history of mankind which provide the Church, or more precisely, its catholicity, with its matter. These developments in the history of the first Adam have to be evangelized and therefore first recognized, and they also give a topicality to the Church's message, matter to its mission, and new ways of proclaiming the gospel. At the most, the events taking place in the world that stimulate the consciousness of Christians, enabling them to hope and to act energetically, can be seen as a genuine "word" of God.[128]

Christian service in the world is essentially *diakonia*. Christianity inspires a new order in the world, not by force or dominance but by a new

---

themselves to be called and yoked to the same task: the laity are no longer mere passengers in a ship navigated by the clergy alone: they are, in their own place, part of the ship's company." Congar, *Priest and Layman*, 246.

126. Congar, *Faith and the Spiritual Life*, 204.

127. Congar, *Lay People*, 400.

128. Congar, *I Believe*, 2:32.

attitude: agapic service.[129] As a result of the Spirit's action, Christian disciples see with new eyes and encounter the other no longer as stranger, but neighbor.[130] Jesus is the sole inspiration of the servants of God. His refusal to engage in tactics of domination or political intrigue marks out a transformative path characterized by humility, obedience, and fidelity.[131] Sharing in the life of Christ means not simply mimicking his actions; it is a genuine embrace of the path of self-giving and surrender that Jesus walked.

> Diakonia, ministry, the position, behavior and activity of a servant, appears throughout the whole of the New Testament to be as it were coextensive and practically identical with the character of disciple—a man possessed by Christ and living in subjection to him. The title "doulos," slave, servant (of God), which had no religious significance in the pagan world, best expresses this complete belonging to Christ, in which we become also the servants of all our brothers.[132]

While the way of humble service is the path marked for all disciples, Congar makes it very clear in several of his texts that disciples entrusted with the charism of authority must particularly attend to the servant nature of their ministry. Authority for Congar is functional, serving to orchestrate the life of the community and to further the influence of the faith community in the world.

> This return to the sources has already begun to emphasize the necessity of a certain rediscovery of the two religious realities by reference to which authority must find out the truth about itself. They are the living God active among us through his grace, and the holy community and brotherhood of the faithful. It is by setting authority in an authentic relationship with these two Christian realities that we shall be able to go beyond legalism which consists in seeing the formal validity of phenomena to penetrating to their meaning. The movement back to the sources must go forward until it restores a completely evangelical concept of authority, a concept that will be both fully supernatural and fully communal.[133]

---

129. Congar, *Priest and Layman*, 6.

130. Congar, *Lay People*, 383.

131. "Le messianisme de Jésus n'est pas celui de la puissance dominatrice, mais celui du Serviteur." Congar, *Un Peuple*, 95.

132. Congar, *Power and Poverty*, 25.

133. Ibid., 78.

Authority does not exist for itself or by itself; it exists within the community. While relations of dominance exist in ordered society, Congar notes that Christ rejects the practices of domination, tyranny, and lording-over.[134] Authority is a duty of service, a charism that furthers the life the community and secures the authenticity of its apostolic witness.[135] Authority as service does not eliminate the element of power; authority as service is situated in the context of the life of the community. Christianity comes first, authority follows.[136]

By the power of the Spirit and the witness of Christ, we are made sharers in God's own life. This invitation to the fullness of life is both a gift and a task. How does Congar understand service as agapic love realized in the life of the individual disciple?

### Agapic Service and the Other as Neighbor

The love of God sent into the hearts of believers transforms their existence by sharing in God's own life. The love that unites humans to God is the first gift, the foremost expression of grace. This love transforms everything about the disciple; thus, human relationships are radically altered in the light of the Christian mystery.

> The first fruit of the Spirit is love. It is more than simply the first in the order of the list. It is the all-embracing and creative principle and is in fact all. "He who loves has fulfilled the law" (Rom 13:8). Paul, however, goes even further than this and teaches that the holy life is a communication of the holiness of God. The love of which he speaks is the love of God which "has been poured into our hearts through the Holy Spirit which has been given to us" (Rom 5:5). This Spirit also makes us sons of God.[137]

The love that makes us children of God draws us into communion with God and with all people.[138] The agapic love of God creates within the human heart the conditions of the possibility of that love among

---

134. Congar, *Un Peuple Messianique*, 134.

135. Congar, *Power and Poverty*, 91–92.

136. "We must not posit authority first and in itself, and then say that it is wielded over Christians for spiritual ends, and must be used impartially, in a spirit of service. Christianity must be posited first, and then the fact of authority in it. . . . In this way, it is qualified as Christian from its very roots; it is service, because the Christian life is service." Congar, *Priest and Layman*, 260.

137. Congar, *I Believe*, 1:31.

138. Congar, *Mystery of the Church*, 127.

human beings; only by the power of this divine love is a disciple able to enter into the fullness of the Christian mystery: the surrender of self for love of the other.[139]

The agapic love of God in Jesus Christ transforms the human experience of otherness (*exteriorité*) and orders human relationships such that, for Christians, the other is no longer stranger, but neighbor. "Christianity could not but inspire a new order in the world, since it involved a new way of looking at life and the regarding of others as one's neighbors."[140] Created for relationship with the divine, the children of God become the means by which God's love continues to flow into the world; disciples enter into a genuine religious relationship whereby their lives become the channels of God's life to the world.[141] Discipleship is not possible unless faith and love are lived in the context of a freely chosen commitment to agapic service of our neighbor.

> When we speak of being God's channels, it should be obvious that our freedom is not in the least suppressed. We are not mechanized channels; we act freely, we commit ourselves freely to his love and service; it is through faith that we become the channels of the living God.[142]

The agapic nature of a disciple's service expresses the depth to which God's love penetrates the life of the disciple. Faith opens the disciple to the perspective of another and love invites the disciple to consider the new point of view with openness, respect, and genuine welcome.[143] Christian service is other-centered in a manner that gives precedence to the good of the other; that is, the good of the other is guarded as the disciple's own deepest good.

> This will mean, in practice, deepening and purifying our love, a love which is really love; not, that is, asserting ourselves, even in the

---

139. "In one way or other the conduct of the Christian, and especially the apostolate, because they lie in the realm of agape, of self-giving love, self-sacrificing love, pledge the Christian and especially the apostle to sacrifice, and ultimately to the surrender of life itself." Congar, *Power and Poverty*, 35.

140. Congar, *Lay People*, 383.

141. Congar, *Faith and the Spiritual Life*, 176. "Our work is not only to be recipients of God's glory; it is also the splendid and important task of becoming irrigation channels flowing from the river that streams from God for the warmth and enlightenment of the world and for the life of man" (175).

142. Ibid., 176.

143. Congar, *Mystery of the Church*, 71.

masked and apparently disinterested form of serving our Church, but seeking the good of the other person and, to that end, accepting the other, with a total respect for that profoundest movement in which he is truly himself. And we must do so as if it concerned ourselves and our own good, and that deepest movement which expresses ourselves, and which we accept with so profound an agreement.[144]

In this manner, Christian service can approach, in however small a measure, the agapic quality of divine love, a "love that seeks not itself but gives itself, and for this very reason is directed towards the weakest and the most wretched."[145] Congar recalls that from the beginning the Christian community sought to care for bodies as well as souls and "to succor everywhere whatever is lost . . ."[146] The works of mercy express outward-moving, other-centered acts of communion and solidarity with those most in need. Disciples need to "be with these people, not just beside them or in front of them, but with them."[147]

The Christian disciple, as servant, knows that her fate is intimately bound to that of the other and encounters in the mystery of the other a grace of communion. This is the lesson of agapic love that Jesus preached and witnessed to in his own paschal mystery. By the grace of the paschal event the reality of agapic love is realized and the power of that event reverberates throughout time and space, creating through the Spirit the means by which strangers become neighbors. The Christian disciple serves the purposes of the Spirit towards this end: that all might become neighbor.

> The way leading to God who is "all in all," leading that is to mankind in communion, is a state where others are not destroyed to sustain life, but where life, coming from God shines out on all men; it is the way of love in humble service.[148]

## Congar and Discipleship

One way of approaching Yves Congar's notion of discipleship involves a thorough review of his works in search of the various ways he speaks

---

144. Congar, *Priest and Layman*, 40.
145. Ibid., 6.
146. Ibid.
147. Ibid., 7.
148. Congar, *Power and Poverty*, 30.

of the "messianic and eschatological way of living in community . . . received from the Lord."[149] This review yields three significant aspects of the "Christian mystery": ecclesial fellowship, witness, and service. This review also illuminates certain commitments that inform Congar's theology. Seemingly, Congar is a thoroughly modern theologian. While he acknowledges the disjunctive and interruptive aspects of historical life, he expresses a consistent confidence regarding the progress of history towards its *telos*. Particularly in works written during the years immediately preceding and following Vatican II, Congar exhibits a positive orientation towards all things human, a characteristic that marks much theological reflection of the 1960s. From the 20/20 vision of hindsight, it is difficult not to miss the naiveté of maintaining a position that "the order of things" participates in "the absolute character" of the divine authority.[150] However, within the ecclesial context of the late 1940s and early 1950s, this assertion may be more clearly understood as a plea to an entrenched and insulated hierarchy to pay attention to a world it resolutely dismissed. Moreover, it could be argued that these theological attempts to link the divine with the social order prepared the way for the quintessential phrase of Vatican II: "reading the signs of the times."[151] Yet, even in later works Congar maintains theological positions that have definite foundational commitments. His ontology of grace, a position he maintains from his earliest to his latest writings, is firmly grounded in an Alexandrian Christology.

A critical awareness of Congar's own historical location and context helps towards understanding how he describes discipleship in the life of the individual believer. Congar's entire theological project was directed towards the recovery of the fullness of ecclesial life, lost to encroaching papalism and an overemphasis on the role of the hierarchy. In order to promote the recovery of the full ecclesial witness of the church, Congar

149. Congar, *I Believe*, 2:39.

150. Congar, *Lay People*, 415.

151. "At all times the Church carries the responsibility of reading the signs of the time and of interpreting them in the light of the Gospel, if it is to carry out its task." Second Vatican Council, *Gaudium et Spes*, no. 4. Peter Hebblethwaite notes that the phrase originated from John XXIII in *Humanae Salutis*, a solemn apostolic constitution. "In a single sentence, Pope John provided the Council with a method and commentators with material that could last a lifetime. He spoke of the need to 'discern the signs of the times': 'We should make our own Jesus' advice that we should know how to discern 'the signs of the times' (Matthew 16:4), and we seem to see now, in the midst of so much darkness, a few hints which augur well for the fate of the Church and humanity." Hebblethwaite, "John XXIII," 29.

engaged in the delicate work of de-emphasizing the structural elements of the faith community. His careful analysis of Christian ecclesial life revealed the historical influences that precipitated the gross overemphasis of the institutional and hierarchical without denying the central role that the apostolic charism plays in the life of the church.[152] By focusing on the charisms given to the church, Congar is able to show how the Spirit structures the Christian community for the sake of its mission.[153]

## Communal Praxes of Discipleship: Contemporary Markers of the Ecclesial Identity

In this final section, I propose and describe three contemporary markers of ecclesial identity derived from an analysis of Congar's understanding of Christian discipleship. This attempt at a thick description of Christian social identity from the particularity of Congar's perspective offers possible answer to the question he himself raised concerning ecclesial identity, but does not pretend to be pseudo-Congar in voice. Rather, it is an interpretation of the gospel arising from an immersion in Congar's theology and focused towards the pressing questions and signs of our times.

> The church's presence in the world "can be reduced to three terms, compact with the greatest possible spiritual meaning: "Koinonia, Diakonia, Marturia" (Fellowship, Service, Witness).[154]

Each of these three dimensions explored in this section is qualified by a particular *praxis*, proposed as possible responses to Congar's query, "How are the requirements of discipleship to be applied to the church as a social entity"? The use of the word *praxis* is intended to highlight the dynamic engagement that so marks Congar's understanding of Christian discipleship: "the sign and at the same time the means of God's intervention in our

---

152. See Congar, *L'Église*, esp. chs. 8–15.

153. Congar maintains throughout his theological project that the *ecclesia* receives its structure from God and this structure is hierarchical. However, Congar situates the hierarchical structure within the larger context of Christian service and mission. Hierarchical gifts are not given for their own sake; their essential purpose is service, as are all the gifts of grace bestowed on the community of faith. Congar notes that Paul speaks of two principles that shape the assembly of God: the diversity of gifts found in the members and the single source from which all gifts flow and eventually return. "[T]out vient du même Esprit, tout est ordonné à la construction du Corps du Christ." The charisms are given to the entire church for the sake of the mutual life of all; where one lives for others in the manner that Christ lives for us. Congar, *Un Peuple Messianique*, 78.

154. Congar, *Power and Poverty*, 138.

world and our history."[155] Thus, the requirements of Christian discipleship demand an active, or more correctly, a *proactive* engagement of "the signs of the times" that continue to present themselves.

> These "signs of the times" are not always clearly defined, but they are sufficiently clear. They are to be found in the situation in which the Church, as the people of God, has to carry out its mission. This situation somehow conveys the presence and the plan and therefore the activity of God.[156]

How then can the church apply to itself the requirements of discipleship normally prescribed for individual Christians?

## *Ecclesial: Praxis of Communion*

Congar's notion of discipleship is centered in what he calls "the Christian mystery." The heart of this mystery is the affirmation that disciples do more than imitate the life of Christ; the Christian mystery is relational mystery between God and creation. In Jesus, God is revealed as one who creates and draws all things into the divine life, realizing creation's deepest longings and fullest potentials. How does this aspect of Congar's notion of discipleship best find its social ecclesial expression in the light of the "signs of the times"? This question cuts to the soul of Congar's ecclesiological passion. "Forms designed to inspire respect . . . still persist today and their effect today is the opposite of what one would wish. Not only do they keep men at a distance from us, they us keep us at a distance from men, so the real world . . . is inaccessible."[157] Congar's life was devoted to recovering and promulgating a theology of church that reflected this understanding: Christ and the Spirit are the true sources of the church, not the hierarchy.[158]

At Vatican II, the church reclaimed in a new way its identity as a particular locus of the saving intention of God in the world. Retrieving the notion of sacraments from a juridical, extrinsic, rite-focused perspective, Vatican II situated all ritual life within the fundamental sacramental character of the entire ecclesial community; the church in the world is a sacramental presence of God. The People of God exist in the world for the single

---

155. Congar, *I Believe*, 2:6.
156. Ibid., 2:31.
157. Congar, *Power and Poverty*, 139.
158. "I am therefore in complete agreement with Walter Kasper in his claim that 'the Church is the specific place in which God's saving work in Jesus Christ is made present by the Holy Spirit." Congar, *I Believe*, 2:46.

purpose of making God's Word and God's ways known in creation.[159] The gift of God dwelling in the church is an eschatological gift given to humanity, affirming that "the regenerating power that will finally operate is already at work in our world, transiently, precariously, fragmentarily and generally unperceived."[160] The sacramental character of the church's life is not effected by the good will and hard work of the community, although without these God's intentions are undeniably frustrated.[161]

The sacramental character of the community is reflected in its total life: *ad intra* and *ad extra*. Thus the very structure of the church and the relationships that sustain and challenge these structures are of exceeding importance as potential means of the saving Presence of God. As members bonded to each other and God through a sacramental covenant, the whole church forms a structured people, institutionally organized for the mission entrusted to them by the Spirit.

> The whole Church—its people, its ministers, its treasure of the means of grace and its institution—is that sacrament of salvation. So far from the comings of the Holy Spirit to the Church challenging and questioning its institutional character, they establish it in truth. The Church is, after all, an institution of a very special kind. It acts in the present on the basis of past events and in the prospect of a future which is nothing less than the kingdom of God, the eschatological City and eternal life in communion with God himself. This is undoubtedly a sacramental structure, containing a memory of the event of foundation, a prophetic sign of the absolute future, and present grace coming from the first and preparing the way for the latter.[162]

Yet, unresolved internal issues often threaten the prophetic mission of the church. Specifically, although a hierarchically structured group is often best suited for carrying out long-term missions, these same organizations often have difficulty integrating new data, particularly data perceived as a threat to the very structure that affords such mission effectiveness (cf.

---

159. "La sacramentalité est la forme que Dieu prend en venant à nous comme grâce, et celle dans laquelle nous pouvons le rencontrer. Cette qualité s'applique d'abord à l'Église, elle est le sacrement primordial, global, enveloppant." Congar, *Un Peuple Messianique*, 64.

160. Congar, *Lay People*, 86.

161. "There is a 'Christ that is to be' (the words of Tennyson's), and this through a power that comes from his historical incarnation and passion; but also through contributions and a 'doing' which are—we hardly dare say it—our part in his mystery." Ibid., 312.

162. Congar, *I Believe*, 3:271.

Mary Douglas, ch. 3). Whether cast in the terms of periphery vs. center, laity vs. clerics, or charism vs. institution, the forces of stability and innovation that shape human social existence are often portrayed as inherently adversarial, oppositional, and a fundamental threat, one to the other. The entrenchment of institutionalism is as disastrous for the church's mission as the uncritical appropriation of innovations, particularly those that fail to "issue from the heart of the tradition."[163]

If the church as a community of disciples is to be faithful to the gift of revelation and its historical expression, the church must attend to and nurture the creative interplay between charism and institution. Since both aspects of the social dimension function sacramentally as potentially revelatory of God's Presence, they must be properly understood and fostered as indispensable dimensions of the messianic People of God.

> I know that it is wrong to oppose charism and institution and to rewrite the history of the Church as a history of opposition between these two elements. The fact is that each of these two realities is the source of a different kind of order in the Church, with the result that they are often in a state of tension. That tension is normal and can even be beneficial. Grace has frequently gone beyond the fixed institutional forms of the Church. Both are required in the life of the Church.[164]

Thus, a proactive *praxis of communion* will engage the current structural challenges of the ecclesial community and not ignore this critical dimension of the church's sacramental identity. These internal concerns include a wide range of significant issues: women's role and the reality of sexism in the church; inculturation and the often-unacknowledged racism that informs the church's missionary efforts and mistakes unity as adherence to forms of catholic identity shaped primarily by a single Christian cultural experience; pluralism and the resistance obstructing any meaningful engagement of the principles of subsidiarity and collegiality.

Each of these areas of concerns (not an exhaustive list by any means) results from significant social change. The "irruption of the poor into his-

---

163. Congar, *Revelation of God*, 166. "Les institutions veulent durer. Elles appellent la stabilité. Il est donc presque fatal que, du Projet et de la Sagesse de Dieu, elles traduisent de préférences les aspects d'ordre assuré, de hiérarchie. L'evangélisme qui sans cesse ressurgit a souvent connu un mauvais accueil." Congar, *Un Peuple Messianique*, 98.

164. Congar, *I Believe*, 2:152.

tory" has initiated a "turn to the other" and places new emphasis on the presence of the Spirit in the local and the particular.[165]

> [A]nd there are also original collective gifts and resources—those of the different peoples and cultures and of historical experiences and traditions. The Holy Spirit is also at work in all of these. In the greater Church, there are countless local and particular Churches, faithful to the Spirit and respectful of Christian freedom. In this pluralism, the Church must recognize the "signs of the times."[166]

Given the more immediate historical context from which our present is emerging, a praxis of communion calls for dramatic shift from an ecclesiology in which the Roman pontiff serves as the primary symbol of unity to an ecclesiology that makes the interrelational communion of the various local churches the prominent symbol of Christian unity. Since the unity of the many churches derives from the triunity of God, the praxis of communion today becomes the intentional work of promoting diversity-in-unity: creating ecclesial environments, governance structures, and communicative networks that engage the profound complexity of our current polycentric situation. Certainly, a critical skill related to this praxis is the ability to engage in ongoing ecumenical dialogue. Promoting a social environment of respectful exchange, particularly in areas where differences reach a conflictual pitch, makes the possibility of a truly catholic communion more viable.

Another critical aspect of the praxis of communion is the relationship between the local and universal church. What would the community of disciples be like if both the local and universal church engaged in the praxis of communion by their eagerness to secure the other's rightful and appropriate place in governance? What would it look like if pontifical authority actively advanced and protected the full, appropriate self-governance of the local church? Conversely, what would it look like if local churches made decisions conscious of the universal mission and witness of the church? A praxis of communion from this perspective calls for a critical retrieval and

---

165. "What we have often called the 'major fact' in the life of the Latin American church—the participation of Christians in the process of liberation—is simply an expression of a far-reaching historical event: *the irruption of the poor*. Our time bears the imprint of the new presence of those who in fact used to be 'absent' from our society and from the church. By 'absent' I mean: of little or no importance, and with the opportunity to expression themselves to their sufferings, their comraderies, their plans, their hopes." Gutierrez, *Theology of Liberation*, xx.

166. Congar, *I Believe*, 2:129.

reinterpretation of the fiduciary responsibilities incumbent upon disciples entrusted with a universal mission, expressed and known within a particular local church.

### *Witness: Praxis of Reconciliation*

For Congar, Christian witness testifies to the living God, present and active in the now. The words of Elizabeth Johnson aptly reflect Congar's view; Christians attest to the "livingness of God" in all the circumstances of human life.[167] Ecclesial witness to the God of Jesus, the one who is, who was, and who will be, can never be reduced to a static formula or rote practice, although important creeds, teachings, and disciplines continue to guide and direct the community's ongoing historical witness. The witness to the God who sent Jesus "for us and for our salvation" is challenged in every age to be faithful, intelligible, and empowering.

As witnesses to God's saving action in the present moment, the Christian community attests to God's plan for the well-being of all peoples. God desires the good, the fulfillment of all, yet sin undermines God's intention. In Jesus, Christians affirm that the eschatological realization of God's reign is already present in the world, however partial and fragmentary.[168]

Christians are impelled to share the intention of God to subvert sin and to reconcile all things to Godself in Jesus the Christ.

Thus, the love of God is forwarded in the world through a proactive *praxis of reconciliation*. Christian witness is always a living memory, testifying that what God effected in Jesus is equally present today, and directed towards the absolute future of God's reign.[169] It pleases God to effect the salvation of the world, the very cosmos, by inviting human beings to cooperate in God's design. In a world where our differences threaten us more readily than they delight and intrigue us, Christian fellowship becomes a human expression of the divine grace of reconciliation.[170]

---

167. Johnson, *She Who Is*, 224–45.

168. "[R]ien de moins que la Paix eschatologique, rien de moins que la justice de Dieu qui, étant le Père de tous, veut que tous aient leur chance de bien, d'estime, d'amour, de communion. Il faut que le peuple de Dieu pense, parle, agisse à ce plan." Congar, *Un Peuple Messianique*, 96.

169. "The specific point of the apostolic message and of the Christian faith is the forgiveness and newness of life that come from the sacrificed and conquering Lamb. . . . The essence of Christianity consists in participation in this forgiveness and newness of life, in making the work done for us by the Lamb of God a practical reality within us." Congar, *Revelation of God*, 107.

170. "To be in conformity with [God], means to be carrying out his plan. Since the

A praxis of reconciliation invariably brings the ecclesial community into the heart of Jesus' paschal mystery, particularly when violence rages in families, communities, and nations. This suffering encompasses not only the horrific violations that make the evening news, but also the insidiously unacknowledged affronts to human dignity: sexism, racism, classism, and other social and culturally embedded oppressions. Christian witness fails when it does not engage, condemn, and counteract the suffering of those denied that which God desires for them. The ecclesial community that will not risk the costs of discipleship and the inevitable consequences of such witness ultimately offers a counter witness to God's intentions.[171] Jon Sobrino amplifies this sentiment, exploring how the failure of Christian witness can undermine Christian faith itself.

> [W]e humans must make a choice not only between faith and atheism but between faith and idolatry. In a world of victims, little can be known about a person simply because he calls himself a believer or a nonbeliever. It is imperative to know in which God she believes and against which idols she does battle. . . . I have learned that faith is difficult but entirely possible, that it is very costly but deeply humanizing.[172]

What would happen to the church's witness if Christian communities were primarily experienced as loci of reconciliation and fellowships of repentance? What changes would have to be made within the church's own internal life to offer this credible witness to the God of Jesus? Such a witness could call the world to recognize its sinfulness, even as it acknowledges that the church itself is "made up of sinners . . . who do penance and try to lead a life of conversion."[173] A praxis of reconciliation, engaging in the active pursuit and practice of forgiveness, straining towards the eschatological accomplishment of justice in human social life, poses the Christian church's greatest contemporary challenge and offers the world a singular hope.

---

world proceeds from him, God has a purpose for it, a purpose and a plan . . . it is the preparation for the Kingdom of God, that is, an attempt, aided by God's grace, to make the world conform to his will. It is a communal plan, and therefore a plan of reconciliation, brotherhood, assistance to all who are suffering and are lost." Congar, *Faith and the Spiritual Life*, 175.

171. "If you are my witnesses, that is if you proclaim my will, if you ensure that what I want becomes an effective reality in the world, then, in that world, I shall be God . . . through your witness I become what I want to be in the world: its God." Ibid., 177.

172. Sobrino, *Principle of Mercy*, 9.

173. Congar, *This Church*, 27.

## Service: Praxis of Solidarity

It is helpful to approach Congar's ecclesial expression of gospel service from within an active awareness of his own historical moment, particularly the factors that informed the evolution of the church-world relationship. The dominant ecclesiology of Congar's time continued to describe the church in Counter-Reformation terms of *societas perfecta*, a complete society, containing within itself all that was necessary to bring to fruition its God-ordained mission. "This [notion] arose because of the struggle that the Church—and above all the Popes—had conducted against the absolute and lay claims made by the secular power."[174] Following Vatican I and the modernist crisis, the magisterium promoted the notion of the church as a *societas inaequalis, hierarchica*, amplifying the self-sufficiency of the church by emphasizing the hierarchy as God's means for the sure completion of the church's mission. These notions of church dominated the Catholic ecclesial imagination for the better part of two centuries and fostered an antagonistic, isolationist view of the church-world relationship. Although the care of the poor, the suffering, and the uneducated were always significant elements in the church's mission, these works of mercy occurred within and fostered a "meaning, which implied that the Church, as Catholics living together and forming a cultural world of their own, was quite self-sufficient."[175]

The refusal to engage the world, its questions and answers, actually resulted in a failure on the part of the Roman Catholic Church to realize its mission. Congar maintains that an ahistorical, juridical notion of church, combined with a poor knowledge of scripture, resulted in an impoverished eschatology.

> One of the greatest deficiencies of classical religion has therefore been its failure to inspire the world as such with hope. The hope that it provided as part of the "last things" was individual. It was not cosmic, social or historical. There is an almost complete absence of documentation on this aspect of hope produced by the Roman magisterium.[176]

---

174. Congar, "Moving Towards," 130.

175. Ibid., 138. "I was personally familiar with that Church which undoubtedly had a certain power and grandeur. It constituted a Catholic replica of the framework and structures of the whole of life, having its own schools, universities, hospitals, clubs, trade and professional associations, newspapers, journals and books. Catholics had a defensive, siege mentality."

176. Ibid., 143.

The momentous shift in the Roman Catholic Church's understanding of its role in the world heralded the emergence of an ecclesiology that had been developing in the thirty years before Vatican II and would become a springboard for various future ecclesiological reflections regarding how the church exists in the world.[177] Congar, reflecting some twenty years later on Vatican II, characterized this as "*une ecclésiologie en gestation*" and masterfully limns the transition of the church from a *societas perfecta* to the pilgrim People of God.[178]

God's pilgrim people exist in the world as witnessing signs of agapic love, and this love is effective: at its very heart are the transforming energies of the Spirit. Thus, the community of faith receives the world in a new way, "as the eschatological People of God, on pilgrimage through time and proclaiming the death and resurrection of the Lord until he comes again."[179] Far from rejecting the world and retreating into isolationism, the church today expresses its servant nature through a *praxis of solidarity*, particularly with those who are most threatened by powers of death and oppression. Foregoing any safehaven within an ahistorical triumphalism, the church risks the consequences of contingency; where both the forces that oppose God's purposes as well as the Spirit are likely to be encountered.

For Congar, the revelation of God's agapic love is both gift and task. Jesus, Servant of God, sought out the forgotten, the unwanted, and the despised, modeling a praxis of solidarity with the least and affirming God's commitment to their ultimate good. Engaging in table fellowship with sinners and the unclean, Jesus validates the privileged place where God chooses to dwell with humanity, expressing the depth of agapic love. As a community of disciples, Christians can do no less . . . or they do so at the peril of their authentic witness the Christian mystery, for "his mystery becomes our mystery."[180]

---

177. Congar is explicit in his assertion of the Second Vatican Council's continuity with Vatican I. "Something happened at the Council and the dominant values in our way of looking at the Church were changed by the Council. That will become clear in my analysis; but I am bound to stress that such a plan is simplistic. Vatican II was intentionally in continuity with the previous councils of the Church and Tradition. Paul VI himself insisted on its continuity with Vatican I. As every historian knows, everything is always changing and at the same time there is in many ways a deep continuity." Ibid., 129.

178. Ibid., 129–52. See also Congar, "D'une 'ecclésiologie en gestation.'"

179. Congar, "Moving Towards," 144, quoting Msg. László on the schema *De Ecclesia*.

180. Congar, *Lay People*, 57.

> [The Church] must, if she is to be fully missionary, begin to exist in a new way. She must be with these people, not just beside them or in front of them, but with them. Think for a moment what it means to be not only beside someone, but with him and for him; ask yourself whether, in our modern societies, in which the Church indeed erects her steeples everywhere and celebrates her age-old ceremonies, there are not whole sections of humanity that the Church is not truly with, although she is just by their side.[181]

Because God's love "is directed towards the weakest and most wretched," [182] the Christian community directs its energies of compassion towards the least ones, and, as the years following Vatican II have shown, this solidarity has opened the church to the cries of the Spirit mourning the subversion of God's intention, particularly in the lives of those subjected to death-dealing poverty.

This stance has already impacted the task of theology, expanding and extending the loci of theology to the historical and social conditions of human beings and forwarding "an option for the poor."[183] Congar notes that the church's involvement with these realities has already made it necessary to rethink important conciliar and postconciliar documents.[184]

---

181. Congar, *Priest and Layman*, 7.

182. Ibid., 6.

183. "The problem of poverty is an ancient one in Christian thought, but the new presence of the poor to which I have referred gives it a new urgency. An essential clue to the understanding of poverty in liberation theology is the distinction, made in the Medellín document 'Poverty of the Church,' between three meanings of the term 'poverty': real poverty as an evil—that is something that God does not want; spiritual poverty, in the sense of a readiness to do God's will; and solidarity with the poor, along with protest against the conditions under which they suffer. This is the context of a theme that is central in liberation theology and has now been widely accepted in the universal church: the preferential option for the poor." Gutierrez, *Theology of Liberation*, xxv.

184. "Since the pontificate of Leo XIII and Pius XII, the Popes have frequently spoken of the dignity of the human person. There is a clear connection between these earlier Popes' way of thinking and the Council's Declaration on Religious Freedom which Paul VI valued so highly. In *Gaudium et Spes*, that dignity takes the form of man on the one hand made in the image of God and called to sonship, but on the other as a sinner and destined to bodily death. The danger or the limitation of these considerations is that man is seen simply as an individual and as existing outside of time. Christians influenced to a greater or lesser extent by Marxism have often expressed this criticism. This is a relatively new way of thinking that was, if I am not mistaken, not followed either by the Council or by Paul VI. The historical and social dimensions of the conciliar documents will have to be carefully considered." Congar, "Moving Towards," 147.

> This synthesis will be made in tears and in the blood shed by Mgr. Oscar Romero and many others. A Church of the people is being reborn and it promises to be both serious and lasting because it has its martyrs. It is no longer, as it did in the past, claiming priestly power in the sphere of political power. It is trying to let the Gospel, as experienced in the lives of Christians, be effective and influential. How should I define the new form that this Church takes? I would say that it is that of the Gospel lived in the realities of human lives on earth or their "temporal" experience. It is in that life that the Gospel is spread and is able to act in souls.[185]

An ecclesial praxis of solidarity continues to refigure the church-world relationship. Today, the notion of the non-poor "taking care of" the poor, providing for the needy without working to change the systems that create such conditions, is simply unacceptable. Furthermore, a praxis of solidarity has liberated "other," poor Christian churches to challenge the dominant, white, Northern church's complicity with a social order that subverts theological voices as well as economic power. What do the poor say of God, that only they can tell? What conversions are necessary to hear the God of life issuing from their broken lives? Truly, Congar's sense that this is "*une ecclésiologie en gestation*" could not be more correct.

## Conclusion

> [I]f we listed all their most valid claims on the Church we should find that they amount to this: that she be less "of" the world and more "in" the world; that she be simply the Church of Jesus Christ, the conscience of men in the light of the Gospel . . .[186]

This chapter offers a possible answer to Congar's query regarding how the requirements of individual discipleship might be applied to the church as an ecclesial community. For Congar, discipleship, communal and individual, is forever a gift and a task, marked primarily by three factors: ecclesial fellowship, witness, and service. More specifically, when these markers are considered in the context of the present signs of the times, they can be expressed as praxes of communion, reconciliation, and solidarity.

Each of these praxes involves specific behaviors and represents a particular interpretation of the Christian mystery. While the historical expressions of Christian faith and discipleship are not timeless entities, they are

---

185. Ibid., 148.
186. Congar, *Power and Poverty*, 137.

sacred to the community because of the revelatory encounter they afford. Since encounters between the church and God's Spirit are symbolically mediated, they must be interpreted within the historical and cultural ground in which they occur. At the same time, these mediating symbols are not neutral; they come into any encounter with a history of use. The critical question facing the church at any time is whether or not the symbol system continues to mediate transformative encounters with the living God. There are dead symbols; signs made univocal in an effort to impose a false fidelity, staving off the insecurity of change. Thus, the very means that mediate religious experience must be critiqued for their effectiveness, or run the risk of collapsing living symbols into idols.

The premise that guides this study is that the functional effectiveness of the Christian tradition lies in its ability to form and transform Christian disciples. The following chapter explores the potential fruitfulness of a symbolic, interpretative approach to tradition for Roman Catholicism.

5

# Traditioning Disciples

*Ecclesial Identity and Refiguring Tradition*

SOCIAL IDENTITY, AS IT is conceived within an integrated notion of culture, cohesive and binding, seemingly can no longer account for the data both communally and individually. Historical research indicates that the complexities of membership are not a new phenomenon; identity has always been a relatively diverse and conflictual enterprise.[1] It appears safe to say that notions of identity have received a much-needed ideological critique, resulting in heightened consciousness of the way power-knowledge functions within the asymmetrical relations that are forged daily within social life. Social identities, simultaneously a relational matrix (context) and the relations themselves, are porous and open-ended, even while affirming their rootedness within specific locales.

Given this, there is no question that the role of traditions in social identity needs to be seriously reconsidered. This question takes on an even graver import within the theological context of religion founded on the premise of encounter with divine revelation. Within Roman Catholicism, the gift of divine revelation is intrinsically tied to the church's understanding of tradition. What has been "handed down," whether ontologized as "the deposit of faith" or theologized as a salvific encounter with God mediated through Jesus, Roman Catholic tradition functions as a touchstone for divine revelation.

The notion of tradition functioning within the church at any one time reflects the particular historical time and the predominant self-understanding of the church. The Enlightenment posed particular challenges to Christian tradition, both in its Protestant and Catholic manifestations.

---

1. To what extent, however, our own postmodern sensitivity to difference has been "naturalized" by our global context remains to be seen.

The current crisis of tradition extends the Enlightenment critique exposing the way in which the Christian tradition functions to sustain the status quo and resists alternative interpretative frameworks. Tradition is a suspect entity, easily bent to the will of those who make authoritative, though often fictive, claims.

Despite these credible critiques, however, there are clear indications that the Christian tradition remains a vital source of a transformative encounter with the Living God. Recent debates concerning the Christian tradition, touched off by much of the critique that would jettison the very possibility of tradition, point to the potential fruitfulness, however inchoate, lurking within the ripening question. Tradition, once considered a dead end, is now commanding a significant amount of attention within various academic disciplines.[2] Within this climate of recent ferment, a notion of tradition refigured from the insights of interpretative anthropology offers a critical hermeneutic from which to assess the congruence of Christian identity with its historical expressions and its authoritative past: faithful, intelligible, empowering. The premise of this work asserts that when ecclesial social identity is located within the theological category of discipleship, the dialogical and dialectical relationship between the tradition and its ability to create, sustain, and transform Christian disciples becomes the basis of determining the fecundity of the tradition.

Refiguring tradition from interpretative cultural anthropology, three ideas emerge: the *constructed practices of remembrance* utilized by social groups, amounting to a selective traditioning process; the *provocative polyvalency* of symbols, affording a more nuanced view of the converging interplay of multiple meanings available with the religious symbols; and the need to practice a method of *juxtaposed thick description*, construing the contrastive incomparables of specific forms of Christian discipleship such that their available light might be more clearly illuminated. Furthermore, from the Congarian case study in discipleship, three praxes point towards a thriving ecclesial identity embedded within a particular notion of discipleship: communion, reconciliation, and solidarity. The purpose of this chapter is to bring the material presented thus far into a mutual critical correlation such that the learnings of both cultural anthropology and theology may be brought to bear on the present dilemma regarding tradition, social identity, and their relationship in Roman Catholicism.

---

2. See Tilley, *Inventing Catholic Tradition*; and Thiel, *Senses of Tradition*.

Since this study locates Christian identity within the theological category of discipleship and posits that the functional effectiveness of the tradition should be judged by the tradition's ability to form the church's self-understanding in terms of discipleship, the question invariably arises: Whose discipleship? Who determines the form and shape of authentic Christian discipleship? The renewed interest in discipleship as a theological category, noted earlier in chapter 4, particularly among the theologies of liberation and social justice, has refocused the attention of believers on the gospel practices of Jesus. While there are many contested understandings of Christian discipleship, each base their particular interpretation of Jesus in the light of the questions of ultimacy that confront the world. Since these questions of ultimacy are embedded within cultural and social contexts that are not identical, they demand a multiplicity of responses. The question of whose discipleship points out the need for many and varied responses to the question.

Limning the contours of a specific notion of discipleship, this study points out the potentials residing within a perspective that might be made to speak to larger issues confronting the Roman Catholic Church. Should the correlation prove fruitful, it may be possible to bring other notions of discipleship into critical correlation towards a practice of juxtaposed thick descriptions in critical dialogue with each other and other disciplines engaging the dilemma of traditions and social identities.

## A Method of Correlation

Before proceeding, it is important to reflect upon the methodology employed in this chapter. A method of mutual critical correlation implies that the correlates share some points of comparison that, on the basis of apparent similarity, make it possible to place the correlates into dialogue. This correlation is truly reflective of the theological method of David Tracy in that, via a hermeneutical approach to both tradition and identity, meanings within the disciplines of cultural anthropology and theology are correlated to forward a more relatively adequate understanding of tradition's role in Christian identity.

Clearly the correlation of these meanings resists any attempt to impose a simple one-to-one correspondence. Instead, the correlation of meanings is directed towards a heuristic middle ground—the question of how to refigure tradition—so that the meanings derived from dissimilar perspectives might be allowed to question and inform each other even as they respond to the central question of tradition/identity/transformation.

An underlying commitment that informs this theological method is the symbolic character of all God-talk, which therefore demands a hermeneutical, interpretative approach to theology. More specifically, Christian theology, as the community's God-talk, is the articulation of the community's mediated revelatory experience of God.[3] Communal traditions provide the (privileged) symbolic context within which religious meanings are construed, debated, and authorized. While the reservoir of religious symbols is a fairly established matrix, the currents of construed meanings potentially available reflect their "tensive, dynamic and dialectical" character.[4] Symbols are both tenacious and malleable. Although they do not have a "shelf-life," symbols do exhibit a range of vitality such that Mary Douglas and Paul Tillich can both speak of dead symbols.[5] The dying and rising of

---

3. "Theology is not revelation. Beliefs, doctrines, and dogmas are theological statements and as such cannot be simply identified with revelation. Although doctrines may share a status of general acceptance within the community different from more theological opinions, generically doctrines are theological statements. As such they are not revelation. There are no revealed doctrines as such, for revelation is personal encounter with a personal God and not an historically relative interpretation of that encounter in the form of an objective proposition. . . . Theology consists in the interpretation of revelation; theological statements are interpretative expressions of reality, God, the world, and ourselves under the impact and on the basis of the experience of revelation. Revelation is the initiative and activity of God within the human subject. Relative to this revelatory dimension of experience the human subject is first of all passive. Stimulated by the revealing contact with God, theology is active, a human endeavor, a human activity. . . . Within the experience of revelation itself these dimensions can scarcely be distinguished because there is no revelation without response; impression and interpretation run together. Yet in the exercise of theology as a discipline, in the deliberate expression of revelation, in second and third reflection on its content, the distinction is clear. Theology depends on experience; it has no direct access to God. It is totally dependent on revelational experience and all its assertions have their meaning through and on the basis of this existential encounter." Haight, *Dynamics of Theology*, 83–84.

4. Haight, *Jesus*, 11.

5. See Mary Douglas quoted earlier at p. 119. Paul Tillich notes, "A religious symbol can die only if the correlation of which it is an adequate expression of dies. This occurs whenever the revelatory situation changes and former symbols become obsolete. The history of religion, right up to our own time, is full of dead symbols which have been killed not by a scientific criticism of assumed superstitions but by a religious criticism of religion. The judgment that a religious symbol *is* true is identical with the judgment that the revelation of which it is the adequate expression is true. This double meaning of the truth of a symbol must be kept in mind. A symbol *has* truth: it is adequate to the revelation it expresses. A symbol *is* true: it is the expression of a true revelation." Tillich, *Systematic Theology* 1:240.

religious symbols within a community reflects the questions and concerns that the group holds, particularly those questions that point out the limits of current interpretations to effectively stave off encroaching anomaly and ambiguity. No matter how venerated the religious symbol may be, changing circumstances demand that religious meanings be renegotiated.

A method of correlation provides for the necessary revision of religious meanings. Although this method continues to be debated, the contextual character of all rationality seemingly makes it impossible to avoid the hermeneutical task of theology.[6] Moreover, a method of correlation more effectively accounts for the Christian understanding of revelation as not mere information about God, but an actual encounter of God. If Christian revelation is a present existential encounter of the divine Spirit mediated and disclosed by Jesus, and not simply data about God passed down through time, then there can be no true communication of the divine Spirit without engaging and using the cultural meanings already flourishing and contending within the culture. Moreover there may be new, yet-to-be disclosed meanings that the Christian church needs to attend to and nurture. In his christological "essay," Roger Haight notes that the hermeneutical-historical task of theologians cannot be ignored, nor can theological assertions fail to address their present context. "The meaning of Jesus is not as it were, a given, a substance that takes on new accidental connotations in new relationships. Rather, the new relationships themselves constitute new meanings and relevancies of *Jesus*."[7] A method of correlation provides the context within which the questions and answers of the present moment can be brought into critical dialogue with the questions and answers of the tradition, affording the place where the new relationships, forged by encounters with new situations, peoples, and dilemmas, yield new meanings.

## Critically Correlating Interpretative Anthropology

In this section the three gleanings of interpretative anthropology will provide the context within which to discuss important issues and questions that impact a refigured notion of tradition in Roman Catholicism. The selective traditioning process generated by constructed practices of remembrance raises the question of ideology and its pervasive presence in

---

6. Lindbeck, *Nature of Doctrine*; Placher, *Unapologetic Theology*.
7. Haight, *Jesus*, 56.

the asymmetries of social life. Provocative polyvalency extends this discussion exploring the question of the theological significance of subjugated knowledges within a tradition and how continuity is possible. Finally, the practice of juxtaposed thick descriptions explores the risky business of intercultural hermeneutics and the implications of such exchanges for future theological reflection.

## Constructed Practices of Remembrance

Mary Douglas's anthropological insight that institutions "think" in such a manner so as to secure both the knowledge (classification) and the relations of knowledge (social ties) that generate and sustain the social group does not appear to be too far afield from the postmodern mind and Michel Foucault's observation that power is relational, present only in its exercise, which is fundamentally the production of knowledge. While Mary Douglas and Michel Foucault seemingly occupy parallel universes when the scope of their commitments are compared, one cannot but notice the striking resonance of their respective insights regarding the function of tradition in social identity.[8]

Douglas, rooted in a Durkheimian vision of the social, describes how individuals within institutions formulate classification systems that simultaneously foster allegiances based on mutually agreed cognitive fit: sameness. The category of sameness is itself a negotiated entity. Sameness is construed, assigned to objects, experiences, interpretations perceived and agreed to be relatable in a social process that all the while constructs the social distinctions of "us" and "them." There is much more invested in cognitive definitions than simply the assigning of identity to discrete objects and entities. The preconditions for this classification process according to Douglas are the social relations in which peoples are born and raised. Human rationality, embedded in specific cultures and social relations, receives a worldview of the "really real" that corresponds to social

---

8. Foucault's application of a Nietzschean analysis of historical data works to excavate suppressed and delegitimated knowledges discarded by the normative tradition. Convinced that the exercise of power is the production of knowledge, Foucault engages in a genealogical deconstruction of power/knowledge by focusing on local, hidden, and subjugated knowledges in order to unmask "the claims of a unitary body of theory which would filter hierarchies and order them in the name of some true knowledge." Foucault, *Power/Knowledge*, 83. While Foucault is often associated with postmodernism, it is no less important to acknowledge that poststructuralism informs his attention to the breaks and fissures in historical data.

relations that re-create and sustain the established order. But this is never a static reality; there are constant challenges to the "really real." Anomaly and ambiguity pose an ever-present threat to the semblance of established order, generated and sustained by a selective traditioning process. Through constructed practices of remembrance, social groups stave off encroaching cognitive dissonance by employing interpretative strategies that diminish group shame and promote group prestige.[9] The function of these social processes is to preserve the relations that both keep the system of knowledge and the system of ordered roles and relationships in place. The very need for social groups to establish practices that promote social amnesia points to the contested character of social identities and the reality of what Foucault called "subjugated knowledges." The practice of social groups to promote certain memories while delegitimizing other memories poses important questions for religious traditions.

## No Innocent Traditions

First and foremost, religious traditions can no longer rest easy in an ahistorical, ideologically absolved space. Nor can the adepts of specific religious traditions engage in non-critical retrievals of symbols and practices in order to make claims for an essentially benign social identity. There are no innocent traditions. To be human is to engage in social practices that name the world and all within it via socially embedded rationalities that construct both knowledge and relations. These constructions are inherently asymmetrical, recalling J. Comoroff's insight that social identity is the product of relations between "ethnicizers" and the "ethnicized."[10] To make claims that certain religious institutions are freed from this fate, or that their constructions are singularly exempt from the limits of human

---

9. The events of September 11, 2001, serve as a remarkable case in point. As the U.S. grieved over the horror of the attack on the World Trade Center towers, the central symbol that dominated was the American flag. News networks crafted videologs of U.S. citizens (predominantly white) and monuments of U.S. identity: the Washington Memorial, Mt. Rushmore, the White House, golden plains, and shining seas. The message clearly conjured all that is great and admirable about the U.S. even as hundreds of its citizens were harassed, threatened, beaten, even killed because they did not "look" like Americans. The reticence of leaders to acknowledge hate crimes committed against citizens slowly changed as messages of tolerance were broadcast. The country was told that these attacks were not committed by "true Americans." Even as reports of attacks against Arab, Sikh, and Indian citizens increased, the reality that some Americans equate patriotism with xenophobic acts of violence has not been allowed to quell the dominant theme of the U.S. as the arbiter of freedom and justice.

10. See ch. 3, p. 165.

institutional life, is to make the oldest religious mistake: idolatry, claiming for the human that which alone is the province of the divine.

## A Counterintuitive Hermeneutical Task

Therefore, Christianity, as a religion based on special revelation and entrusted with a hermeneutical mission, must constantly examine its present faith articulations against the self-serving ideological tendencies that threaten the integrity of the church's message. The Roman Church, as an ecclesial community that maintains the sacral dimension of its tradition, must be particularly vigilant and engage in a counterintuitive hermeneutical task: actively questioning how and where its tradition fosters something other than the "dangerous memory of Jesus."[11] The standards for addressing the responses to this question are equally important and must also share in ideological critique. The selective traditioning process that should guide the Christian church's self-understanding will still involve a process of inclusion and exclusion, but the final arbiter of how a present practice or faith statement fits in relation to the normative (read dangerous) Christian memory of Jesus will be less tied to propositional correctness and more connected to the observed fruitfulness of Christian life. Of particular concern will be the critical appraisal of what informs a community's decision to exclude certain symbols, practices, interpretations and those who adhere to them. A critical knowledge of how human communities use selective traditioning processes to solidify and validate their own communal perspective offers an important self-corrective to Christian communities and demands that they ask themselves difficult questions regarding the motives informing a particular decision to exclude. This does not mean that decisions to exclude cannot or should not be made, but it does demand that the group become communally conscious of who and what this decision serves. This ideological consciousness can no longer be understated or ignored in Christian communal life and witness.

---

11. "The *memoria Jesu Christi* is not a memory which deceptively dispenses Christians from the risks involved in the future. It is not a middle-class counter-figure to hope. On the contrary, it anticipates the future as a future of those who are oppressed, without hope and doomed to fail. It is therefore a dangerous and at the same time liberating memory that oppresses and questions the present because it reminds us not of some open future, but precisely this future and because it compels Christians constantly to change themselves so that they are able to take this future into account. This memory breaks through the magic circle of the prevailing consciousness. It regards history as something more than a screen for contemporary interests. It mobilizes tradition as a dangerous tradition and therefore a liberating force. . . . Christian faith can and must, in my opinion, be seen in this way a subversive memory." Metz, *Faith in History*, 90.

## A Critical Process of Traditioning

Finally, since all traditions engage in a process of selective memory, calling into the present moment that which promotes the group's intentional existence, Roman Catholicism most authentically pursues its true purposes when it engages in the task of bringing into view those symbols that nurture the community's self-understanding through transformative encounter with the divine Spirit. The community's faithful engagement with a critical process of traditioning, as described above, simultaneously manifests authentic witness even as it reiterates the ongoing need for conversion within the community itself. The church as communities of disciples engages multiple loci of conversion both *ad extra* and *ad intra*. Conversion serves as a functional norm that remains eschatologically distant, yet heralds the goal towards which Christian life seeks to approach; truly there is no point of arrival. The transformative presence of the Spirit in the world expressed by the Christian community is always and everywhere first an act of the Spirit; it is the Spirit that creates the community, not the community that commands the presence of the Divine. Neither is the Christian community the only means by which God's Spirit encounters the world. Yet, the gift of revelation encountered in Jesus is the privileged proclamation entrusted to the Christian community and, as noted earlier, the nature of revelation enjoins the community to seek out the new meanings of Jesus that are both consistent with tradition and intelligible in the current context. The revelation of God in Jesus is not less or partial; who God reveals God to be in Jesus is truly God. But the historical articulation of the mystery of God revealed in Jesus is incomplete, partial, and awaiting the eschatological completion of God's reign. Christian religious symbols afford for those so disposed an existential (hermeneutical) encounter that both reveals and conceals. Like the good steward who knows when to bring out the old and the new, the Christian community, entrusted with a sacred tradition, best serves the gospel when it critically engages the tradition's potential to most effectively communicate the saving Presence of God in the midst of present questions of ultimacy.

## Provocative Polyvalency

A reconsideration of Victor Turner's understanding of symbolic action has led to the proposal that the complexities of human social identity can only be adequately attended to through an analysis of the symbol system's *provocative polyvalency*. This requires that those who dwell with a tradition pay attention to the confluence of multiple viewpoints and commitments that symbol systems can and do support. Relinquishing an integrated notion of culture, the polyvalent character of tradition as both arbiter and traitor needs to be recovered.[12]

The inherent ambiguity of traditions as symbol systems can both support the status quo of a given social structure while simultaneously providing the resources to disrupt, and even upend, the existing social order. As human beings pursue intelligibility through a process of responsible decision making, the contextual backdrop of particular traditions provides both the interior cognitive landscape as well as the exterior field of social interaction. Human rationality, understood as contextualized, interactive social practice, thoroughly embedded in specific traditions, is limited but *not determined* by its local character. Thus, according to J. Wentzel van Huyssteen, the traditioned character of a refigured notion of human rationality (that encompasses cognitive, affective, pragmatic, and evaluative domains) creates knowledge that is *conditioned* but not determined.[13] This is critical because traditions function within social life in a formative and transformative manner. "Although conditioned by its context, human thought is nonetheless able to transcend the particularities of its social and historical contexts. Thus it is that we can critique our traditions while standing in them."[14] Van Huyssteen's assertion that humans pursue "intelligibility and optimal understanding" within a contested context of cultural and social life supports the notion that the symbolic resources of a tradition offer a broad range of legitimate, diverse, even conflictual con-

---

12. Terrence Tilley notes, "In Latin, the word *traditio* means not only what was handed on but also *treason*. In fact, early Christian leaders who *handed on* the Sacred Scriptures to the Roman authorities were branded *traditores*. They were traitors. This etymological note is preserved in an Italian motto, *Tradutore, tradditore*, which is usually rendered in English as "the translator is a traitor"—whoever hands on a text from one language to another is a traitor to the original text. What all this means, of course, is not that those who transmit tradition are traitors, but that attending merely to the barest concept of tradition as *id quod traditur* without close attention to context and particular circumstances of the practice of *traditio* is bound to fail to explicate the rich meanings of the concept of tradition. And while it may seem Derrida-esque or quixotic to do so, I will argue later that it is not only necessary but good that, from one perspective, a *traditor* is a traitor." Tilley, *Inventing Catholic Tradition*, 10.

13. Van Huyssteen, *Shaping of Rationality*, 147.

14. Ibid. He continues, ". . . and this refusal to be determined by a particular tradition, a particular conceptual system, or a particular form of behavior, enables a standpoint of critique that delivers us from the kind of relativism in which all interpretations and perspectives are granted an equal claim to thrive."

stellations of interpretations that are constantly, dynamically shaping both social thought and social relations.

From a perspective that respects the provocative polyvalency of a tradition, it is important to address two questions. First, what is the theological significance of "subjugated knowledges" within a religious tradition? In other words, what does the multivocal character of religious traditions say about the theological task of construing religious meanings adequate to the challenges of the present context? The second question follows from this. What is the nature of continuity within multivocal religious traditions, subject to the reality of historical contingency? This is an important question for Christian tradition, and particularly for Roman Catholic tradition given its understanding of the incarnational character of God's revelatory Presence. If God communicates Godself through the medium of human history, what is the authoritative character of the monuments of tradition, particularly when traditions are understood to be both multivocal and multifunctional?

## Theological Significance of Subjugated Knowledges

The first question regarding the theological significance of "subjugated knowledges" points out that traditions necessarily contain within themselves the seeds for their own revision. Because traditions are not univocal, but contain a broad field of multiple points of interpretation, there is significant potential to respond to various conditions of social life in a manner that supports certain values, strategies, and outcomes, while rebuking others as inconsistent with the original genius of the religious tradition. African-American Catholics of the nineteenth-century discovered this to be the case when they engaged the social teaching of the Roman Catholic magisterium and used the Church's tradition to instruct bishops and priests in the evils of racism, particularly as it operated to erase black Catholic presence in the ecclesial memory of Roman Catholicism.[15]

---

15. "To speak about tradition and the traditions of African American Catholicism is not without contention. Almost from the beginning, indeed, even now, the faith praxis of African American Catholics has been met with arrogance and suspicion. These reactions stem chiefly from the notion that African American Christianity is restricted to, if not identical with, a certain form of Protestantism. This misconception has been absorbed not only into our religious, cultural, and social commonsense, but has been formalized in scholarship, that is, in the prevailing American religious and social historiography. On the one hand, authoritative voices among Catholic historians, sociologists, and theologians treat the notion of the immigrant church as the primary interpretative paradigm for Catholic life and thought in the United States. But since African Americans are not

M. Shawn Copeland describes the creative contribution of these African Americans who gathered for four congresses (1890, 1892, 1893, 1894) and organized to discuss the "political and economic, social and religious issues of national and international scope: civil rights at home, the abolition of slavery in Brazil, the back to Africa movement, just and equal treatment in church and society."

> Delegates appealed to their White bishops and pastors for the admission of Black youngsters to Catholic high schools and barring that, proposed the establishment of a national Catholic high school to meet their need. They called for ongoing religious education so that Black Catholics might be well grounded in the faith and the support of vocations to the priesthood and religious life. Moreover, these laypeople exhorted themselves to greater respect for family life, and to the cultivation of thrift, frugality, honesty, industry and virtue.[16]

The participants of these congresses formulated and issued concluding addresses intended for the whole Catholic community. Of particular interest is the concluding statement issued at the end of the fourth African-American congress. Clearly, the participants were conversant with the social teaching, *Rerum Novarum*, promulgated by Pope Leo XIII in 1891. From a magisterium that asserted "all men are equal; there is no difference between rich and poor; master and servant, rule and ruled,"[17] African-American Catholics gleaned that "the Catholic Church, guided by the spirit of truth, must always preserve inviolate the deposit of faith, and thus she cannot err in proclaiming the rights of man."[18] In the following passage from the fourth congress, a reappropriation of ecclesial tradition, quite different from ecclesial practice (Roman Catholics owned slaves without ecclesial censure), renders a new interpretation of the Christian message in terms of its teachings with regard to human rights.

> For ages the Church has labored to break down the walls of race prejudice, to teach the world the doctrine of the meek and hum-

---

immigrants, this paradigm is not only insufficient to mediate the experience of African American Catholics and, thus, cannot account for their appropriation and transmission of the faith, but reduces African American Catholicism to a 20th-century phenomenon." Copeland, "Tradition," 632–33.

16. Ibid., 638.
17. Quoted in ibid., 643. *Rerum novarum* 32.
18. Ibid., 638.

ble Christ, that man should be gauged by his moral worth; that virtue alone, springing from grace, truly elevates a man, and that vice alone, springing from the malice of the heart, degrades him. Though the practice of the Church is consistent with her divine doctrine, we must deplore the fact that some of her members in various parts of the country have, in the words of our very distinguished friend, the Most. Rev. John Ireland, "departed from the teaching of the Church in the treatment of the colored Catholics and yielded right to popular prejudice." As children of the true Church, we are anxious to witness the extension of our beloved religion among those of our brethren who as yet are not blessed with the true Faith, and therefore we consider it a duty, not only to ourselves but to the Church and to God, that we draw the attention of every member of the learned Roman hierarchy to such violations from Catholic law and Catholic practice.[19]

The above aptly points out both the multivocal character of religious traditions and the ability of suppressed currents within a tradition to engage the symbol system towards new, prophetic expressions of the original message. This highlights a significant feature of polyvalent symbol systems. The ambiguity of the Christian tradition provides within itself the potential for new relationships emanating from the contingencies of history; new meanings are forged, shedding light on liberating potentials available within the tradition. The fact that these new meanings are historically unwelcomed and often pass through a time of significant suspicion also highlights how traditions function is social life. In many domains of knowledge yesterday's heresy becomes today's orthodoxy. The process by which traditions adjust to new information, new relationships, and new disruptions involves a complicated, interactive play between conserving forces and innovating forces, raising the question of how continuity is understood in the light of the provocative polyvalency of religious symbol systems.

## The Question of Continuity

A significant aspect of postmodern sensibilities is a particular bias against traditions, a bias that betrays, for some, postmodern critique's thoroughly modern nature. Recall Foucault's "methodical precaution . . . not to regard the point in where we are now standing as the outcome of a teleological

---

19. Ibid., 639. "The address of the Fourth Black Catholic Congress was published in the Boston *Pilot* (September 23, 1893) under the caption 'The Colored Catholic Memorial: The Eloquent Expression of Their Fourth Congress.'" Ibid., 639n23.

progression."[20] Yet, the dissolution of universalism does not necessarily herald the demise of traditions as inherently ideological or, more importantly, relegate traditions to the isolation of time-bound cultural specificity without any real relation to a past or a future. Continuity does emerge, albeit ragged, messy, and truly not as coherent and integrated as some traditioning processes would impose. Continuity is not only an achievement of the dominant social discourse that actively secures social amnesia as well as social greatness; it results from a critical hermeneutical process in which the authoritative locus of a tradition is received and challenged through cultural processes of identity formation/transformation, and where change plays a constructive role.

Many theologians have engaged the question of continuity from a variety of perspectives. In each, there is a critical examination of the religious tradition to ascertain the locus of authority or the center of gravity that serves as a touchstone for the community's ongoing reflection on the meaning and present significance of the founding event. While the ideological function of traditions must be readily acknowledged, it is simply incorrect to reduce the function of traditions to this limited frame. Traditions, and religious traditions in particular, have a locus of authority, however negotiated the communal construals of this field may be. Whether we speak of Tracy's religious classic,[21] Lindbeck's rules,[22] Haight's "genetic structures of understanding,"[23] or Brown's understanding of canons within traditions, there is a considerable amount of scholarship devoted to describing authority within religious traditions and how this factor functions within the hermeneutical task of construing religious meaning that is both relevant (cognitively responsible) and faithful (in dynamic relationship to an authoritative past).

Talal Asad notes that an appeal to certain essentials within a tradition is not necessarily a fall into essentialism; it is to affirm that there are critical components to social projects that when lost or eliminated fundamentally change identity.

> [T]o those who have been taught to regard essentialism as the gravest of intellectual sins, it is necessary to explain that certain things are *essential* to that project—as indeed there are to "India"

---

20. Foucault, *Power/Knowledge*, 89.
21. Tracy, *Analogical Imagination*, 99–153.
22. Lindbeck, *Nature of Doctrine*, 73–88.
23. Haight, *Jesus*, 40.

as a nation-state. To say this is not equivalent to saying that the project (or "India") can never be changed; it is to say that each historical phenomenon is determined by the way it is constituted, that some of its constitutive elements are essential to its historical identity and some are not.[24]

Therefore the challenge that presents itself is how to responsibly assert the phenomenon of shared sources of identity located in contested traditions without resorting to an ontological identity impervious to historical contingency and cultural infiltration. Delwin Brown's notion of canonical fields within traditions offers a helpful view toward considering how provocative polyvalency functions within a non-essential understanding of tradition.

## Canons and Traditions

Delwin Brown maintains that canons both legitimate and subvert social order. "What a canon gives it usually can take away, for canons, voluminous contemporary studies now agree, are inherently polyphonic and plurivocal."[25] Yet this multivocal reality of canons does not result in a dissolution or dissipation of symbolic sources. While canons are contested and fluid, Brown maintains that canons are *not* "best described as an *infinitude* of meanings" or "an endless play of difference."[26] Thus, while canons are never univocal, neither are they the momentary play of language captured for an already-departed present. "A canon is a contest of varied visions and voices. Its diversity may not be infinite, but it is expansive and substantial."[27]

Brown describes five features of canons: they are bounded realities,[28] display a curatorial character,[29] make normative claims,[30] are inherently contestable,[31] and exhibit contemporaneity.[32] Canons are bounded in the sense that they are circumscribed fields that establish identity. The content of the canon "may be defined as a list of documents, a set of stories, a complex of myths, a body of doctrine or concepts, a cluster of symbols,

24. Asad, *Genealogies of Religion*, 18.
25. Brown, *Boundaries of Our Habitations*, 72.
26. Ibid.
27. Ibid., 74.
28. Ibid., 77.
29. Ibid., 78.
30. Ibid., 79.
31. Ibid., 80.
32. Ibid., 81.

a group of rituals, a pattern of cultivated sensibilities, and so forth, or combinations of these."[33] The limitation that a canon imposes does not establish unity within the canon, but it does establish the play within which social identity is negotiated. The curatorial character of canons highlights the selection process that establishes their existence. "A canon is a unity and a diversity in interdependence, for every canon is *a* preservation, *a* collection" of contrastive meanings. In this sense canons are never monolithic but "multilithic."[34] The normative character of canons describes their "gravitational pull" because canons make claims. "Canons are agents, alleging their adequacy, indeed their indispensability, for accomplishing something essential to human well-being."[35] As a contested reality, canons never offer a single answer. That canons are multivocal has an important impact on the notion of normativity. Because canons are multilithic and not monolithic, the character of normativity shifts from the primacy of a single view to the intersecting play of many potentially harmonious views. This parallels Haight's assertion, "The problem of revelation is not its scarcity, but the plurality of its manifestations."[36] Thus, a new criterion for normativity comes into view. "The normative character of a canon is the depth of its fecundity."[37] Finally, canons are contemporaneous in the sense that they are the symbolic sources from which social lives are lived today. Their ability to be retrieved from past usages for present concerns speaks to the generativity of these sources.[38]

Brown's description of canons as loci of authority within religious traditions attempts to describe the process of creating social identity within a tradition. Accordingly, the "pragmatic behavior of traditions takes the form of creating, sustaining and recreating viable communal and individual identities."[39] But this is a dialectical process that engages social identity, tradition, and the loci of authority within the tradition. The canon is never monolithic in its relationship to the religious tradition.

> The relationship of a canon, that is, an authoritative locus, and a tradition is dialectical. . . . Tradition derives from canon and canon

33. Ibid., 77.
34. Ibid., 78.
35. Ibid., 79.
36. Haight, *Jesus*, 7.
37. Brown, *Boundaries of Our Habitations*, 80.
38. Ibid., 81.
39. Ibid., 28.

derives from tradition. Tradition creates canon and canon creates tradition. A corollary is that each is fluid. In some sense, canon and tradition are each open to change, and the change in either affects the definition of the other.[40]

I would add that the relationship is not only dialectical but also *dialogical*, in much the same sense that Mary Ann Donovan described Irenaeus' understanding of the relationship between scripture and the rule of faith: tradition and canon are dialogue partners within ever-changing historical circumstances.

Brown's notion of canons and their function within tradition in the negotiated processes of social identity allows for the provocative, contested character of symbolic resources while acknowledging the reality that some shared sources function towards establishing a relatively distinctive identity. Brown construes canons as both loci of authority as well as the boundaries that circumscribe the cultural negotiation of identity. As a bounded reality, canons impose limits, not unity. Within this circumscribed field of play, voices, visions, and stories interact constantly within a negotiated cultural process of social identity that is "tentative and proximate."[41] Thus, people inhabit traditions and engage therein with the canons that give a tradition its identity. The process is both one of reception and construction and is therefore necessarily ambiguous. Individuals within a tradition both receive tradition as a gift and engage in the task of questioning, refuting and contesting aspects of the tradition that are seemingly irrelevant. The experience of inhabiting a tradition is never a matter of pure receptivity or pure challenge.

> There is no pure receptivity because every inheritance within a canon is perspectival; every experience of canon is a particular construal of it. Nor is there pure challenge because each confrontation with a tradition requires some acceptance of its terms in order to communicate at all. The only pure departure from tradition, the only complete rejection of its canon, is indifference to it.[42]

Given the insights discussed above, a nuanced understanding of provocative polyvalency within religious traditions comes into view. Traditions are more than inert reservoirs of symbols. Traditions are inherently dynamic, working at a variety of social levels and loci, providing

40. Ibid., 29.
41. Ibid., 77.
42. Ibid., 86.

symbolic resources by which individuals engage in social processes of identity formation and transformation. Although the boundaries of traditions are porous and their contents contested, traditions are traditions precisely because they possess a certain gravitation pull which is in some sense both received and refuted as individuals inhabit the living tradition. The provocative polyvalency of symbol systems describes both the sense of embeddedness within a tradition and the ability to transcend the limits of our habitations. While the stretch that can be achieved in this transcendence remains debatable, the conditioned (not determined) character of social living accounts more adequately for the reality of cross-cultural communication. How we are cross-cultural may be more conditioned that we have admitted in the past, yet the "boundaries our habitations" are regularly transgressed, and this is of particular import for a church with a mandate to bring the Good News of God's reign to all the nations.

The present postmodern critique asks how continuity is possible, and poses that it is not. This is true: it is no longer possible to think about continuity as we have in the past. This is, in great part, because our notion of continuity flowed from an integrated notion of culture. In this understanding, continuity figures largely as a check for *sameness*; that which passes on relatively intact becomes the touchstone for continuity in an integrated notion of culture.

But in a postmodern milieu, where culture is thought of as a contest of meanings, constantly vying within a relatively bounded field, the notion of continuity itself must be refigured. Sameness cannot function as a primary criterion for continuity because, as we have uncovered, sameness functions ambiguously within traditions and is easily manipulated towards hegemonic ends. Fidelity to the tradition therefore must also be reconsidered from this viewpoint because fidelity can never be understood as mere repetition or recapitulation of the initial genius of the tradition. Fidelity might be refigured such that *resonance*, not sameness, functions as the key to continuity.

Resonance, in physics and music, is a stirring, a movement caused by energies emanating from sources such that motion is incited within another. Resonance is triggered by complementary wavelengths and involves a transfer of energies that incites new motion. The response triggered is not identical to the source. The transfer of energy stirs responses that are unique to the character of the receptors. Therefore, the result is not sameness or repetition, but a harmony. In the next section of this chapter, the fruitfulness of a refigured notion of continuity as resonance and potential harmonies will be explored.

## *Juxtaposed Thick Description*

In theology, particularly Roman Catholic theology, the notion of tradition is fundamentally linked to revelation.[43] Therefore, the notion of fidelity to an original gift, a founding encounter, plays a dominant role in the Christian understanding of tradition. If revelation is more than a weak impulse emanating from a distant starting point, Christian theology must provide the needed reflection on how it is that people continue to encounter Jesus in a living way today.

Yet clearly, without a Christian tradition, without a community devoted to the saving, dangerous memory of Jesus, there can be no encounter with God-revealed-in-Jesus. This diachronic journey of faith over time (and synchronic through cultural and social life) provides a record of faith expressions: a historical tradition rich in texts, practices, rituals, and central figures (saints, leaders, holy women and men). For the life of the community and its mission of gospel witness, the historical memory, the traditions of faith, are critical resources of revelation.

As described earlier, the current state of crisis in traditions poses particular difficulty for Roman Catholicism precisely because of its immediate history and the notion of tradition that developed from its failed attempt to root out modernism. Clinging to an ahistorical perspective while attempting to legitimate a propositional notion of revelation, Ultramontane Roman Catholicism made remarkable claims for papal primacy and linked tradition with the teaching magisterium in a manner that remains contested today.[44]

It was John XXIII's unanticipated move in calling the Second Vatican Council that forever changed the church's relationship to the modern world. Desiring a church that was more like a living garden than an airtight museum, John XXIII's oft-quoted opening speech heralded a long-awaited new season in the Roman Catholic Church, putting all museum keepers on notice. "The substance of the ancient doctrine of the deposit of faith is one thing, and the way in which it is presented in another."[45]

The struggle to understand the meaning of revelation and its relationship to history became even more complicated in the immediate years

---

43. Tilley notes, "For Roman Catholic thinkers, the concept of tradition is theologically very important because it is associated with disputes concerning divine revelation, its sources and its bearers . . ." Tilley, *Inventing Catholic Tradition*, 8.

44. See Stagaman, *Authority in the Church*.

45. Vatical Council, *Vatican Council II*, 715.

following Vatican II as the realization dawned that the Roman Catholic Church had opened itself to a world already gone postmodern. The ensuing crisis continues into the present as multiple worldviews (premodern, modern, postmodern) interact, argue, and make conflictual claims to authority. Given this multivocal climate, how is it possible to speak responsibly about the faith conviction that the Divine Presence continues to be encountered in Jesus through the symbols of the Christian tradition? This is the dilemma facing Christian theologians of tradition.

Tradition and Risk

The notion of tradition remains suspect in a postmodern world. Prone to ideological manipulation in the social processes that create both knowledge and relationships, traditions are not neutral or innocent; neither are they phantasms, illusions generated by peculiar cultural logics. Symbolic sources function; traditions are dynamic, suspect entities. To live with tradition is to live at risk.[46] An Ultramontane notion of tradition attempts to eliminate the element of uncertainty, and it is precisely the recovery of risk that is essential to a refigured Roman Catholic understanding of tradition. What, then, can a practice of juxtaposed thick description do towards forwarding such an engagement of the tradition?

To set the stage for this question, a critical dimension of the risk involved in a new approach to tradition needs to be addressed. In an article written for the Society for Comparative Study of Society and History, Corinne Kratz problematizes the notion of tradition itself, noting that "its usages in the English language carry values and perspectives that may have no correspondences in other cultures and their languages."[47] All too often tradition is used in scholarly articles and discussions without reference to how "representations of time, history, and identity within particular political contexts"[48] are organized and understood contextually. Advocating

---

46 "Christian systematic theology is a personal risk of interpretation of the event (including the tradition and symbols which mediate it) and the risk of an interpretation of the situation. Ordinarily, both risks of interpretation will be guided by the belief that that theologian must correlate these two interpretations or collapse into rough coherence. More, exactly, the systematic theologian articulates mutually critical correlations between the interpretation of the situation and the interpretation of the event. The structure of systematic theology is the structure of a personal, risk-ridden response of participatory and critical interpretations of both situation and event." Tracy, *Analogical Imagination*, 375. See also Brown, *Boundaries of Our Habitations*, 82.

47. Kratz, "'We've Always,'" 31.

48. Ibid., 61.

a method that opens the concept of tradition beyond a *narrow* universalism (one cultural understanding writ large), Kratz encourages the study of tradition as a "cultural concept which shapes and is shaped by different perspectives and processes."[49] The result is an enlightening study that juxtaposes Western and Okiek notions of tradition, exposing both assumptions and potentials for further reflection.

Kratz skillfully demonstrates three dominant approaches to tradition in the West. *Tradition as representation* understands symbolic sources to function in social differentiation. This focus tends to literalize cultural practices, grounding them in a history that may or may not have actually been the case. Concern for how change undermines or contaminates (from the outside) a "traditional" life dominates this perspective. In the light of Okiek traditioning practices Kratz notes that this concern fails to explore "the way in which new circumstances are made into tradition."[50] *Tradition as ideology*, with its emphasis on the asymmetries of political and economic relations, can actually blind observers to all the other relations that inform local knowledge. "Concentrating on control and power in a single domain, they have less regard for interpretative aspects of shifts in tradition and their influences."[51] Finally, while *tradition as cultural creation* focuses on forms considered traditional and the multiple meanings that emerge from their interactions, this perspective often celebrates adaptations without paying attention to the "connections between imaginative reshapings and material circumstances."[52] These insights are gleaned from Kratz's contrastive description of Okiek traditioning strategies, where innovations in ceremonial practices are incorporated through a connecting relationship to the past.[53]

49. Ibid., 30.
50. Ibid., 42.
51. Ibid.
52. Ibid.

53. "Okiek ceremonial tradition is predicated on the image of overriding continuity, undisturbed by changes in certain elements of ceremonial practice. This broad, encompassing continuity is in fact a historically and culturally differentiated mosaic. There is no memory of an alternative or origin for certain practices. Some new practices have well-known, widely recognized, and discussed beginnings; but others have a novelty that is passed over silently unless questioned. The last, which are rarely noted or questioned, are well on the way to becoming practices the origins and alternatives of which are lost to memory. The broad view resembles the image of tradition projected by differentiating Western approach, but a more particular focus shows the dynamic mixture of representations and memories that the ideological approach stresses. Okiek notions of tradition are

While there is much in Kratz's work that demands further consideration and study within a theological question of religious tradition, her insights are introduced here to emphasize the nature of the shift that is called for in a rehabilitated notion of tradition. Her work calls for a "reorientation" in the study of tradition; one that engages in-depth the local situation "in order to focus on the ways in which tradition is both an outcome of daily life and a means through which it is understood."[54] Furthermore, this analysis extends beyond the intricacies of daily life into the larger, broader social, political, and historical domains. The interpenetration and mutual influence of these micro- and macro-levels of social life function "in the cultural dynamics of tradition and cannot be neglected."[55] Given the range of analysis recommended by this study, there is a broad expanse of perspectives that can be brought to bear on the cultural inquiry into tradition. Multivocal traditions are embodied realities; they have human faces and occupy diverse geographies of experience, education, and interest. "As a cultural resource, tradition can figure in issues and interactions in many ways. No one social group or individual has a monopoly over its particular forms and meanings, as they are changeable and at times contested."[56]

If a central tenet of Christian faith is the affirmation that Jesus reveals God-with-us, then the incarnational potential of human culture must be attended to in new ways. Christian faith affirms that discipleship is gift and task; and this engaged existential encounter takes on new dimensions of meaning when Christian identity is viewed from the contested ground of cultural life.[57] Since traditions are intimately connected to human identity and how social groups understand themselves in relation to time and place, there is no small need to reconsider (and reshape) the monolithic notion of tradition/identity that pervades Roman Catholic religious imaginations.

---

not reducible or identical to either, however. The latter image is turned into the former in ways that this section analyzes, but both aspects of tradition continue to inform and influence each other in the process." Ibid., 53.

54. Ibid., 61.
55. Ibid.
56. Ibid.

57. "'Culture' means that any religious sign language is produced by human beings independently of the fact that religions understand themselves as the result of divine action. The association of particular material elements with meanings and the organization of these meanings in a system of meaning is human action; above all it is social action. For only through the participation of whole groups and communities can a sign system become effective. Religions are socio-cultural sign systems." Theissen, *Religion of the Earliest Churches*, 6.

When the plural character of human life is read through incarnational eyes, the need for juxtaposed thick description as a *multi-dimensional hermeneutic,* practiced both *inside and outside* the local church, becomes quite evident. The result of these interpretative layers is a *revisable record* of Christian life and practice, the documentation of a living tradition of discipleship.

## Juxtaposed Thick Description as a Multidimensional Hermeneutic

Thick descriptions attempt to get at the meanings that people say they are about.[58] As second- or third-person narratives, thick descriptions are multilayered interpretative exercises in which the participant observer seeks to "elaborate a language of significant contrast."[59] The result of good thick description is not the reduction of particulars into abstracted wholes, but the distinctiveness of perspectives made known: a nuanced juxtaposition of seeming incomparables. Although Geertz is adamant that juxtaposed thick descriptions are not attempts to impose a prior unity on the diversity encountered in the local, nonetheless, this methodology would not work unless there were enough shared elements to evoke a sense of resonance with or interest in (cognitive curiosity) the perspective the juxtaposition creates. While the wholes contrasted are represented in their contested diversity, thick description orders these relations into a descriptive picture that may be affirmed or disputed by others engaged in similar analyses. Thus, a practice of thick description focused on a local Christian community's identity construed as discipleship would attend to the religious meanings generated by the community's gospel-framed encounter with the circumstances of its context, including the asymmetries that may have

58. While others have borrowed the notion of thick description from Geertz and applied it to theological discourse, what I propose stands in significant contrast. Thick description figures in the works of a number of postcritical theologians. Among them, Ronald Theimann's *Constructing a Public Theology* proposes an application of Geertz's notion of thick description that makes the elements of Christian life and worship (Bible, practices of prayer and devotion) the central focus of theological discourse. Only from this internally informed theological ground do Christians authentically enter into public discourse. As Van Huyssteen points out, this approach fails in the public realm because it does not enter into a public debate around the soundness of its own epistemological commitments. By begging the question of rationality, Theimann falls into a form of contextualism that reinforces a notion of incommensurable local discourses. My use of thick description is in direct contrast to this, proposing that juxtaposed thick descriptions more adequately serve the purposes of intercultural hermeneutics. For Van Huyssteen's critique of Theimann's proposal see *Shaping of Rationality*, 74–77.

59. Geertz, *After the Fact,* 20.

suppressed or even delegitimated particular local expressions. This type of thick description would give attention to the factors that Kratz identified: the micro- and macro-levels of Christian life within a particular culture, allowing for the possibility of new, emerging Christian meanings.

Juxtaposed Thick Descriptions Inside and Outside

The new meanings generated in the local scene are simultaneously engaging the larger world of the universal church. A practice of juxtaposed thick description calls for a revised understanding of how local traditions fit together in a worldwide witness to the reign of God.

Robert Schreiter has aptly described the present reality of the local-global ecclesial relationship, noting that often local (particularly younger) churches are in a hearer-speaker relationship with the universal (older) church. The universal church functions as a speaker and in this role has a primary concern for the clear and full transmission of the message. Younger churches, as hearers, are more concerned with how the message can be intelligibly incorporated within an already well-established cultural/social context.[60] When the validation of the local church lies in the authoritative domain of the universal church, paternalism threatens to undermine local expressions of the gospel and even subvert new gospel meanings and relevancies.[61] Juxtaposed thick description calls for a decentering that puts the local churches in global relationship, each contributing and contending within a worldwide field of interaction and response that results in the ongoing expression of Roman Catholic ecclesial identity.

The decentering afforded by the practice of juxtaposed thick description does not ignore or undervalue the original genius of Christian life. On the contrary, the decentering works to reorient the relationship between the faith communities toward a collegiality that is intelligible, responsible, and prophetic in a globalized world. In the end, this reorientation places even greater emphasis on the sources of Christian tradition and the accountability that the whole church shares as each local church contributes to the possible prophetic meanings of Jesus and Christian life.

Questions arising from the new global context require a respect for and even an anticipation of the Holy Spirit's presence, thus calling for a certain ecclesial expectancy, a hope of hearing the gospel once again. The decentering recommended by the practice of juxtaposed thick description

---

60. Schreiter, *Constructing Local Theologies*, 59.
61. Ibid., 99.

does not negate the truth or significance of previous gospel forms; it does invite the possibility of new gospel forms, or in the words of Geertz, makes "available to us answers that others, guarding other sheep in other valleys, have given, and include them in the consultable record."[62] When the answers to proverbial questions are allowed to come into gospel view, new potentials for catholicity may be realized.

Since all cultural "answers" are really negotiated discourses, they require both analyses from within and without. Above I have discussed the approach needed to bring to light the multiple meanings generated in the local scene. In a global world these meanings can never be fully insulated from the interpretations of those outside the tradition(s) and culture(s) of a particular place. Gerd Theissen notes, "Today we can no longer take up one tradition without entering into dialogue with others. The 'external perspective' is increasingly becoming part of the 'internal perspective.' Dialogue with others is part of a dialogue with ourselves."[63] Moreover, Schreiter's description of global theological flows demonstrates the porous character of cultural boundaries.[64] Thus, the theological practice of juxtaposed thick description proposes that local answers can and do have global significance.[65]

## Juxtaposed Thick Descriptions as Revisable Records

A practice of juxtaposed thick description brings the polyvalent discourse on Christian discipleship to a level of intentional global interaction, allowing the insights of local churches to contribute and contend towards the pressing questions of Christian identity in a global world. As the answers of the local churches are brought forward, the gospel tradition becomes gospel *traditions*, richly multiple, widely divergent, and engaged in issues of such significance that conflictual assessments and interpretations are more the common case than the exception.

This brings out the importance of the *revisability* of juxtaposed thick descriptions. The ability of local traditions to speak beyond their immediate contexts assumes the possibility of global conversations where ideas,

62. Geertz, *Interpretation of Cultures*, 30.
63. Theissen, *Religion of the Earliest Churches*, xiv.
64. Schreiter, *New Catholicity*, 15–27.
65. "Theology must also have a universalizing function, by which is meant an ability to speak beyond its own context, and an openness to hear voices from beyond its boundaries. Universalizing is not totalizing, which entails a suppression of difference and a claim to be the sole voice. Theology cannot restrict itself only to its own and immediate context, if the message of what God has done in Christ is indeed Good News for all people, then the occurrence of grace in any setting has relevance for the rest of humanity." Ibid., 4.

practices, and teachings are subjected to critical review from other perspectives. The polyvalency of the local scene increases exponentially as churches engage in cross-cultural disputations/intercultural hermeneutics of global ultimacy. Once again the element of risk enters in. The global conversation needs to allow for the processes of change and revision that the larger forum may stimulate locally. As stories and expressions of discipleship are described from within the dynamic contexts of local traditions, interlocutors must forestall hasty judgments to allow the play/work of tradition-identity within particular historical-material circumstances. Forestalling judgment does not eliminate critical questions and disputation. When these strategies are focused toward the overarching question being engaged, meanings are challenged and positions are clarified (or shown to be in need of clarification), which serves both the communities of faith and the faith of the communities. Given this, juxtaposed thick descriptions are never meant to be immutable expressions. They are hermeneutically framed descriptions that attempt to say something of import regarding the particular manifestations of the Spirit made present to a local church. If tradition is construed as a series of local traditions,[66] juxtaposed thick description offers a means to make the multidimensional, historically conditioned stories and practices of faith available for the world church, thus expanding the theological discourse around the question, "What does it mean to be a follower of Jesus"?

As a proposal towards refiguring the Roman Catholic notion of tradition, juxtaposed thick descriptions make the contest of meanings within the traditioning process more readily accessible to the churches and the global theological discourse. Juxtaposed thick descriptions become one possible means towards an understanding of continuity as a critical hermeneutical process where the authoritative locus of a tradition is both received and questioned through cultural processes of identity formation and transformation. The effort to produce and critique thick descriptions of Christian discipleship affirms that human pluralism is not simply the result of accidental embellishments on a generic human model; how we are different is matter for grace. Bringing to light the meanings available in both the congruencies and incongruencies of Christian social identity, juxtaposed thick description offers a theological door into the much-needed elaboration of the graced significance of our diversity.[67] Accordingly, the play

---

66. Ibid., 2.

67. "[W]hat is the theological significance of difference? Are we to understand difference

within traditions between consensus and dissensus is of considerable importance. While there is much to commend the social processes that help groups to overcome communication blocks and the debilitating effects of misinformation, any resulting consensus does not guarantee the "true." J. W. Van Huyssteen advises against linking contextual consensus with the rational and thereby relegating dissensus to the irrational.[68] Dissensus plays as significant a role as consensus in the making of meanings and social traditioning. Dissensus within a tradition, often the stirrings of subjugated voices, offers potential energies for prophetic reorientations of a group, a transformative function.

By arguing that theological reflection must take difference into serious consideration and work with the complex interaction of consensus and dissensus, the risk of tradition becomes evident. Since the sure foundations of an immutable tradition have dissolved in a postmodern world, what keeps the threat of relativism at bay?

No longer is it possible to think about continuity within traditions from a foundational perspective. The move from the former security of modern notions of culture, tradition and history represents a true paradigm shift, still producing no small amount of "Cartesian anxiety." The strategy offered here, juxtaposed thick descriptions, is very much a pro-

---

in God's creation as merely decorative or is it something revelatory? Is the plenitude of difference simply a display of God's power or does it tell us something about being itself? We need a much more profound and thoroughgoing theology of culture and of grace in order to be able to probe that question." Ibid., 43.

68. "The fact that different human minds, in and across different domains and disciplines, share in the same resources of human rationality does not therefore mean that rational agents must ultimately reach agreement on all meaningful issues. Rescher convincingly argues that rationality ultimately consists in effecting an appropriate alignment between our beliefs and the way we experience 'bodies of evidence' differently: different individuals will generally confront different bodies of evidence and will accordingly—through responsible judgment—evaluate it differently. This kind of 'perspectival pluralism' thus reveals consensus or agreement as at most an ideal, but as not morally or epistemically necessary for our commitment to rationality. The diversity of our traditions, our experiences, our epistemic situations, and cognitive values, of our disciplinary domains, and methodologies, all make for a difference in beliefs, judgments, and evaluations of otherwise perfectly rational people. Our moral obligation is therefore not first of all to coordinate our beliefs with those of others, but rather with what we, through ongoing critical conversation, have come to accept as correct, right, or true. This kind of intellectual honesty may of course lead to agreement with others; agreement, as such, however, is not something to which we are morally—or rationally—obligated." Van Huyssteen, *Shaping of Rationality*, 272. Van Huyssteen here quotes from Nicholas Rescher, *Pluralism: Against the Demand for Consensus*.

visional, perspectival practice for the "between time": the transition we continue to experience within an ongoing paradigm shift. We have yet to exhaust the conversation on the nature of human rationality and how traditioned epistemologies can understand each other, let alone engage in argumentation over truth claims. These critical global conversations cannot be fruitfully entered into without considerable attention to how the dominant discourse and its categories continue to be challenged, deconstructed, and reconstructed through encounters with and assertion of "the other."

Given this social global climate, a more descriptive account of local theologies is a preliminary step before judgments of theological orthodoxy can be addressed. If traditions are in constant, dynamic interaction with an internal authoritative locus, the practice of juxtaposed thick description attempts to expand the breadth and depth of the traditioning voices contending with and shaping the authoritative locus (understood here as Brown's notion of a bound, curatorial, normative, contestable, and contemporaneous canon). A local theology must engage in the task of explaining in its own terms how its truth claims authentically represent a gospel perspective, that is, "faithful" to the authoritative locus of the Christian tradition. Yet, in a world newly awakened to the theological significance of difference, the Western notion of fidelity is problematized by its association with sameness. How can this understanding of fidelity be addressed?

## Fidelity or Harmony?

One possible approach may be Peter Phan's suggestion that Catholic theology consider the Asian notion of *harmony* in contrast to fidelity.[69] Phan suggests that the Western notion of fidelity is not expansive enough to anticipate what the Spirit may be about in local theologies. Speaking from the perspective of Asian theologies, developing since Vatican II and in conversation with the Federation of Asian Bishops Conference, Phan notes that the church in Asia is involved in a "triple-intertwined dialogue": the suffering poor, Asian cultures, and Asian religions. This intertwined dialogue takes into account these three indispensable components as they mutually condition each other. "Just to limit ourselves to inculturation, without the work of liberation, inculturation turns into archeologism and elitism, and without interreligious dialogue, it becomes religious vandalism, pillaging this or that element of other religions for Christian use."

---

69. Phan, response to Roger Haight, 2001. I am deeply grateful for Dr. Phan's generosity in sharing the text of his response with me. All quotes in this section come from this unpublished manuscript. See also Eilers, *For All the Peoples*, 2:229–98.

The result of the dialogue leads Phan to suggest that Western tests for orthodoxy, whether they are based on "propositional conformity" or "conceptual and terminological conformity," are not adequate to the present task. When Christian faith encounters totally new cultures, as it does in Asia, "one must entertain the possibility that something genuinely new will emerge."[70]

Phan's notion of harmony is based on "the notion of yin and yang as complementary contraries (not contradictories) of all beings." Harmony can also be construed as a type of resonance offering a wider metaphorical field of play where both sameness and difference have a place. Particularities and their relationships to wholes are accounted for more dynamically, allowing for multiple, potentially harmonious combinations. Here, the criterion for normativity is not sameness, but fruitfulness. Juxtaposed thick descriptions function towards resonance; they are not attempts at glossing over differences or erasing distinctiveness.

The juxtaposition of seemingly discordant gospel expressions offers a view that could not be known outside the collision of competing viewpoints. Yet, the practice of juxtaposed thick description will not result in non-critical acceptance of all possible interpretations of the gospel. Critical discernment and exercise of judgment will continue to function in the communal praxis of engaged discourse. In fact, since the process of responsible judgment is a contextual social practice, the potential for greater critical attention is significantly increased. Ultimately, since all God-talk is symbolic and therefore always partial and incomplete in expression, the contest of meanings that juxtaposed thick description promotes frees all interlocutors involved from the extravagant claim of possessing a universal truth that simply needs to be translated into other languages.

When the original witness of faith (a thoroughly interpreted witness) is allowed to enter a broader hermeneutical field where potential harmonies are sought, a far more fruitful gospel potential may be realized. If the revelation of God in Jesus is to be a light to all the nations in a postmodern world, Western Christian tradition can no longer function as a theological export.[71] To say that the Word is made flesh in a postmodern

---

70. In his response to Haight, Phan gives the example of the Chinese Rites Controversy where new "concepts, terminologies, theologies and practices" were introduced and subsequently rejected by Rome as "religiously superstitious and practically immoral."

71. "But one can see clearly that despite the implied contradiction to its essence, the actual concrete activity of the Church in its relation to the world outside of Europe was in fact (if you will pardon the expression) the activity of an export firm which exported a

world invites reflection on how profoundly diverse God incarnate is. Human diversity is no small existential, and therefore theological, fact.[72] To paraphrase Geertz, although human beings have the potential to live a thousand different kinds of lives, in the end they only live one: a life lived within a conditioning particularity that expresses certain potentials, not all possible potentials. If this is true, our diversity is one of the most mysterious, significant, interesting, and graced dimensions of our existence. Continued reflection on the theological meaning of human diversity may indeed lead to the conviction that the dynamism of the tradition expresses itself most powerfully in its fecundity. The saving encounter of God mediated through Jesus continues to flourish, not in spite of, but because of the ambiguity of the historical tradition that is, in the end, the only means to encounter the God revealed in Jesus.

## Critically Correlating the Meanings of Theology

The work of correlating Congar's understanding of ecclesial discipleship began in chapter 4 when his three essential elements (ecclesial fellowship, witness, and service) were put into conversation with the current situation (signs of the times) and resulted in a particular construal of Roman Catholic ecclesial identity as praxes of communion, reconciliation, and solidarity. In this final section of chapter 5, three questions will be addressed in order to extend the insights of the critical correlation in the light of what has been discussed in the previous pages. The first question explores how local ecclesial identities, construed in terms of discipleship, contribute towards a refigured notion of tradition. Then, more specifically, the second question examines Congar's notion of discipleship and its contributions towards a refigured notion of tradition. The final section will consider how local thick descriptions of Christian discipleship provide a perspectival critique of *tiempos mixtos* and current assumptions and assertions regarding human traditions and social identity.

---

European religion as a commodity it did not really want to change but sent throughout the world together with the rest of the culture and civilization it considered superior." Rahner, "Fundamental Theological Interpretation," 717.

72. "Pluralism means real, solid and persistent differences prevail between people, between their views, between who they think they are as human beings, between ways in which they act and thus between people themselves." Haight, *Jesus*, 425.

## *Local Ecclesial Identities and Tradition*

### Local Discipleship and Tradition from Below

How, then, does a specific ecclesial identity, construed as discipleship, contribute towards a refigured notion of tradition? I propose three ways in which local construals of discipleship help in this regard. First, when the question of tradition is addressed from the place of local discipleship, there is a significant shift in the point of entry into the question. Instead of emphasizing the descent of tradition from God to humanity, mediated through a divinely inspired magisterium, this approach starts from the ground up, focusing on the vitality of the witness of Christian life. When tradition is approached "from below" through a hermeneutic of discipleship, the result is an approach that is pragmatic and oriented towards mission. This does not undervalue the "received" aspect of Christian tradition, but it does demand certain gospel suspicion of any naïve acceptance of tradition for tradition's sake. As has been thoroughly documented, human traditions exhibit an ambiguous character. Since traditions are considerably oriented towards social concerns of survival, power, and legitimation, their pragmatic behavior of forming, sustaining, and transforming social (and individual identities) must be critically evaluated.[73] If the Christian tradition is forming, sustaining, and transforming other social identities besides (or even instead of) discipleship, this must be challenged and possibly refuted. Evoking tradition itself does not guarantee against the possibility of a Christian counterwitness to the gospel.[74] Ultimately, the tradition functions, and it is the community's risky engagement of tradition in particular historical contexts that more or less forwards God's intentions or frustrates them.

### Local Discipleship, an Itinerant Experience

Second, all construals of discipleship are embedded within specific historical and cultural contexts. At their best, these construals capture something of the gospel genius, and their classic forms are remembered and passed down as exemplary symbolic expressions of Christian life and mission. Although thoroughly bound in time and place, these exceptional writings, practices, and persons continue to speak beyond their contexts. Examples of discipleship that remain within the community's memory testify less to immutable creeds and practices and more to the livingness of the tradition

---

73. Brown, *Boundaries of Our Habitation*, 27–28.
74. Ch. 4, p. 219.

within particular cultural/social circumstances; the fecundity of creating, sustaining, and transforming a thoroughly inculturated gospel witness.

Yet, even at their best, these expressions of Christian life are partial and limited. Moreover, no expression of Christian discipleship is unambiguous. Even as certain expressions of Christian life are promoted and valorized, other views recede and may even be eclipsed to the detriment of Christian witness. Moreover, given the polyvalency of religious symbols, multiple meanings construed from a single symbol can simultaneously fuel divergent, conflictual social means and ends. As good and as true as particular interpretations of the gospel maybe, the character of human traditions as cultural and historical products makes even the best articulations of the Christian mystery capable of being complicit with and co-opted by the vilest human designs.

This reality will be dealt with more specifically in the next section on Congar's view of discipleship, but it does require a dual respect for and "holy suspicion" of the forms of religion. Because symbols rise and die within a community, it is critical that believers become more aware of how social processes of selective memory function to subjugate voices within a tradition in the supposed service of orthodoxy. While a critical view is always a necessary tool in religious/theological reflection, an uncritical, undialectical approach to symbols threatens to collapse the distance between transcendent revelation and mediating symbols, resulting not in worship but idolatry.

These cautions alert us that living in a religious tradition is not impossible, just dangerous. Far less a comfortable home, and much more a critical, negotiated journey of faith, living responsibly within a religious tradition calls for a particular sense of itinerancy. In the face of historical contingency where new questions of ultimacy figure within changing political and material circumstances, the refusal to "move on" threatens to reduce a particular symbol of Christian life to a univocal sign; an archival treasure, but far too fragile and implausible to withstand the current assaults to faith. Thus, within the very ambiguity that makes religious traditions suspect lies their power for renewal and rejuvenation. The vitality of the Christian tradition lies in the community's ability to reinterpret its symbol system and practices in the light of current social, political, and economic challenges.

## Local Discipleship and Accountability to Daily Life

Although traditions are received by virtue of being born into time and culture, the reality is that traditions are constantly being made and remade within the demands, dilemmas, and dramas of day-to-day existence. Traditions, as Kratz points out, are formed out of the stuff of daily life, even as they provide the means by which people make sense of their existence.[75] When traditions are approached from the ground of the daily, there is a greater demand for accountability to the present circumstances. The challenges of the present are encountered and understood through the mediation of a community's symbol system: its contested, yet real "sacred canopy."[76] When anomaly sets in, there is a sense of cognitive dissonance; if the current interpretations of the religious tradition fail to adequately account for the complexities and dilemmas of current situation, new alternatives are sought. Since there is no true escaping the traditioned character of the social, new interpretations are fashioned and fought over in a traditioning process that is always a negotiation between present dilemmas and the most recent canonical expressions of the religious tradition. Engaging the tradition is always at some level a negotiation with its authoritative locus, the canon that is "received and cherished, and challenged and changed."[77]

> Negotiating identity in relationship to a canon is a process of employing the materials of canon—which necessarily means construing the canon in this way or that—as a framework in terms of which one understands one self, one's own social world and natural world and one's place in it. But canonical negotiation can also be a process of advocating the revision of canon in the name of expanding or diminishing its potentials.[78]

A rehabilitated notion of tradition works with the vital fruitfulness of the tradition over time and space, not in defense of an exaggerated claim to immutability.

### *Congar, Ecclesial Identity, and Tradition*

Given that the local notion of discipleship offers a perspectival view of how the fruitfulness of the tradition may be manifest in a community's engage-

---

75. Kratz, "'We've Always,'" 61.
76. Berger, *Sacred Canopy.*
77. Brown, *Boundaries of Our Habitation*, 86.
78. Ibid., 90.

ment of its historical circumstances, what does the specific description of Congar's notion of discipleship contribute towards a refigured notion of tradition? When the markers of the social identity of the church as a community of disciples are construed as praxes of communion, reconciliation, and solidarity, what view of tradition comes to light?

### Tradition from Praxis of Communion

When a praxis of communion, described as the recovery of the right relationship between the local churches and the universal church, is taken up, a significant shift in the understanding of tradition occurs. Major changes in ecclesiology instigate new understandings of tradition. Thus, from the view of a praxis of communion, the tradition is no longer an immutable deposit of faith jealously guarded by the "Roman" church in the name of the universal church. The tradition is the sacred trust of the universal church, the shared custodial legacy and fiduciary responsibility of the local churches. A praxis of communion in a globally diversified world refigures the notion of fidelity to the tradition; the churches share authority and responsibility for the *fruitful* transmission of the gospel. Since this criterion involves both right speech and right action about God and God's world, the ability to recognize gospel life in human cultures offers new challenges and opportunities for those engaged in the praxis of communion. There is no one inculturated symbol of Christian faith that fully embodies the depth and breadth of the mystery. Each cultural expression, as a symbolic representation holds potentials for both revelatory encounter and blasphemous idolatry. The theological expressions of the Christian faith, because they are thoroughly human creations, must be continually challenged, revised, and renewed in pursuit of the fruitful transmission of the gospel. Do the blind see? Do the lame walk? Are lepers cleansed? Do the deaf hear? Are the dead raised to life? Is the Good News preached to the poor? (Luke 7:22). The tradition is the living matrix of contested symbols, practices, and interpretations that requires a global forum devoted to the praxis of communion in the pursuit of viable, transformative articulations of the Good News. Because the tradition is the only means believers have to encounter the God revealed in Jesus, with John the Baptist, the churches must ask, "Are you the one who is to come or have we to wait for someone else"? (Luke 7:20).

## Tradition from a Praxis of Reconciliation

Because Christians are as diverse as any group of human beings, the potential for difference to degenerate to rupture is a constant fact of life. A praxis of reconciliation speaks to the ongoing need in human communities to acknowledge the ways in which the asymmetries of social living offend the dignity of human beings. The task of building a social life with all the components of economics, politics, culture, and social structures is never an innocent project. Christians engage in the task of world building as a sacred work in cooperation with the Spirit of Jesus, yet the reign of God is never a human achievement. Christian discipleship is a covenant relationship in which the gift and task of forwarding God's intention in creation is a central baptismal commitment. We do not effect the reign of God; but neither are we mere tourists on this earth.[79] As limited as we are by sin, we are impelled to seek God's reign, pursue its purposes, foster the conditions for its flourishing among all people, and grieve its absence. This is the heart of Congar's notion of discipleship: the Godward orientation of the disciple and the community of disciples in history.

There is a radical dimension to the praxis of reconciliation that elicits a prophetic expression of the Christian tradition. As a messianic, pilgrim people committed to the praxis of communion, good Christians will disagree over the ways in which an authentic gospel life should be expressed, even to the point of breaches in relationship.[80] Christians who pray "forgive us as we forgive" are invited to show what that existentially looks like in their particular historical situation. While reconciliation (and communion and solidarity as well) is always the first act of the Spirit and never a human achievement, nonetheless, without intentional engagement in a praxis of reconciliation, this grace has no material expression; grace is refused. Tradition from this perspective is a gift and task that results from the interplay of dissensus and consensus, the contest of meanings that any really good theological question will provoke. Tradition stands under judgment

---

79. "Christian freedom is not the freedom of a man [sic] without responsibility or of a tourist—we are pilgrims, travelers, in the world, but not in that sense. Ours is the position of one who, delivered from bond-service, is given a new task, or simply the same one, as a vocation and labour of love." Congar, *Lay People*, 411.

80. As with all other social identities, Christian discipleship is a contested identity. Kathryn Tanner maintains that the diverse and provocative character of discipleship "suggest . . . the possibility of genuinely conflicting understandings of discipleship among equally 'good' Christians," potentially leading "to a genuine fight." Tanner, *Theories of Culture*, 159.

not because it is inherently evil, but because it is inherently ambiguous, capable of great good and great harm. Even so, the tradition itself will be an important source as Christians, informed by a praxis of reconciliation, develop strategies to disagree without calling down *anathema* or unleashing sectarian conflicts to the detriment of the witness of the universal church and the peace of the planet. From a praxis of reconciliation, the contested aspects of the tradition do not require resolution for the sake of a coherent, albeit coerced, witness to Christ. Disagreement within a praxis of reconciliation shows the vitality of a tradition able to respond to changing circumstances, even as the disputants witness to the possibility of dissensus without diminishing or dismissing the human dignity of the contesting parties.

### Tradition from a Praxis of Solidarity

Finally, what does a praxis of solidarity contribute towards a refigured notion of tradition? From this perspective, the tradition expands and deepens as voices long relegated to the fringes of theological reflection are brought into the conversation. At a gathering of Dominican women theologians in Lima, Peru, Gustavo Gutierrez was asked to comment on the most important issues in theology today. The first point he made was the dual need for the essentials of Christian faith to be expressed in contemporary terms *and* for minority voices to enter into this important theological task.[81] The perspective of those who are in solidarity with the insignificant, who are insignificant themselves, is a critical gospel witness that must be articulated. Solidarity breaks up the monologue of Western Christian theology and makes the faith perspectives of those who believe in the promises of God despite all historical evidence to the contrary a potent *locus theologicus*. The significance of these voices is not their marginality or the fact that they are often the victims of life-threatening asymmetries. Their import is their faith; their belief in the God revealed in Jesus and their hope, in spite of all evidence to the contrary, that the reign of God is at work in the world.

Tradition from this perspective includes the practices of prayer and devotion within popular religions that have sustained the dignity and faith of peoples caught in the deadly trap of insignificance and expendability. Tradition expands to include the local voices of resistance and dignity that resonate with the gospel experience of liberation in Jesus. Martin Luther King's "I Have a Dream," Jose María Arguedas's "Todas las sangres," and Chung Hyun Kyung's plenary address to the 1991 World Council of

---

81. Gutierrez, informal talk, 2001.

Churches' Canberra Assembly on the Holy Spirit are all expressions connected to the tradition even as they speak beyond it. The tradition has revolutionary potential; traditions can critique themselves even as they seemingly offer a secure house of meaning.

Solidarity is a frontier space, a boundary experience where questions of *social* ultimacy are encountered. Does God intend the systematic evil of oppression that keeps countries so poor there is no hope of securing the governmental structures, infrastructures, and economic transparency necessary for global existence? Does God will the subjugation of races, women, and the rejection and revilement of lesbian and homosexual persons? What are the cultural and social values that these questions offend, and can an embedded religious consciousness transcend these limits to explore the underlying question of human dignity? The tradition itself allows this move. However conditioned, the ambiguity and malleability of symbols within new contexts and relations introduces new meanings and values into the matrix of contending interpretations. From the perspective of solidarity, the process of traditioning does not just secure "the way we were"; it also opens the door to "the way we could be."

## *What One View of Christian Discipleship Might Say beyond Its Particularity*

Given this description of how the three praxes of communion, reconciliation, and solidarity might contribute towards a refigured notion of tradition, how do these three praxes speak beyond a theological domain, to the assumptions and assertions of the present age? Much of postmodern discourse is focused on the experience of difference, the incommensurability of social groups, and the rejection of a Western universalizing logic that erases, homogenizes, and subverts particularity. While diversity discourse has funded some measure of tolerance, recent studies on globalization indicates that there is both increased tolerance and intolerance; globalization has spawned both new integrations and new particularities.

The three praxes that mark ecclesial identity gleaned from a study of Congar's theology take this critique seriously, but reject any extreme postmodern assertions that mistake insulated provincialism for local knowledge. The fact that conversation across social, cultural, political, and religious boundaries is risky business does not make such conversations undesirable, let alone impossible.

While Congar's theological work is thoroughly modern, somewhat innocent of the postmodern complexities of difference, when his notion of Christian life as unity-in-diversity is made to speak beyond his own time and place as praxes of communion, reconciliation, and solidarity, an important critique of the present age presents itself. Although some would label Congar's God's-eye view of unity-in-diversity as abstract and foundational, it is also true that his perspective is thoroughly grounded in the insight that the celebration of diversity often eclipses *how* real, protracted differences between human communities rarely exist without a history of violence. An a global world where time and space are compressed and boundaries of difference can be as close as a next door neighbor, the potential for particular, proximate, and vicious enmities is much more the case than ever before in history.

From the ground of this particular vision of discipleship issues an important critique of the present global situation. A nuclearized world cannot afford to undermine completely the image of a common humanity. Whether the arguments are cast in terms of shared sources of rationality or anthropological constants, human beings face a global situation in which the well-being of the other is no longer a tangential concern. In a nuclear world we do share a global fate; plutonium radiation annihilates all differences, killing equally across boundaries so jealously guarded, infiltrating food webs and water cycles, threatening all life. The wisdom of the Christian tradition, fundamentally expressed in Jesus and the stories of faith that center around the mystery of his life, death, and resurrection, is a wisdom that knows the depths of human treachery and the heights of human agapic love. The tradition participates in the limits and potentials that human social living express. Moreover, Christian tradition witnesses to the revelatory glimpses that continue to stir up within peoples the ancient longings, the desire to thrive.

A world without a *telos* is very dangerous place, indeed. However conflicted and disputed the notion of "the purpose of human life," the stories and traditions that offer such views tap into a shared desire for significance and identity that power the relations of our common lives. To live without these stories is to lose the only real compass worthy of our diverse yet common humanity. "What we need are metaphors and stories that will help us imagine a world in which we really change and yet really remain the same thing."[82]

---

82. Bynum, *Metamorphosis*, 188.

## Conclusion

The correlation of meanings generated from cultural anthropology and theology has opened new directions for understanding how traditions function in Christian identity. Refiguring a notion of tradition within Roman Catholicism through a functional appraisal of the tradition's ability to form and sustain disciples is one approach that attempts to promote a relevant witness of Christ in a globalized world. The insights of cultural anthropology highlight how communities engage in social practices of memory and forgetfulness to legitimate and sustain social relations and knowledges, often at the expense of other voices. This chapter, however, has also shown that suppressed voices, though marginalized, agitate within a tradition and make energies of resistance and dissensus available in a limited yet real way. The presence of prophets and martyrs within traditions affirms that you can kill the messenger, but rarely does the message die.

In a refigured notion of tradition focused toward discipleship formation the ideological tendencies of traditions must be attended to without reducing traditions to mere epiphenomena of economic choices. Traditions express a continuity that can be authoritatively imposed through discipline, but coercion is not the only means; continuity happens in a hermeneutical process where the authoritative locus of the tradition is received and contested by those who inhabit the tradition. Here the local experience of contingent life is interpreted and understood within the frame of tradition, even as these same historical events potentially subvert past understandings and demand new interpretations.

In the face of local contingencies, tradition is always at risk. Both anchor and wave, tradition provides the means to both establish a life-world and to adapt to the challenges that assail it. The provocative polyvalency of traditions requires a multidimensional hermeneutic to get at the local interpretations and those beyond the local situation. A practice of juxtaposed thick description offers a method to bring out the various meanings of discipleship at play within a local ecclesial tradition and produces a revisable record of what people say they are about as a people of faith. When multiple juxtaposed thick descriptions are allowed to interact, question, and respond to each other, new potentials for catholicity are expressed. To be catholic in this sense is less the unveiling of a fully framed ecclesial identity and more a process of becoming catholic, allowing the multiple elements of tradition and the reality of historical circumstances to converge, resulting in new relationships and meanings of Christian life and mission.

The insights gleaned from a particular thick description of Christian discipleship also contribute towards a new construal of tradition. When Christian tradition is evaluated in terms of its ability to form and transform the members who inhabit the tradition, the resulting shift makes the historical existence of the local church a *locus theologicus*. The stories of faith and gospel practice that inform the discipleship of a local church allow aspects of the Good News to find a transforming resonance within a particular culture. When the theological significance of human diversity is explored from a question of fruitfulness within a local culture, the catholic potentials in Christian faith are attended to with renewed energies.

Evidence of this is found in the three praxes of communion, reconciliation, and solidarity construed from Congar's theology. Juxtaposed thick descriptions such as these offer a view into the multiple dimensions that inform Christian identity and other human identities. Praxes of communion, reconciliation, and solidarity, though rooted in specific ecclesial concerns, speak beyond their context to larger concerns of human flourishing in the face of violence and oppression. For instance, when disagreement or disputes arise within or among specific traditions, Congar's thick description recommends that strategies for reconciliation, however locally conditioned, be a major consideration in any discussion of discipleship. The grace and challenge of diversity demands that we expect conflict and suspect any easy unity. What would the witness of the Christian churches be to the world if Christians were renowned for their will to enter into disputes without violence?

The correlation of meanings gleaned from cultural anthropology and theology do support a refigured notion of tradition, where the resulting identities as Christian disciples serve as a test for the fruitfulness of the tradition's transmission of gospel faith. In this view orthodoxy and orthopraxis are linked in an integral manner, as a vital Christian life becomes the touchstone for a community's right use of the sacred tradition entrusted to its care.

# Conclusion

THE QUESTION OF TRADITION and social identity in current discourse remains thoroughly contested. When the categories "religion," "culture," "history," and "tradition" are exposed to be thoroughly inculturated concepts, where does one begin? The embeddedness of human epistemologies points to the local as the only reasonable starting point.

Human embeddedness within particular contexts imposes limits and constricts the capacity to transcend.[1] The human ability to designate and assign social identity to self and others is fundamentally an interpretative enterprise in which the perimeters of experience are already delineated by some sense of shared social history.[2] While the extent to which cultural embeddedness functions remains a highly debated argument, it appears that, in spite of the limits, persons engage in cross-cultural exchanges and challenge the assertion that radical determinism and incommensurability are our singular fate.

What has come to light is the manner in which Western universalism functions towards erasing difference: promoting a single cultural genius as the normative standard and setting the terms of discourse for global interaction. The hegemonic propensities of the West over the "rest" saturate the very categories at play within the various discourses. For some the only safe haven from the tentacles of Western incursion is a flight to essentialism in a fundamentalist pursuit of a society pure and uninfiltrated by the West. For others, there is a similar move towards incommensurability, but here difference, celebrated and embraced as *fluxus quo*, so dominates the social that traditions are rendered as just so much symbolic debris:

---

1. In the words of Van Huyssteen, "Because we relate to our world epistemically only through the mediation of interpreted experience, the observer or the knower is always in a relationship to what is known, and thus, always limited in perspective, in focus, and in experiential scope." Van Huyssteen, *Shaping of Rationality*, 191.

2. "If we always relate to our world epistemically through the mediation of interpreted experience, then our experience will always be theory-ladened and tradition-specific." Ibid., 191–92.

disjointed, discontinuous, and dismissed.³ Yet, both continuity and discontinuity are recognizable as peoples engage the past for the purposes of the present. "In this sense, tradition is not something we can presume as an ontological datum, but it is rather something we create out of the phenomenon of history."⁴

The decentering of Western meanings has significant consequences for Christian theological discourse and mission, heralding a new global context for a world church. How do Roman Catholics speak competently and responsibly of sacred tradition in this new situation? Moreover, who/what makes a Roman Catholic and authorizes that identity?

Two significant threads run the historical length of the Roman Catholic notion of tradition. First and foremost, the tradition is intimately related to the church's experience of revelation: an experience of encounter with the saving Presence of God revealed in Jesus.⁵ Each experience of faith is singular, but believers do share a symbol system within which religious experience is interpreted as having ultimate meaning. Thus, the community is impelled to relate the story of Jesus in all its revelatory potential so that the intentions of God for all creation might be realized.

Second, given the mediated character of all revelatory encounters with the Divine Presence, how does a human community speak a divine word? How is the ineffable articulated and adequately expressed in contingent, historical reality? Roman Catholicism has struggled with these questions through attention to sound doctrine and apostolic authority, contributing towards a particular and enduring form of ecclesial governance.⁶

---

3. In the words of Michel Foucault, "I adopt the methodical precaution and the radical but unaggressive skepticism which makes it a principle not to regard the point in where we are now standing as the outcome of a teleological progression which it would be one's business to reconstruct historically." Foucault, *Power/Knowledge*, 89, quoted in Van Huyssteen, *Shaping of Rationality*, 253.

4. Van Huyssteen, *Shaping of Rationality*, 253–54. See also Byrne, "Foucault on Continuity."

5. This experience is common in the sense that it is recognized and named as an encounter of ultimacy. As Roger Haight points out, believers do not reconstruct and enter into the religious consciousness of our ancestors in the faith. Haight, *Dynamics of Theology*, 75–78.

6. Raymond Brown, noting the range of New Testament ecclesiological diversity, makes the observation that the Roman Catholic Church mirrors the communities of the Pastoral Epistles with their "concomitant instruction to silence those who are upsetting the church (Titus 1:10–11)." Brown, *Churches*, 149. This is in contrast to other Christian churches that emphasize John and the Spirit as indwelling teacher within all believers. Right doctrine has certainly dominated Roman Catholic tradition, and concerns for revelation continue to translate into reverence for orthodox teaching and those who possess it.

These two threads, the conviction of God's revelation and the church's responsibility for the gift of revelation, are woven throughout the cultural, social, and political history of the Roman Catholic Church. This history shapes the present discussion of tradition and revelation because most Catholics and non-Catholics alike are informed by relatively recent Roman Catholic claims to an infallible papal authority in matters of faith. When questions of historical contingency and cultural embeddedness are raised, the perceived threat is a serious one: what/who validates the promises of God to humanity through special revelation? In the recent past, the clear, unambiguous assertion of the Roman Catholic Church that it alone secured the correct expression of the true faith through the sacred teachings of its magisterium served a powerful purpose for the faith community. Besides authoritative teaching, such claims functioned to create a cross-cultural allegiance to the central authority of the Roman Church, powerfully symbolized in the Roman pontiff.[7] In the light of the current pluralistic situation and the ever-increasing variety of perspectives and assertions forwarded on significant moral and ethical questions, it is not difficult to imagine the power that a claim to divine authority, however ahistorical, can have on those who experience pluralism as confusion and not opportunity.[8] At the same time, it must be acknowledged that Roman Catholic ecclesiocentrism frames tradition in a way that raises serious concerns. Is the Church eclipsing the message it so dearly hopes to preserve?

This study engages the question of tradition within Roman Catholicism by attending to both the revelatory potential of the tradition and the limits of contingency on this potential. Mining the ambiguity of the religious tradition and the theological implications of this ambiguity drives these reflections. Insights from interpretative anthropology have been placed into critical correlation with theology by exploring how one particular construal of Christian social identity as discipleship might speak to the current dilemma of tradition and identity within Roman Catholicism.

From a critical appropriation of the works of Mary Douglas, Victor Turner, and Clifford Geertz, three strategies for refiguring tradition within

---

7. Some have pointed out that no pope has better understood and used the symbolic power of the papacy more effectively than John Paul II.

8. This raises the question of power/knowledge and Comoroff's asymmetrical relationships. Who experiences the present pluralism as confusion and who experiences it as opportunity? I venture to say that, for the most part, confusion abounds for those who benefited from status quo and opportunity lives for those finding voice in the decentering of dominance.

Roman Catholicism emerge. Mary Douglas's approach to how institutions function raises important questions; particularly, how social identity is fostered through traditioning practices that promote social amnesia or instigate social memory depending on the relation of the events to group prestige. A reconsideration of Victor Turner's symbol theory leads to the proposal that traditions function within social life in a provocative, polyvalent manner such that it is not possible to say only one thing within a tradition. This raises questions around the theological meaning of multivocality in religious traditions and how continuity is possible. Clifford Geertz's hermeneutical approach, dedicated to thick descriptions that "elaborate a language of significant contrast," suggests that there may be a more fruitful way of approaching human diversity than the imposition of "bloodless universals." This offers a universally Romanized church a possible methodology for attending to the theological significance of diversity while engaging questions about the adequacy of cultural construals of the Christian mystery.

In order to consider how a particular construal of Christian discipleship might contribute towards a refigured notion of tradition, Yves Congar's works in theology were carefully reviewed. For Congar, "the Christian Mystery," the heart of discipleship, is the gift and task of divine encounter that transforms human life into Christ-life. This mystery, explored within Congar's corpus, yields three aspects of the messianic, eschatological way of living together: the Christian life is an ecclesial *fellowship* devoted to *witness* and *service*. Furthermore, these three elements, considered from a perspective of the social identity of the church, suggest three praxes that mark the church corporately as disciple: *communion, reconciliation,* and *solidarity*. When these three praxes are considered within the "signs of the times," specific consequences appear to follow. Communion highlights the appropriate relationship between the local and universal church, and calls for a reconsideration of the theological meaning of diversity in a postmodern, globalized world. Reconciliation acknowledges how the reality of finitude and sin obstruct the church's witness and leads to a proactive praxis of reconciliation as the most authentic witness to a broken world and wounded humanity. Solidarity promotes a repositioning of the church with those who are denied all that God desires for them. Standing with those who walk in the shadow of death amplifies Christian witness in the world and opens the church to a new depth of communion with Jesus in his death and resurrection. The worldwide church has yet to plumb the theological riches of such solidarity. What do those who believe in spite of all odds know of the mystery of God?

The correlation of the meanings of cultural anthropology and theology does help to refigure a notion of tradition within Roman Catholicism. Meanings derived from interpretative anthropology have particular consequences for an ecclesial identity construed from the praxes of communion, reconciliation, and solidarity. Selective traditioning processes that promote both social memory and social amnesia demand that Christians pay attention to the perspectives and voices that are dismissed in these social processes. This counterintuitive hermeneutic may be more readily attained if it is focused towards the question raised in the consideration of the provocative polyvalency of the tradition. What is the theological significance of subjugated voices in the tradition—blasphemy or prophecy, or both? The complexity of interpretation, given perspective, orientation, and purpose, will require that the polyvalency of symbolic forms be attended to with ever more responsibility and patience.

Since traditions are traditions because they remain in a dialectical and dialogical relationship with authoritative loci, the provocative polyvalency of a tradition's symbol system occurs within a contest of meanings that interact around, within, and about a gravitational force that serves as both boundary and field where social identity is received and refuted. The continuity that this hermeneutical process fosters is not one of sameness but fruitfulness. Does the tradition flourish in spite of historical factors that impinge and anomalies that threaten? Although it is certainly possible to avoid the risk of contingent historical life by employing coercive means to secure continuity-as-sameness, continuity is not limited to sameness. As the lessons of history teach, no mere repetition of the forms of religion will guarantee the fruitful expression of "the messianic and eschatological way of life received from the Lord."[9]

Even more pressing is the question of how to respond to multiple, diverse, potentially harmonious forms of the Christian tradition. If it is true that the gospel is an inexhaustible source of divine encounter, then the possibility of multiple orthodoxies and orthopraxes is great; diverse truths that are context-specific, yet capable of speaking beyond their particularity. A practice of juxtaposed thick description could foster the kind of ecclesial exchange both within and between the churches that engage the tradition in order to articulate intelligent, harmonious, and fruitful forms

9. Congar, *I Believe*, 2:39.

of Christian discipleship within ever-changing local contexts. Yet the question of fidelity to the tradition, in contrast to seeking harmony among the traditions, remains an important question. What happens to the concern for sound doctrine when the test for accountability to the tradition shifts from sameness of expression to fruitfulness of gospel living? How can this be addressed from the context of diverse local churches? Again, the praxis of juxtaposed thick description, bringing the various local expressions of discipleship forward to a global exchange, could help to expand the Western notion of fidelity through a new emphasis on orthopraxis, simultaneously rehabilitating notions of orthodoxy.

If the functional effectiveness of the tradition is its ability to form and transform disciples, and if the process of becoming a disciple is ultimately open-ended, never attaining completion, historical contingency offers both risk and opportunity as believers affirm and refute a multilithic tradition, the only means of revelatory encounter with the Divine Presence in time and space. *Semper ecclesia reformanda per traditionem.*

# Bibliography

Aberigo, Giuseppe, and Joseph Komanchak. *History of Vatican II*. Vol. 2. Maryknoll, NY: Orbis, 1997.
Anderson, Benedict. *Imagined Communities: Reflections on the Origin and Spread of Nationalism*. London: Verso, 1991.
Appadurai, Arjun. "Disjuncture and Difference in the Global Cultural Economy." In *Modernity at Large: Cultural Dimensions of Globalization*, 27–47. Minneapolis: University of Minnesota Press, 1996.
Aquino, Maria Pilar. *Our Cry for Life*. Translated by Dinah Livingstone. Maryknoll, NY: Orbis, 1994.
Arendt, Hannah. *The Origin of Totalitarianism*. New York: Harcourt Brace, 1951.
Asad, Talal. *Genealogies of Religion: Discipline and Reasons of Power in Christianity and Islam*. Baltimore: Johns Hopkins University Press, 1993.
Ashley, Kathleen M. *Victor Turner and the Construction of Cultural Criticism*. Bloomington: Indiana University Press, 1990.
Augustine. *De Baptismo contra Donatistas*. Translated by J. R. King. London: T. & T. Clark, 1956.
Bell, Catherine. "The Ritual Body and the Dynamics of Ritual Power." *Journal of Ritual Studies* 4.2 (1990) 299–313.
Berger, Peter. *The Sacred Canopy: Elements of a Sociological Theory of Religion*. New York: Doubleday, 1967.
Beyer, Peter. *Religion and Globalization*. London: SAGE, 1994.
Biemer, Günter. *Newman on Tradition*. Translated by Kevin Smythe. New York: Herder, 1967.
Boudewijnes, H. Barabara. "The Ritual Studies of Victor Turner: An Anthropological Approach and Its Psychological Impact." In *Current Studies on Rituals: Perspectives for the Psychology of Religion,* edited by Hans-Gunther Heimbock and H. Barabara Boudewijnes, 1–18. Atlanta: Rodopi, 1990.
Bowerstock, G. W., et al. *Late Antiquity: A Guide to the Postclassical World*. Oxford: Clarendon, 1999.
Brett, Annabel S. Introduction to *On the Power of Emperors and Popes*, by William of Ockham. Edited and Translated by Annabel S. Brett. London: Thoemmes, 1998.
Brown, Delwin. *Boundaries of Our Habitations: Tradition and Theological Construction*. Albany, NY: SUNY Press, 1994.
Brown, Peter. *The Making of Late Antiquity*. Cambridge, MA: Harvard University Press, 1978.
———. *Power and Persuasion in Late Antiquity*. Madison: University of Wisconsin Press, 1992.
———. *The Rise of Western Christendom*. Malden, MA: Blackwell, 1996.

Brown, Raymond. *The Churches the Apostles Left Behind.* New York: Paulist, 1984.
Bynum, Caroline Walker. *Fragmentation and Redemption: Essays on Gender and the Human Body in Medieval Religion.* New York: Zone Books, 1991.
———. *Metamorphosis and Identity.* New York: Zone Books, 2001.
Byrne, James M. "Foucault on Continuity: The Postmodern Challenge to Tradition." *Faith and Philosophy* 9.3 (1992) 335–52.
Calderon, Fernando. "America Latina, identidad y tiempos mixtos, o cómo de ser boliviano." In *Imagenes desconocidas,* 225–39. Buenos Aires: CLASCO, 1988.
Cameron, Averil. "Remaking the Past." In *Late Antiquity: A Guide to the Postclassical World,* edited by G. W. Bowerstock et al., 1–20. Oxford: Clarendon, 1999.
*Canons and Decrees of the Council of Trent.* Translated by H. J. Schroeder, OP. St. Louis: Herder, 1950.
Chadwick, Henry. *The Early Church.* Middlesex, UK: Penguin, 1967.
Chadwick, Owen. *From Bossuet to Newman.* Cambridge: Cambridge University Press, 1987.
———. *Newman.* Oxford: Oxford University Press, 1983.
Chemnitz, Martin. *Examination of the Council of Trent.* Translated by Fred Krammer. St. Louis: Concordia, 1971.
Chenu, Marie Dominic. *Nature, Man and Society in the Twelfth Century.* Chicago: University of Chicago Press, 1957.
Clement, Keith. *Schleiermacher: Pioneer of Modern Theology.* London: Collins Liturgical, 1987.
Clifford, James. *The Predicament of Culture.* Cambridge, MA: Harvard University Press, 1988.
Clifford, James, and George Marcus, editors. *Writing Culture.* Berkeley: University of California Press, 1986.
Comaroff, John. "Ethnicity, Nationalism, and the Politics of Difference in an Age of Revolution." In *The Politics of Difference: Ethnic Premises in a World of Power,* edited by Edwin N. Wilmsen and Patrick McAllister, 162–83. Chicago: University of Chicago Press, 1996.
Congar, Yves. "D'une 'ecclésiologie en gestation' à Lumen Gentium chap. I et II." In *Le Concile de Vatican II: Son Église Peuple de Dieu et Corps du Christ,* 123–36. Paris: Beauchesne Éditeur, 1984.
———. *Faith and the Spiritual Life.* Translated by A. Manson and L. C. Sheppard. New York: Herder, 1968.
———. *I Believe in the Holy Spirit.* Translated by David Smith. 3 vols. New York: Seabury, 1983.
———. *Journal d'un théologien 1946–1956.* Edited by Étienne Fouilloux. Paris: Cerf, 2001.
———. *Lay People in the Church.* Translated by Donald Atwater. Westminster, MD: Newman, 1957.
———. *Le Concile de Vatican II: Son Église Peuple de Dieu et Corps du Christ.* Paris: Beauchesne Éditeur, 1984.
———. *L'Élise: De saint Augustin á l'épogue moderne.* Paris: Éditions du Cerf, 1970.
———. "Moving Towards a Pilgrim Church." In *Vatican II Revisited: By Those Who Were There,* edited by Alberic Stacpoole, 129–52. Minneapolis: Winston, 1986.
———. *The Mystery of the Church.* Translated by A. V. Littledale. Baltimore: Helicon, 1960.

———. *Power and Poverty in the Church*. Translated by Jennifer Nicholson. London: G. Chapman, 1965.

———. *Priest and Layman*. Translated by P. J. Hepburne-Scott. London: Darton, Longman & Todd, 1967.

———. *The Revelation of God*. Translated by A. Manson and L. C. Sheppard. New York: Herder, 1968.

———. "Theologians and the Magisterium of the West," *Chicago Studies* 17.2 (1978) 210–24.

———. *This Church That I Love*. Translated by Lucien Delafuente. Denville, NJ: Dimension Books, 1969.

———. *Thomas d'Aquin: sa vision de théologie et de l'Église*. London: Variorum Reprints, 1983.

———. *Tradition and Traditions*. Needham Heights, MA: Simon & Schuster, 1966.

———. *Un Peuple Messianique: L'Église sacrement du salut, Salut et liberation*. Paris: Cerf, 1975.

———. *Vraie et Fausse Réforme dans l'Église: 2édition revue et corrigeé*. Paris: Cerf, 1975.

———. *The Word and the Spirit*. Translated by David Smith. London: G. Chapman, 1986.

Copeland, M. Shawn. "Tradition and the Traditions of African American Catholicism." *Theological Studies* 60 (2000) 632–55.

Davis, Leo Donald. *The First Seven Ecumenical Councils (325–787): Their History and Theology*. Collegeville, MN: Liturgical, 1983.

Deflem, Mathieu. "Ritual, Anti-Structure, and Religion: A Discussion of Victor Turner's Processual Symbolic Analysis." *Journal for the Scientific Study of Religion* 30.1 (1991) 1–25.

Dietrich, Donald J., and Michael J. Himes, editors. *The Legacy of the Tübingen School: The Relevance of Nineteenth-Century Theology for the Twenty-First Century*. New York: Crossroad, 1997.

Donovan, Mary Ann. *One Right Reading?* Collegeville, MN: Liturgical, 1997.

Douglas, Mary. *Essays in the Sociology of Perception*. London: Routledge & Kegan Paul, 1982.

———. *How Institutions Think*. Syracuse: Syracuse University Press, 1986.

———. *Natural Symbols: Explorations in Cosmology*. London: Routledge, 1970.

———. *Purity and Danger: An Analysis of the Concepts of Pollution and Taboo*. London: Routledge, 1966.

———. "Response to Ninan Smart." In Review Colloquium of *In the Wilderness: The Doctrine of Defilement in the Book of Numbers*, by Mary Douglas. *Religion* 26 (1996) 69–89.

Drey, Johann Sebastian. *Brief Introduction to the Study of Theology with Reference to the Scientific Standpoint and the Catholic System*. Translated by Michael J. Himes. Notre Dame: Notre Dame University Press, 1994.

———."Towards the Revision of the Present State of Theology." Translated by Joseph Fitzer. In *Romance and the Rock: Nineteenth-Century Catholics on Faith and Reason*, 60–73. Minneapolis: Fortress, 1989.

Dulles, Avery. "Yves Congar: In Appreciation." *America* 173.2 (1995) 6–7.

Eilers, Franz-Josef, editor. *For All the Peoples of Asia: Federation of Asian Bishops' Conferences Documents from 1992 to 1996*. Vol. 2. Quezon City, Philippines: Claretian, 1997.

Eno, Robert. "Doctrinal Authority in Saint Augustine." *Augustine Studies* 12 (1981) 133–72.

Eusebius. *Life of Constantine*. Translated by Averil Cameron and Stuart G. Hall. Oxford: Clarendon, 1999.
Featherstone, Michael. *Global Culture: Nationalism, Globalization, and Modernity.* London: SAGE, 1990.
———. *Undoing Culture: Globalization, Postmodernism and Identity*. London: SAGE, 1995.
Featherstone, Michael, Scott Lash, and Roland Robertson, editors. *Global Modernities*. London: SAGE, 1995.
Fitzer, Joseph, editor. *Romance and the Rock: Nineteenth-Century Catholics on Faith and Reason*. Minneapolis: Fortress, 1989.
Ford, David. *The Modern Theologians*. Cambridge, MA: Blackwell, 1997.
Foucault, Michel. *Power/Knowledge*. Edited and Translated by Colin Gordon. New York: Pantheon, 1980.
Freud, Sigmund. *The Interpretation of Dreams*. Translated by James Strachey. New York: Avon Books, 1998.
Friedman, Jonathan. *Cultural Identity and Global Process*. London: SAGE, 1994.
Geertz, Clifford. *After the Fact: Two Countries, Four Decades, One Anthropologist*. Cambridge, MA: Harvard University Press, 1995.
———. *Available Light: Anthropological Reflections on Philosophical Topics*. Princeton: Princeton University Press, 2000.
———. *The Interpretation of Cultures: Selected Essays*. New York: Basic Books, 1973.
———. *Local Knowledge: Further Essays in Interpretative Anthropology*. New York: Basic Books, 1983.
———. *Works and Lives: The Anthropologist as Author*. Stanford: Stanford University Press, 1988.
Giles, Anthony. *The People of Anguish: The Story behind the Reformation*. Cincinatti: St. Anthony Messenger, 1987.
Greenblatt, Stephen J. *Renaissance Self-Fashioning: From More to Shakespeare*. Chicago: University of Chicago Press, 1980.
Gutierrez, Gustavo. Informal talk, Inter-American Meeting of Dominican Women Theologians, Colegio Jesus, Lima, Peru, October 6, 2001.
———. *A Theology of Liberation: History, Politics and Salvation*. Translated by Sister Caridad Inda and John Eagleson. Maryknoll, NY: Orbis, 1996.
———. *We Drink From Our Own Wells: The Spiritual Journey of a People*. Translated by Matthew O'Connell. Maryknoll, NY: Orbis, 1984.
Haight, Roger. *Dynamics of Theology*. Mahwah, NJ: Paulist, 1990.
———. *Jesus, Symbol of God*. Maryknoll, NY: Orbis, 1999.
Harris, Carl V. *Origin of Alexandria's Interpretation of the Teacher's Function in Early Christian Hierarchy and Community*. New York: American Press, 1966.
Hastings, Adrian, editor. *Modern Catholicism*. New York: Oxford University Press, 1991.
Hebblethwaite, Peter. "John XXIII." In *Modern Catholicism*, edited by Adrian Hastings, 27–34. New York: Oxford University Press, 1991.
Heimbock, Gunther, and H. Barbara Boudewijnes, editors. *Current Studies on Rituals: Perspectives for the Psychology of Religion*. Atlanta: Rodopi, 1990.
Himes, Michael J. *Ongoing Incarnation: Johann Adam Möhler and the Beginnings of Modern Ecclesiology*. New York: Crossroad, 1997.
Hinze, Bradford. "J. S. Drey's Critique of Schleiermacher's Theology." *Heythrop Journal* 37.1 (1996) 1–23.

Hobsbawn, Eric, and Terence Ranger, editors. *The Invention of Tradition*. Cambridge: Cambridge University Press 1983.
Irenaeus of Lyons. *Adversus Haereses*. In *The Writings of Irenaeus*, translated by Alexander Roberts and W. H. Rambaut. Edinburgh: T. & T. Clark, 1868.
Jay, Eric G. *The Church: Its Changing Image through Twenty Centuries*. 2 vols. London: SPCK, 1977.
Jedin, Hubert. *A History of the Council of Trent*. Translated by Ernest Graf. 2 vols. London: T. Nelson, 1957.
Johnson, Elizabeth. *She Who Is: The Mystery of God in Feminist Theological Discourse*. New York: Crossroad, 1994.
Kelly, J. N. D. *Early Christian Doctrines*. New York: HarperCollins, 1978.
Ker, Ian. *John Henry Newman: A Biography*. Oxford: Clarendon, 1988.
Ker, Ian, and Alan G. Hill, editors. *Newman after a Hundred Years*. Oxford: Clarendon, 1990.
———. *Newman on Being a Christian*. Notre Dame: University of Notre Dame Press, 1990.
King, Anthony. "The Times and Spaces of Modernity (or Who Needs Postmodernism?)." In *Global Modernities*, edited by Michael Featherstone et al., 108–23. London: SAGE, 1995.
Kittleson, Richard. *Luther: The Reformer*. Minneapolis: Augsburg, 1986.
Komonchak, Joseph. "The Return of Yves Congar," *Commonweal* 110 (1983) 402.
Kratz, Corinne A. *Affecting Performance: Meaning, Movement, and Experience in Okiek Women's Initiation*. Washington, DC: Smithsonian Institution Press, 1994.
———. "'We've Always Done It Like This . . . Except for a Few Details': 'Tradition' and 'Innovation' in Okiek Ceremonies." *Comparative Studies in Society and History* 35.1 (1993) 30–65.
Lindbeck, George. *The Nature of Doctrine: Religion and Theology in a Postliberal Age*. Philadelphia: Westminster, 1984.
Luther, Martin. "Against Latomus." In *Luther's Works*, vol. 32, edited by George W. Forell. Philadelphia: Muhlenberg, 1958.
———. "The Babylonian Captivity of the Church." In *Luther's Works*, vol. 36, edited by Abdel Ross Wentz. Philadelphia: Muhlenberg, 1959.
———. "That a Christian Assembly or Congregation Has the Right and Power to Judge All Teaching." In *Luther's Works*, vol. 39, edited by Eric W. Gritsch. Philadelphia: Muhlenberg, 1970.
———. "Confession Concerning Christ's Supper." In *Luther's Works*, vol. 37, edited by Robert H. Fischer. Philadelphia: Muhlenberg, 1970.
Malanowski, Gregory E. "Pneumatology: The Growth of a Theological Perspective." *Living Light* 26 (1990) 227–37.
Marcus, George. *Ethnography through Thick and Thin*. Princeton: Princeton University Press, 1998.
Mauss, Marcel. "Body Techniques." In *Sociology and Psychology: Essays by Marcel Mauss*, translated by Ben Brewster, 95–123. London: Routledge and Kegan Paul, 1979.
McBrien, Richard P. *Lives of the Popes*. San Francisco: HarperSanFrancisco, 1997.
Metz, Johann Baptist. *Faith in History and Society*. Translated by David Smith. New York: Seabury, 1980.
Möhler, Johann Adam. *Symbolism: Exposition of the Doctrinal Differences between Catholics and Protestants as Evidenced by Their Symbolical Writings*. Translated by James Burton Robertson. New York: Crossroad, 1997.

———. *Unity in the Church, or, The Principle of Catholicism Presented in the Spirit of the Church Fathers of the First Three Centuries.* Translated by Peter C. Erb. Washington, DC: Catholic University of America Press, 1996.

Newman, John Henry. *The Arians of the Fourth Century.* New York: Longmans, Green, 1897.

———. *An Essay in Aid of a Grammar of Assent.* New York: Longmans, Green, 1947.

———. *An Essay on the Development of Christian Doctrine.* Notre Dame: University of Notre Dame Press, 1989.

———. *On Consulting the Faithful in Matters of Doctrine.* Edited by John Coulson. New York: Sheed & Ward, 1961.

O'Connell, Marvin R. *Critics on Trial: Introduction to the Catholic Modernist Crisis.* Washington, DC: Catholic University of America Press, 1994.

O'Meara, Thomas. "'Raid on the Dominicans': The Repression of 1954." *America* 170.4 (1994) 8–16.

———. *Romantic Idealism and Roman Catholicism: Schelling and the Theologians.* Notre Dame: University of Notre Dame Press, 1982.

Ockham. *On the Power of Emperors and Popes.* Edited and Translated by Annabel S. Brett. London: Thoemmes, 1998.

Oliver, Mary. "The Summer Day." In *New and Selected Poems*, 94. Boston: Beacon, 1992.

Origen. *On First Principles: Being Koetschau's Text of the De principiis.* Translated by G. W. Butterworth. New York: Harper & Row, 1966.

Oring, Elliot. "Victor Turner, Sigmund Freud, and the Return of the Repressed." *Ethos* 21.3 (1993) 273–94.

Phan, Peter. E-mail to the author, September 12, 2001.

———. Response to a paper presented by Roger Haight, Catholic Theological Society of America, Milwaukee, June 2001.

Pieterse, Jan Nederveen. "Varieties of Ethnic Politics and Ethnicity Discourse." In *The Politics of Difference: Ethnic Premises in a World of Power*, edited by Edwin N. Wilmsen and Patrick McAllister, 25–44. Chicago: University of Chicago Press, 1996.

Placher, William. *Unapologetic Theology: A Christian Voice in a Pluralistic Conversation.* Louisville: Westminster John Knox, 1989.

Rahner, Karl. "Towards a Fundamental Theological Interpretation of Vatican II." *Theological Studies* 79 (1979) 716–27.

Ricoeur, Paul. *The Symbolism of Evil.* Translated by Emerson Buckanan. Boston: Beacon, 1967.

Roberts, Alexander, and W. H. Rambaut, editors. *The Writings of Irenaeus.* Edinburgh: T. & T. Clark, 1868.

Sanks, T. Howland. "David Tracy's Theological Project: An Overview and Some Implications," *Theological Studies* 53 (1993) 698–727.

———. *Salt, Leaven, and Light: The Community Called Church.* New York: Crossroad, 1992.

Schneiders, Sandra. *The Revelatory Text: Interpreting the New Testament as Sacred Scripture.* Collegeville, MN: Liturgical, 1999.

Schreiter, Robert J. *Constructing Local Theologies.* Maryknoll, NY: Orbis, 1996.

———. *The New Catholicity: Theology between the Global and Local.* Maryknoll, NY: Orbis, 1997.

Sobrino, Jon. *The Principle of Mercy: Taking the Crucified People from the Cross.* Maryknoll, NY: Orbis, 1999.

Spickard, James. "A Guide to Mary Douglas's Three Versions of Grid/Group Theory." *Sociological Analysis* 50.2 (1989) 151–70.
Stacpoole, Alberic, editor. *Vatican II Revisited: By Those Who Were There*. Minneapolis: Winston, 1986.
Stagaman, David J. *Authority in the Church*. Collegeville, MN: Liturgical, 1999.
Strenski, Ivan, and Adrian Cunningham, editors. "Review Symposium: In the Wilderness: The Doctrine of Defilement in the Book of Numbers." *Religion* 26 (1996) 69–89.
Tanner, Kathryn. *Theories of Culture: A New Agenda for Theology*. Minneapolis: Fortress, 1997.
Tarnas, Richard. *The Passion of the Western Mind: Understanding the Ideas That Have Shaped Our World View*. New York: Ballantine, 1991.
Tavard, George. *Holy Writ or Holy Church: The Crisis of the Protestant Reformation*. New York: Harper, 1959.
Theimann, Ronald. *Constructing a Public Theology: The Church in a Pluralistic Culture*. Louisville: Westminster John Knox, 1991.
Theissen, Gerd. *The Religion of the Earliest Churches: Creating a Symbolic World*. Translated by John Bowden. Minneapolis: Fortress, 1999.
Thiel, John E. *Senses of Tradition: Continuity and Development in Catholic Faith*. Oxford: Oxford University Press, 2000.
———. "The Universal in the Particular: Johann Sebastian Drey on the Hermeneutics of Tradition." In *The Legacy of the Tübingen School: The Relevance of Nineteenth-Century Theology for the Twenty-First Century*, edited by Donald J. Dietrich and Michael J. Himes, 56–74. New York: Crossroad, 1997.
Thomas, Aquinas. *Summa Theologiae*. Cambridge: Blackfriars, 1964.
Tilley, Maureen A. *The Bible in Christian North Africa: The Donatist World*. Minneapolis: Fortress, 1997.
Tilley, Terrance W. *Inventing Catholic Tradition*. Maryknoll, NY: Orbis, 2000.
Tillich, Paul. *Systematic Theology*. Vol. 1. Chicago: University of Chicago Press, 1951.
Tracy, David. *The Analogical Imagination: Christian Theology and the Culture of Pluralism*. New York: Crossroad, 1981.
———. *On Naming the Present: Reflections on God, Hermeneutics, and Church*. Maryknoll, NY: Orbis, 1994.
———. *Plurality and Ambiguity*. Chicago: University of Chicago Press, 1987.
———. "Theology, Critical Social Theory and the Public Realm." In *Habermas, Modernity, and Public Theology*, edited by Don S. Browning and Francis Schüssler Fiorenza, 19–42. New York: Crossroad, 1992.
Turner, Frederick. "'Hyperion to a Satyr': Criticism and Anti-structure in the Work of Victor Turner." In *Victor Turner and the Construction of Cultural Criticism*, edited by Kathleen M. Ashley, 147–62. Bloomington: Indiana University Press, 1990.
Turner, Victor. *Blazing the Trail*. Edited by Edith Turner. Tuscon: University of Arizona Press, 1992.
———. "Encounter with Freud: The Making of a Comparative Symbologist." In *Blazing the Trail*, edited by Edith Turner, 3–28. Tuscon: University of Arizona Press, 1992.
———. *The Forest of Symbols: Aspects of Ndembu Ritual*. Ithaca, NY: Cornell University Press, 1970.
———. *The Ritual Process: Structure and Anti-structure*. Ithaca, NY: Cornell University Press, 1969.
———. *Schism and Continuity in an African Society: A Study of Ndembu Village Life*. Herndon, VA: Berg, 1996.

Van Huyssteen, J. Wentzel. *The Shaping of Rationality: Toward Interdisciplinarity in Theology and Science*. Grand Rapids: Eerdmans, 1999.

Vatican Council. *Vatican Council II: The Conciliar and Post Conciliar Documents*. Edited by Austin Flannery, OP. Collegeville, MN: Liturgical, 1975.

Vidler, Alec. *The Church in an Age of Revolution: 1789 to the Present Day*. Baltimore: Penguin, 1961.

Vincent of Lerins. *The Commonitories*. Translated by Rudolph E. Morris. In *The Fathers of the Church*, 257–332. Washington, D.C.: Catholic University of America Press, 1949.

Whale, J. S. *The Protestant Tradition: An Essay in Interpretation*. Cambridge: Cambridge University Press, 1955.

Wilmsen, Edwin N., and Patrick McAllister, editors. *The Politics of Difference: Ethnic Premises in a World of Power*. Chicago: University of Chicago, 1996.

# Index

Aberigo, Giuseppe, 87, 271
Anderson, Benedict, 1, 271
Appadurai, Arjun, 19, 271
Aquino, Maria Pilar, 179, 271
Arendt, Hannah, 24, 271
Asad, Talal, 8, 20–26, 166–67, 169, 238–39, 271
*Aufklärung*, Catholic, 93–94
Augustine of Hippo, 62–65, 82

Bell, Catherine, 118, 271
Bell, Daniel, 15
Bellarmine, Robert, 91–93
Berger, Peter, 257, 271
Beyer, Peter, 45, 47–48, 271
Biemer, Günter, 114, 271
Bossuet, J. B., 88
Boudewijnes, H. Barbara, 133, 271, 274
Brett, Annabel S., 75, 271, 274
Brown, Delwin, 238, 239–41, 244, 252, 255, 257, 271
Brown, Peter, 57, 62, 63, 66, 67, 271
Brown, Raymond, 266, 272
Bynum, Caroline Walker, 164, 262, 272
Byrne, James M., 266, 272

Calderon, Fernando, 7.
Cameron, Averil, 65, 272, 274
Chadwick, Owen, 88, 272
Chemnitz, Martin, 83–84, 272
Chenu, M-D., 69, 181, 187, 272
Clement, Keith, 89, 272
Clifford, James, 8–14, 18, 26, 51, 272
Comaroff, John, 165–67, 267, 272

Congar, Yves, 3–4, 69- 70, 72–76, 82, 85–87, 91, 176, 177–224, 254, 256–62, 268, 272
  influences on, 180–89
  *nouvelle théologie*, 181
  on Christian discipleship, 177–224
  on "the Christian Mystery," 190–92, 268
  on markers of Christian discipleship, 192–211
  on historical method in theology, 181–82
  praxis of communion, 214–18
  praxis of reconciliation, 218–19
  praxis of solidarity, 220–23
  Thomism, influence of, 182, 187–89
Copeland, M. Shawn, 236, 273
crisis of representation, 8, 166

Deflem, Mathieu, 143, 273
Deleuze, Gilles, 11
Dietrich, Donald, 95, 273
Donovan, Mary Ann, 59, 60, 241, 273
Douglas, Mary, 3–4, 118–32, 177, 216, 228, 230, 267–68, 273
  critical assessment of, 164–70
  on anthropological method, 118–20
  on grid-group, 120–30
  on social identity and change, 130–32
Drey, Johann Sebastian, 91, 94–97, 101, 272, 277
Dulles, Avery, 180, 273
Durkheim, Emile, 20, 118, 119, 131

Eilers, Franz-Josef, 252, 273
Eno, Robert, 68, 274
essentialism 23, 158, 238, 265
ethnography, 8–11, 24–25, 129, 150–53, 164–68, 275

Featherstone, Michael, 8, 14–20, 26, 45, 274
Fisher, Mike, 8, 275
Ford, David, 181, 274
Foucault, Michel, 11, 150, 230–31, 237–38, 266, 272, 274
Frei, Hans, 32
Freud, Sigmund, 132, 135, 138–39, 141, 148, 274, 276, 278
Friedman, Jonathan, 49, 274

Geertz, Clifford, 3–4, 29, 117–18, 142, 149–63, 167, 173–74, 247, 249, 254, 268, 274
   critical assessment of, 164–65, 167, 168, 170, 173–75, 267
   on anthropological method, 150–53
   on cultural and social structural processes, 158–60
   on defining culture, 151
   on ethos and worldview, 156–58
   on social change, 158–62
   on social identity, 153–58
   on symbols and religious meaning, 154–56
Giddens, Anthony, 172
Giles, Anthony, 78, 274
Gügler, Alois, 94
global theological flows, 48–49, 249
globalization, 14–20, 25, 27, 43–54, 117, 261, 271, 274
glocal, 46, 49, 54
Gutierrez, Gustavo, 27, 179, 217, 222, 260, 274

Habermas, Jurgen, 29–30, 277
Haight, Roger, 27, 36–43, 54, 228–29, 238, 240, 252–54, 266, 274
Harris, Carl V., 60, 274
Hauerwas, Stanley, 32

Hebblethwaite, Peter, 212, 274
hermeneutics, 42, 51–52, 167, 230, 247, 250
hierarchology, 179, 196
Himes, Michael, 91–103, 274, 278
Hinze, Bradford, 91, 275

Irenaeus of Lyons, 58–60

Jay, Eric 58, 73, 75, 82, 275
Jedin, Hubert, 84, 86, 275
Johnson, Elizabeth, 2, 218, 275

Kant, Immanuel, 90
Kelly, J. N. D., 58, 275
Ker, Ian, 106–7, 275
Kerr, Fergus, 181
King, Anthony, 15
King, Martin Luther, 28
Kittelson, Richard, 78, 275
Komonchak, Joseph, 87, 180, 275
Kratz, Corinne A., 164, 168, 170–72, 244–46, 248, 257, 275

Levi-Strauss, 13, 139, 145, 150
Lindbeck, George, 32, 229, 238, 275
Luther, Martin, 77–82, 275

magisterium, 69–72, 80, 84, 87–88, 114, 181, 220, 235–36, 243, 255, 267
Malanowski, Gregory E., 199, 275
Marcus, George, 8, 272
Mauss, Marcel, 170–71, 275
McBrien, Richard P., 72, 77, 275
method, anthropological
   Clifford Geertz, thick description, 151–52
   ethnographic method, 166–68
   Mary Douglas, 118–19
   Victor Turner, 132–35
method, theological
   juxtaposed thick description, 175, 226, 263
   mutual critical correlation, 28, 227–29

post-liberal, 32–33
Roger Haight on, 27, 36–39
Metz, J. B., 232, 275
Möhler, Johann Adam, 87, 93–106, 114, 276

Newman, John Henry, 106–15

O'Connell, Marvin, R., 114, 276
O'Meara, Thomas, 181, 276
Oliver, Mary, 150, 276
Origen of Alexandria, 60–62
Oring, Elliot, 139, 276

Peirce, C. S., 171
Phan, Peter, 252–53, 276
Pius IX, Pope, 114
Pieterse, Jan Nederveen, 1, 165, 168, 276

Rahner, Karl, 27, 43, 254, 276
religious identity, 45, 49–54
Ricoeur, Paul, 177, 276
Roberston, Roland, 14, 45–46, 274, 276

Sailer, J. M., 94
Sanks, T. Howland, 28, 92, 276
Schelling, Friedrich, 95, 106, 276
Schleiermacher, 90–91, 96, 101
Schneiders, Sandra, 178, 276
Schreiter, Robert, 1, 9, 27, 43–54, 126, 248–49, 276
Simmel, Georg, 18
Sobrino, Jon, 179, 219, 277
social identity 1–4, 7–9, 12, 20, 23, 26–27, 43, 55, 117, 120, 122, 130–36, 143–44, 147–49, 153–56, 162, 165–68, 170, 172, 175, 177, 179, 225, 231, 233, 240–41, 250, 265, 268
social identity, Christian 213–24, 226, 258, 267–69
Sorokin, Pitirim, 159
Spickard, James, 126, 277
Stagaman, David J., 243, 277

symbol
and ambiguity, 116
Roger Haight on, 38–43, 54
symbol systems,
in anthropology, 136–38, 142, 154–56, 161, 167
Christian, 42–43, 54, 116–18, 172, 175, 224, 237, 256–57, 266, 269
syncretism, 15, 49, 52–54

Tanner, Kathryn, 172–73, 259, 277
Tarnas, Richard, 84, 277
Tavard, George, 68, 69, 277
Theimann, Ronald, 247
Theissen, Gerd, 246, 249, 277
Thiel, John, 95–96, 226, 277
Thomas Aquinas, 70–72
Tilley, Maureen, 63, 277
Tilley, Terrance, 226, 234, 243, 277
Tillich, Paul, 228, 277
Tracy, David, 27–35, 55, 116, 227, 238, 244, 277
Trent, Council of, 84–88
Turner, Frederick, 139, 277
Turner, Victor 3–4, 117–18, 132–49
critical assessment of, 164–65, 168, 170–72, 175, 267–68, 271, 276, 277
on anthropological method, 132–35
on dominant and instrumental symbols, 136–42
on ritual action, 142–43
on social change, 143–49
on social drama, 133
on symbolic action, 135–36

Van Gennep, Arnold, 143
Van Huyssteen, J. Wentzel, 34–35, 173, 178, 234, 247, 251, 265–66, 278
Vincent of Lerins, 65–68
von Baader, Franz, 94

Whale, 82, 278
William of Ockham, 74–76

www.ingramcontent.com/pod-product-compliance
Lightning Source LLC
Chambersburg PA
CBHW070238230426
43664CB00014B/2340